MAD SCENES

AND

EXIT ARIAS

MAD SCENES

AND

EXIT ARIAS

The Death of the New York City Opera

and the Future of Opera in America

HEIDI WALESON

METROPOLITAN BOOKS

HENRY HOLT AND COMPANY   NEW YORK

Metropolitan Books
Henry Holt and Company
Publishers since 1866
175 Fifth Avenue
New York, New York 10010
www.henryholt.com

Metropolitan Books® and m® are registered trademarks of
Macmillan Publishing Group, LLC.

Library of Congress Cataloging-in-Publication data

Names: Waleson, Heidi, author.
Title: Mad scenes and exit arias : the death of the New York City Opera
    and the future of opera in America / Heidi Waleson.
Description: First edition. | New York : Henry Holt and Company, 2018. | Includes
    bibliographical references and index.
Identifiers: LCCN 2018002105 | ISBN 9781627794978 (hardcover)
Subjects: LCSH: New York City Opera—History. | Opera—United States—21st century.
Classification: LCC ML28.N3 N384 2018 | DDC 792.509747/1—dc23
LC record available at https://lccn.loc.gov/2018002105

Our books may be purchased in bulk for promotional, educational, or business use. Please contact
your local bookseller or the Macmillan Corporate and Premium Sales Department at (800) 221-7945,
extension 5442, or by e-mail at MacmillanSpecialMarkets@macmillan.com.

First Edition 2018

Designed by Kelly S. Too

Printed in the United States of America

1 3 5 7 9 10 8 6 4 2

For Andy, who loves opera as much as I do

CONTENTS

The only thing more expensive than opera is war.

—Unknown

MAD SCENES
AND
EXIT ARIAS

Introduction

ON SATURDAY NIGHT, September 28, 2013, at the Brooklyn Academy of Music, the New York City Opera dove into Mark-Anthony Turnage's *Anna Nicole*. It's a raunchy, rollicking farce, trashy and splashy in the manner of tabloid headlines and reality TV, about the waitress-turned-bombshell Anna Nicole Smith, who got breast implants, married an elderly oil billionaire, and died of an overdose of pills at age thirty-nine in 2007. Done up in lurid pinks and oranges, sung in burlesque rhythms and suggestive blues backed by a raucous orchestra, it sucked in the audience, entertaining them even as its mockery took aim at their country. "I'm gonna rape that goddamn American dream," sang one of its characters.

But that night, the bigger drama was off the stage. In the beginning of September, City Opera had put out a distress call and a threat: unless it raised $7 million by the end of the month, it would cancel the rest of its season. On Thursday, the board had pulled the trigger, voting to begin bankruptcy proceedings the following week and close down the company entirely. If they could come up with the $7 million by September 30, perhaps the crisis could be averted, but that was now just two short days away. Saviors had rescued City Opera before, but this time, the performers and the audience knew in their heart of hearts that the game was up and that this would most likely be the seventy-year-old company's finale.

After the curtain fell, and the shell-shocked musicians in the pit began packing away their instruments, George Steel, the company's general director, summoned the cast and orchestra onstage. A handful of players complied, but Stewart Rose, the principal hornist and a member of the orchestra for decades, was having none of it. "You killed City Opera," he yelled at Steel. "It's your fault that this is our last performance."

Who killed City Opera? In hindsight, Steel is but one contender for that dubious title. A better question would be, what was City Opera, and were the seeds of its demise sown at the moment of its birth seventy years earlier? Born into wartime New York, the pet project of a populist mayor and a few opera-loving public servants, its very premise was a paradox: it was conceived to be an affordable "opera for the people," yet, as the saying goes, the only endeavor more expensive than opera is war. Over the next seven decades, City Opera's identity morphed with its leadership and in reaction to radically changing times and circumstances. Sentimental attachments notwithstanding, by the time of its death, it was a different creature altogether.

For good and ill, the landscape of opera in America today bears little resemblance to what it was in the middle of the twentieth century. Beginning in the 1950s, opera boomed across the country, a growth that accelerated in subsequent decades. But that expansive time has given way to the straitened twenty-first century, and opera-producing companies have been obliged to retool or die. In many ways, the New York City Opera was unique, but its struggles are excruciatingly familiar to opera company impresarios now doing their best to learn from its example. The New York City Opera led the way for the artistic development of opera as an American art form, performed, produced, written, attended, and loved by Americans. And as it buckled under the pressures of changing times, audiences, tastes, and allegiances, coupled with inexorably rising expenses, it became a more sinister kind of leader—a bellwether, the canary in the coal mine, warning others of a perilous future. Caught in the maelstrom of change, City Opera could neither see the future coming nor adapt to it.

The death of City Opera raises other existential questions as well. Is it still possible to provide a living for a large group of artists by presenting live performances? Who is the audience for this old but still vital art form, and what do they want to see today? Is the creative impulse behind it still evolving? What is opera's place in a country of wildly diverse interests and forms of entertainment that were unimaginable when the New York City Opera was founded? The company's story offers both a history and a glimpse of possibilities that lie ahead.

The Birth of the
"People's Opera"

NEW YORK CITY in the early 1940s was a world center of finance, trade, and communications—but it was also America's cultural mecca. It was home to both the Metropolitan Opera, created by the nouveau riche industrialists of the late nineteenth century, and the New York Philharmonic, America's oldest symphony orchestra. High culture, money, and social status were inextricably linked, and for the city's moneyed upper classes, attendance at the opera or the concert hall, in tuxedos, diamonds, and furs, was a way of broadcasting one's success. However, there were also plenty of people in New York who were interested in culture but couldn't afford to attend these elite temples (an average ticket to the Met cost $3.30), or even Broadway shows, where the average ticket price was $2.50 in 1943, one-tenth of a bookkeeper's weekly salary. In the late 1930s, the Works Progress Administration put on federally funded orchestra concerts at Radio City Music Hall and Carnegie Hall, with tickets priced at 25 cents, which had attracted an enthusiastic public. Furthermore, the war in Europe had flooded the city with now-penniless refugees who had been sophisticated consumers of high culture in their home countries. New York's progressive mayor, Fiorello La Guardia, felt strongly about culture for the masses—he was both a champion of "the little guy" and the son of an immigrant Italian musician who had once accompanied the soprano Adelina Patti on an American tour. La Guardia had long dreamed of founding a center of cultural activity that would be within everyone's reach.

On March 5, 1943, Newbold Morris, president of the New York City Council and a close ally of La Guardia, convened a gathering of civically minded New Yorkers to discuss the creation of a new performing arts center that would present music, dance, and theater at affordable prices. La Guardia's wish had come together with an opportunity: the Mecca Temple on Fifty-Fifth Street, an elaborate and eccentric white elephant of a building, complete with a dome of terra-cotta tile, Moorish inscriptions, and an auditorium seating nearly three thousand. Built and opened with great fanfare in 1924 by the Shriners, the Mecca Temple had fallen on hard times during the Depression and, in 1942, was taken over by the city for nonpayment of taxes. Morris, a New York aristocrat from a prominent family dating back to before the American Revolution, and his close friend Morton Baum, an attorney and former tax counsel for the city, had been tasked by La Guardia with devising some means of putting it to use. Like La Guardia, Morris and Baum were devoted music lovers and were determined to make great art available to people who could not afford to go to the Metropolitan Opera, the New York Philharmonic, or even Broadway. They realized that they could solve two problems at once: turning the dilapidated Mecca Temple into a new arts center for the people would both rescue the building and make La Guardia's dream a reality.

Morris and Baum assembled a high-powered list of forty-six incorporators—philanthropists, theater producers, union representatives, artists, city dignitaries, and others—who pledged to organize the City Center of Music and Drama as a private, nonprofit corporation and guarantee any losses. New York City would provide the building for a nominal $1 per year in rent.

The initial idea was to book different attractions into the theater for back-to-back short runs, but Morris and Baum soon realized that presenting opera would be a tall order. If they wanted to bring opera to the new City Center, it seemed they would have to create their own company—the two smaller opera companies in town were not up to Morris and Baum's standards, and the Metropolitan, which had experimented with popular-priced opera in the 1930s and run up enormous deficits, was not interested in repeating the experience by associating itself with City Center. The board was wary at the idea of forming an opera company. Opera is the most notoriously expensive of all art forms, requiring instrumentalists, singers, scenery, costumes, and numerous other personnel. Low ticket prices would ensure that it would operate at a loss, possibly an enormous one. However, it was reasoned, successful runs of plays and other attractions at City Center would show a profit and help make up those inevitable losses. So, in October 1943, City Center engaged Laszlo Halasz, a Hungarian-born conductor and experienced opera administrator who had one other ace in the hole: he had spent several years as artistic director of the short-lived Saint Louis Opera Company, which had gone out of business in 1942, and that company was willing to make its scenery and costumes available to New York. The first opera season—a single week—was scheduled for February 21–27, 1944, which gave Halasz just four months to put the New York City Center Opera together from scratch.

The principles underlying Halasz's first season were those that would be at the company's core for years to come. There was a mix of repertoire: two well-known pieces (*Tosca* and *Carmen*) and one novelty, Friedrich von Flotow's *Martha*, a romantic comedy about a bored aristocrat who disguises herself as a maidservant. There were different languages: one opera each in Italian and French and, because Halasz was a strong believer in opera in the language of its audience, an English adaptation of *Martha*. Finally, there was a deliberate lack of stars: the Philadelphia-born soprano Dusolina Giannini, who would sing the title role in *Tosca*, was the rare exception—she had sung in Europe and at the Metropolitan and had made recordings. Most of the other singers would be unknowns.

Halasz knew talent, and he knew how to use it. One early arrival at City Center was a young pianist, Julius Rudel, who had emigrated from Vienna in 1938 at the age of seventeen. Recently graduated from the

Mannes School of Music, he was eager to be part of the new company, and Halasz immediately pressed him into service, first as an audition pianist and then as rehearsal accompanist. (Halasz also knew how to stretch a budget: Rudel was paid a total of $60 for the entire audition, rehearsal, and performance period.)

City Center opened with a concert by the New York Philharmonic, conducted by Artur Rodziński, with soloists Bidu Sayao and Lawrence Tibbett and featuring Gershwin's *An American in Paris* on December 11, 1943, Mayor La Guardia's birthday (an impromptu "Happy Birthday" followed his opening remarks). Tickets were $1 tops, and "the people" were out in force: the *New York Times* reported that the capacity crowd was "in ordinary clothes and a happy Saturday night humor and having a wonderful time." The next months were crammed with theater productions and several appearances by tap dance/harmonica duo Paul Draper and Larry Adler, a programming mix assembled through the efforts of City Center's board members and a small staff: Jean Dalrymple, who handled public relations, and Harry Friedgut, who served a brief term as managing director.

On February 21, City Center's brand-new opera company opened with *Tosca*. Again, a sold-out, enthusiastic crowd greeted the performance with bravos. So did the press: the *Times* not only praised the vocal ability of the singers but also commented that Dusolina Giannini and George Czaplicki (Scarpia) acted their parts far better than the famous singers who had recently sung those roles at the Metropolitan. The week continued with *Carmen* starring Jennie Tourel, not yet famous in the United States, but with much experience in the role at the Paris Opera; *Time* magazine declared her "one of the best Carmens in a decade . . . full of Gallic spice and neat as a championship billiard game." *Martha* got a more mixed reception. However, the week of performances—nine, including a student matinee—was deemed a huge success and, thanks to Halasz's careful budgeting, had cost only $30,462.73, which put the losses at a mere $128.82, even with ticket prices ranging from 85 cents to $2.20. The board decided to present a second season right away, in May of the same year. Given two weeks to fill this time, Halasz brought back the original three productions and added three more: *La Bohème*, *Cavalleria Rusticana/Pagliacci*, and *La Traviata*. Critical reception continued to be rapturous and the young Dorothy Kirsten, singing Violetta, was much lauded, though the attendance dropped because a hot spell sent some of the audience to the traveling San Carlo Opera Company, which was playing in an air-conditioned theater.

The first City Center season had also included a profitable visit from the Ballet Russe de Monte Carlo and the launch of another City Center–sponsored entity, the (short-lived) New York City Symphony, conducted by Leopold Stokowski, who donated his services. Financially, the whole operation had, surprisingly, turned a small profit, and it had also generated excellent publicity. At the first annual meeting of the incorporators, in May 1944, Mayor La Guardia declared that the City Center of Music and Drama was no longer an experiment.

When the New York City Opera was born, opera in America was concentrated in a few locations. The Metropolitan Opera, the oldest and most prestigious company, founded in 1883, dominated the landscape, not only in New York but throughout the country as a whole, with enormous national tours each year as well as weekly radio broadcasts. On the West Coast, the San Francisco Opera was building its reputation under the leadership of Gaetano Merola. Apart from those, there were just a handful of small companies in cities such as Cincinnati, Ohio (where the season was played at the Cincinnati Zoo), Central City, Colorado, and Pittsburgh, Pennsylvania. By contrast, many more cities had successfully established symphony orchestras.

Grand opera, with major European stars, was the Met's brand. In the years leading up to the founding of City Opera, the company had begun to engage some American singers, particularly when the war made it difficult for Europeans to travel to the United States, but the international artists were considered the biggest draws. San Francisco also viewed Europe as the source of operatic authenticity and made a practice of giving new European artists their American debuts. Smaller opera companies around the country usually followed in the footsteps of the two big companies—when Halasz ran the Saint Louis Opera, for example, his efforts to engage American singers had often run up against the preferences of his board, which wanted to emulate the Met with European stars.

The identity of the New York City Center Opera, therefore, was a novel one for the American opera landscape. The financial limitations imposed by the mandate to provide affordable "opera for the people" meant that a star-based system was out of the question, opening the field to young unknowns who otherwise had limited opportunities. Without stars, Halasz conceived of his company as an ensemble, for whom acting and creating theater was as important as singing. A few soloists had some experience, but most of the singers hired were young Americans getting their first break on the New York stage. Hundreds of hopefuls trooped through the City Center doors for open auditions, which would remain a hallmark of the company for years to come. The City Opera stage had no prompter's box, so the singers had to know their parts well. Yet this deficiency could also be seen as an advantage: unable to rely on a prompter for words and cues, singers would not be tempted to focus on a single, downstage spot and were thus freer to immerse themselves in the theatrical experience.

Halasz and his collaborators of the early years—the directors Leopold Sachse and Theodore Komisarjevsky, the conductor Joseph Rosenstock, the coach Felix Popper, and Julius Rudel—were all European émigrés or refugees. However, with the New York City Opera, they were creating a company that, while European in origin, was quite different from the Met, where the audiences often cared less about what happened on the stage and more about the prestige of big names or the social milieu of attending the performance and its opportunities for the display of wealth.

"These were people who had no artistic home in Europe any longer and had come here for their lives and their futures," recalled Brenda Lewis, the mezzo-soprano who made her debut with the company in 1945.

I think that Halasz had a vision of creating in New York City an opera theater—not an opera house, but a theater of the kind that he had grown up with in Hungary. Opera theater is the highest form of entertainment. When music and theater are put together on a stage, and that kind of vitality and vigor and honesty is part of the mix, it is far superior to any other theatrical experience. I think that the Europeans took that for granted. [It's very different from what] opera was in this country—it was a plaything for the rich.

Part of the ensemble model was to have singers perform small parts in some operas and large ones in others. The mezzo-soprano Frances Bible—a Juilliard-trained twenty-nine-year-old who would become one of the company's most beloved performers—made her company debut in October 1948 as a contract artist, at $90 a week, responsible for singing or covering (understudying) about a dozen roles. ("I had a part in *Ariadne*; I kept hoping that the girl"—the singer she was covering, that is—"wouldn't get ill because I never learned it.") Her actual debut was as the offstage Shepherd in *Tosca* on opening night; she also sang the Priestess in *Aida* from the pit, Mercédès in *Carmen*, and took over as Cherubino after act 1 of the first *Figaro* because the original singer's English diction was unacceptable to Halasz. Bible remembered that 1948 fall season, a jam-packed eight weeks with forty-one performances of fifteen different operas, as hectic but fun: "You could sing seven performances, start at ten in the morning, go until ten at night, then come back the next morning and do it all over again." The following fall, she got the bigger role of Octavian in *Der Rosenkavalier* added to her portfolio and a raise to $125 a week.

The ensemble model was also efficient for City Opera's repertory system of performing, in which a company offers several different operas in rotation during the same time period. In the alternative model, called "stagione," a company has only one opera in performance at any given time. This is a less stressful method—there is only one physical production to deal with, for example—but it also limits the potential audience. And unlike actors, principal singers cannot perform major operatic roles night after night, so performances of, say, *Tosca* must be spaced out over a week or double cast for the three principal roles. In the repertory system, especially when, as was the case at City Opera, many of the singers take on responsibilities in multiple operas, a company can present an ever-changing array of possibilities.

Brenda Lewis, who got $75 per performance to sing Santuzza in *Cavalleria Rusticana* in her first season and, two years later, had a break-out success in the title role of *Salome*, remembered the working conditions of City Center as challenging, to say the least.

It was a dark place. You went into a dark, dirty hall, with peeling paint and unswept floors and sinks that were green-stained. You carried your own soap and towel and your own toilet paper! There was a big rehearsal room on the third floor. There was a lot of confusion—many times, you were involved in three rehearsals simultaneously, and there was much screaming and anger and loss of temper because you were not in the place where you were supposed to be at the appointed time. You would have coachings with Tommy Martin or Julius Rudel in small rooms on very broken-down, out-of-tune pianos.

The performing conditions were no more luxurious. The theater had no wing space, and the stage had no trapdoor. For many years, sets were improvised, borrowed, or cobbled together—a set for one act of *Traviata* might come from *Rigoletto*. Principal performers often supplied their own costumes—even in 1955, when Beverly Sills made her debut as Rosalinda in *Die Fledermaus*, her mother made all her dresses and bought a white fox stole for $5 in a thrift shop. The peasants in *Cavalleria Rusticana* turned their coats inside out and became the peasants in *Carmen*. Nor were the acoustics ideal. "Nobody really knew how much voice people had," recalled Frances Bible. "We went to Boston," she remembered—to a different theater—"and everyone said, 'Oh, is that what we sound like?'"

Still, Lewis found those early days exhilarating. "Most of us were very, very young. Most of us were inexperienced, and we didn't know how hard it was to be an opera singer, to make a viable living with opera, and we stuck our necks out daily and nightly. I think that excitement translated to our audiences and made the feeling mutual. We were giving greatly of ourselves, and they were absorbing it, with a great deal of love." As she saw it, the audience was of a piece with the creators of the company: "It was a gathering place for Europeans. Many were refugees, people who were hungry for something that they had grown up with, an entirely different audience from what the Met [served] in those days."

Over eight years, Halasz continued to build on the artistic foundation he had laid down in those first seasons. He chose repertoire that balanced standards with less familiar pieces, many of which were not currently in the Metropolitan's repertory, such as *Eugene Onegin*, *Werther*, and *Andrea Chénier*. He mounted *Ariadne auf Naxos* in 1946, a title that the Met would not tackle for another sixteen years, and the New York premiere of Prokofiev's *The Love for Three Oranges*. He presented operas in English by Gian Carlo Menotti, and two world premieres, William Grant Still's *Troubled Island* and David Tamkin's *The Dybbuk*.

The company quickly expanded its seasons, performing around eight weeks in the fall and five in the spring. It was still not a living for its young singers, who were working for minimal fees; most augmented their incomes singing concerts elsewhere, teaching, and performing musicals in summer stock. The company was also able to book paying tours in the Northeast and for several years made regular visits to Chicago, beginning with eighteen performances in December 1948, which helped to position it as a national, rather than a merely local, operation. (The visits to Chicago ceased after the city founded its own opera company in 1954.) Meanwhile, City Center continued to fill its weeks with touring attractions and to develop additional resident companies. The New York City Symphony lasted only five seasons (including three under the very young Leonard Bernstein), but the New York City Theatre Company, run by Jean Dalrymple, took hold, and in 1948, City Center adopted Lincoln Kirstein and George Balanchine's fledgling dance company, which was renamed the New York City Ballet and soon became a major attraction at Fifty-Fifth Street.

For the most part, City Center was able to balance its budget with the profits made on the booked attractions and the Theatre Company, which typically made a profit, along with donations from the guarantors and rental payments for office space in the building. Although the wealthy Kirstein provided some subsidy for his company and underwrote or found sponsors for its new productions, neither the ballet nor the opera paid its own expenses through ticket sales.

Then, beginning with the 1950–51 season, City Center decided to allocate all of its available weeks to its three constituents—the opera, the theater company, and the ballet—and to stop taking the lucrative outside bookings that had helped to subsidize the opera and the ballet. This turned out to be artistically successful but financially problematic, especially since the ballet also undertook two tours—to London and Chicago—which lost even more money than had been anticipated, and the theater seasons were just barely in the black. Newbold Morris and the other board members were obliged to pass the hat in order to have enough funds for the fall 1951 season.

This financial distress was the beginning of the end of Halasz's directorship. He had planned to present the world premiere of *The Dybbuk* as the centerpiece of the spring 1951 season, but the financial shortfalls of fall 1950 made the board nervous about the expense, and he was told that, among other cutbacks, no new productions could be mounted. In January, in the course of a heated meeting to discuss the matter, Halasz complained that his artistic judgment, particularly regarding the new opera, was being second-guessed by the board. He resigned in protest and insisted that the six members of his artistic staff do so as well. But Morton Baum called his bluff. He insisted that *The Dybbuk* had been canceled only for financial reasons and, finances permitting, would be mounted in the fall. Furthermore, he made clear to Halasz and his staff that the spring season would go on with or without them, and he offered them twenty-four hours to rescind their resignations. With *The Dybbuk* reinstated, at least provisionally, Halasz was able to save face and the resignations were withdrawn, but the conflict would have lasting repercussions.

The Dybbuk opened in October 1951 and turned out to be a big hit, selling out all its performances—the original three, and two more that were added due to demand. But Halasz had alienated a number of board members with his threat of resignation. His uncompromising personality and sometimes arbitrary decisions had also created dissension in the artistic ranks. The board began to collect testimony from company artists complaining about his behavior. In December, following the fall season and the Midwest tour (during which the orchestra union complained that Halasz had thrown his baton at the concertmaster during a Chicago performance of *Madama Butterfly*), the board summoned him to lay out its dissatisfaction. Halasz, warned that trouble was afoot, came armed with his own testimonials from company members, but to no avail. The board dismissed him, creating a backlash in the press, which was indignant over the secrecy of the proceedings.

Joseph Rosenstock, a member of the company's conducting staff, was appointed general director, beginning with the spring 1952 season. He continued to build the company as Halasz had established it, presenting operas like the US stage premiere of Bartok's *Bluebeard's Castle*; Marc Blitzstein's savage *Regina*; and William Walton's *Troilus and Cressida*. Phyllis Curtin made her debut with the US premiere of Gottfried von Einem's *The Trial* in October 1953. "I sang all the principal female parts—a different lady in each act," she recalled. "Otto Preminger was the stage director. When we finished the performance, easily a third of the audience had left; those that remained were equally divided between the ones who were hissing and booing, and the ones who were cheering. I've never heard an evening like that in the theater since. It was pretty exhilarating."

But a cloud hung over Rosenstock's directorship. He was no showman, and the press had not forgiven the dismissal of Halasz, so despite the company's solid work and notable premieres, the reviewers seldom raved and audience numbers languished. City Center still sold tickets by the performance—Morton Baum felt that subscriptions would limit their flexibility—so tepid or poor reviews were disastrous for sales. After the spring 1956 season, Rosenstock stepped down. On the recommendation of John White, a former language teacher who joined the company in 1946 (born in Vienna, he had waggishly changed his name from Hans Schwarzkopf) and had been managing its business matters for several years, his replacement was a young star—Erich Leinsdorf. The Viennese-born conductor had already made his mark at the Met and San Francisco, toured internationally, and served as the resident conductor at the Rochester Philharmonic. City Opera offered him the opportunity to run his own opera company.

Leinsdorf's plan was total transformation—fewer operas with more performances of each and no cast changes, more contemporary operas, and only experienced singers in the productions, with a few major European artists to add excitement. He also wanted a single set, designed by Leo Kerz, that would be adapted with lighting to serve for all the operas in the season and would revolve on a turntable to transition between scenes.

Baum resisted Leinsdorf's plans but was overruled by the board. However, he was right to worry. The opening-night production of Offenbach's *Orpheus in the Underworld* was slammed for its witless English translation and bawdy text, which shocked the audience. The revolving-set idea was a disaster—it was more expensive to build than expected, the turntable made noise, and the audience was bored by the sameness of the sets. Worse, the sets for the company's existing repertoire had to be cut down in order to work with it and then could not be used without it. Only one of the fall season's operas was a success: the professional premiere of Carlisle Floyd's *Susannah*, a work that would go on to become an American operatic classic and a staple of that very select canon. *Susannah*, a retelling of the biblical tale of Susannah and the Elders, set in a modern-day mountain town in Tennessee, starred Phyllis Curtin in the title part. The role of the guilt-ridden evangelist Olin Blitch, who rapes her, was a breakout part for the young New Orleans–born bass-baritone Norman Treigle, who had joined the company three years earlier.

But aside from the one bright spot, overall audience numbers that season were worse than those of the Rosenstock years, eight of the thirty-nine scheduled performances were canceled, and the season lost a staggering $157,359 (over $1.4 million in 2017 dollars). Leinsdorf departed in disgrace. Since there was no money to put on the spring season, it was canceled, and for the first time, the company's future was seriously in doubt. Indeed, the Metropolitan Opera began to take an interest, thinking that it might take over City Opera and run it as a satellite.

However, Morton Baum was determined that the company would survive, and he pressed forward with the search for a new leader. This time, John White looked within the ranks and suggested Julius Rudel, a mainstay of the operation since the very beginning. From his initial job as audition pianist, Rudel had graduated not only to conducting performances but also to performing the kinds of tasks that hold an opera company together. He had been the music administrator and rehearsal scheduler, charged with the complex calculus of getting ten or more operas onstage in a handful of weeks. Under Rosenstock, he had taken on even more administrative responsibilities, and he served as the company director when it went on tour. He was not a diva, and he was popular in the ranks. The artists rallied around him, and three singers—Phyllis Curtin, Michael Pollock, and Cornell MacNeil—were delegated to approach Newbold Morris at the Yale Club and persuade him. Morris and the board agreed. Morris later said, "We were tired of prima donna conductors, and Rudel was the only man in the place who knew where all the scenery was buried."

On January 17, 1957, Rudel and his wife, Rita, were getting ready to go to the theater when the phone rang. The caller was Newbold Morris, who asked Rudel his plans for the evening. "I'm going to *Inherit the Wind*," Rudel told him—to which Morris responded, "You just have!"

CHAPTER 2

The Rudel Years

JULIUS RUDEL HAD powerful early memories of opera in Europe. His music-loving parents began taking him to the opera when he was three years old, and in his teenage years, he spent many nights in standing room at the Vienna State Opera, sometimes as a member of the paid claque. It was there, and at the Salzburg Festival, that he acquired his appreciation of opera as total theater—a potent combination of music, scenery, and acting. As a boy, he had built his own cardboard and wooden playhouses and designed opera scenery for them, working out complex scenic transitions. Now, not quite thirty-six years old, he had the real thing.

Rudel had grown up as an artist and strengthened his leadership skills while climbing the ranks at City Opera, absorbing the aesthetics and practices of his predecessors and becoming intimately familiar with the company's operational quirks by performing nearly all of its jobs. Much younger than Halasz and Rosenstock, and more assimilated, having arrived in the United States at age seventeen, Rudel was one of the first American-trained conductors to lead a major American opera

house. (At the time, the only other was the Italian American Nicola
Rescigno, who studied at Juilliard before launching companies in Chicago and Dallas.) Rudel was thus ideally suited to reconfiguring the structure established by his predecessors into a quintessentially American
opera company. It didn't hurt that he was able to interact with his
American ensemble on a more equal basis than more traditionally minded
conductors might have: he was "Julius," not "Maestro." And he inspired
confidence from the pit: "He set a standard for opera conducting that
stayed with me always," Phyllis Curtin said. "Few people were as good.
He knew when to lead and when to follow. . . . We all made wonderful music, and it worked."

Over the next twenty-two years, Rudel would bring the New York
City Opera to the peak of its influence and fame. He was imaginative
and open-minded about opera, tuned in to his singers' strengths, and
eagerly sought new ways to capitalize on their skills and expand the
repertory scope of his company at the same time. He liked the challenge
of creating a season even on a shoestring and, unlike many conductors,
he was not concerned about his own personal glamour and glory. He
could conduct anything, and, if necessary, direct it, too.

However, the most profound influence on the company's future
identity—and possibly the reason that it survived after the Leinsdorf
debacle—was the Ford Foundation, the first American philanthropic
organization to provide significant and consistent support for the arts.
In 1957, the foundation had just instituted a new, small Arts and Human-
ities program, under the direction of W. McNeil Lowry. City Opera was
in dire need of funds, so Lowry and Baum were introduced. Because Ford
would only fund projects, not operating expenses, Lowry and Baum
came up with a plan: Ford, in one of its first five grants to arts organizations, would give $100,000 to underwrite an experimental season of
American operas at NYCO. For practical reasons, and because part of
the plan was to help American operas gain a footing, the works to be
presented would be a mix of premieres, operas that were already in the
company's repertory, and pieces that had been presented elsewhere.

The ten operas of the five-week American Season of spring 1958 displayed a remarkable range. In addition to four titles from its repertory, including *Susannah*, the company added six more. They included Douglas Moore's *The Ballad of Baby Doe*, which had been enormously successful at its 1956 premiere in Central City, Colorado, the location of its Silver Rush–era love story; Leonard Bernstein's brilliant one-act, *Trouble in Tahiti*, about an unhappy couple in contemporary suburbia (Bernstein conducted one performance); and Kurt Weill's wrenching *Lost in the Stars*, based on Alan Paton's *Cry, the Beloved Country*, about apartheid in South Africa, which had already run for nine months on Broadway. There was one world premiere: Robert Kurka's *The Good Soldier Schweik*, a dark comedy about a soldier entangled in a military bureaucracy during World War I. Of the twenty-six performances, most sold only modestly: *Lost in the Stars* was the exception, but when the company attempted to capitalize on its popularity by adding an extra week of performances, attendance fell off. However, the sheer audacity of an all-American season, an unprecedented effort for an opera company, was applauded in the press, and Rudel, Baum, and Lowry felt that their experiment had been a success and deserved to be repeated. In October, Ford awarded the company a second grant, this one for $310,000, which would pay for a second American season in spring 1959 and an American repertory tour in 1960.

Ford's grants for those first American seasons marked the beginning of a relationship that would change the face of City Opera. And in turn, their success, critically speaking if not financially, helped shape the foundation's emerging philosophy of arts funding. In 1958, the year of the first NYCO American season, Ford undertook a study of arts institutions and artists in the United States. One of the most remarkable findings was the discovery of just how Eurocentric the field was. Most major orchestras and opera companies were led by European conductors and artistic directors, performed an almost exclusively European repertoire, and, in the case of the three major opera companies (the Met, San Francisco, and Chicago), employed European singers for most of the lead roles. In response, Lowry redefined the objectives of Ford's arts program: it would advocate for American composers and musicians, attempting to create a new artistic tradition. The NYCO grants were a centerpiece of this strategy.

For the second American season, Rudel revived four of the most successful operas from the previous year—*Susannah*, *Baby Doe*, Marc Blitzstein's *Regina*, and Gian Carlo Menotti's *The Medium*. Seven more titles were added, including *Street Scene*, Kurt Weill's potent fusion of American musical theater and European opera, based on Elmer Rice's play about daily life and tragedy on New York's Lower East Side; Douglas Moore's *The Devil and Daniel Webster*; the New York premiere of Carlisle Floyd's *Wuthering Heights* (which proved less popular than *Susannah*); and the world premiere of Hugo Weisgall's *Six Characters in Search of an Author*. This second American season included a total of twelve operas, up from ten the previous year, and although attendance was again disappointing, with only 41 percent of audience capacity filled, it drew praise from the press for its artistic importance. A critic for the *Nation* wrote, "I shall be surprised if musical history does not record that American opera, as a movement, had its beginnings at the New York City Center in the spring seasons of 1958 and 1959." The following spring, in 1960, the company mounted a two-week New York season to prepare the four American operas (*Susannah*, *Baby Doe*, *Street Scene*, and *Six Characters*) that would be given on the Ford-sponsored, five-week, nineteen-city tour. NYCO also presented a new production of Blitzstein's Brechtian, pro-union piece, *The Cradle Will Rock*, which had been made famous when its 1937 premiere on Broadway was temporarily shut down by the WPA (Works Progress Administration) for its politics; ultimately, as a workaround, the piece was performed with the cast singing their parts from seats in the audience as Blitzstein played the piano onstage. NYCO presented a full staging of *Cradle*, with Blitzstein's original orchestrations.

For City Opera, the Ford Foundation partnership represented financial stability. Ford had put up $410,000 in support of the first three American seasons, a considerable sum, allowing the company to maintain its presence in New York without tumbling into the red. Of course, while City Opera pursued an ambitious program of contemporary and American works in the spring seasons, its fall seasons still included traditional repertory, and the company's focus on young singers made it ideally suited for Mozart operas, which showcase light voices, and were another particular love of Rudel's. One triumph was the company's first *Così fan tutte*, performed in English, in 1959, with Phyllis Curtin, Frances Bible, John Alexander, John Reardon, James Pease, and Judith Raskin in her company debut. It was directed by William Ball, designed by Robert Fletcher (they had a budget of $2,500 for sets and costumes), and conducted by Rudel. Winthrop Sargeant of the *New Yorker* declared it the best *Così* he had ever seen in his life. The fall seasons also included some unusual operas: for example, City Opera reached into the distant past for the New York stage premiere of Monteverdi's *Orfeo* of 1607, which Rudel, intrigued by the idea of juxtaposing one of the earliest operas with a recent one, put on a double bill with Dallapiccola's chilling 1949 drama, *Il Prigioniero*.

In 1959, Ford announced another major initiative that would help City Opera cement its identity as a center for American opera, pledging nearly $1 million to four opera companies specifically for the commissioning and production of new works. Of the four companies selected—the Metropolitan, Lyric Opera of Chicago, the San Francisco Opera, and NYCO—it was NYCO, unsurprisingly, that was most eager to pursue the opportunity. The first two operas it commissioned as part of this effort were Douglas Moore's *The Wings of the Dove* and Robert Ward's *The Crucible*, both premiered in October 1961; over the next ten years, there would be nine more. The Met ultimately produced two new operas as part of the Ford initiative while San Francisco and Chicago did one each, a paltry record that indicated how deeply entrenched the European repertoire remained in these more traditional companies.

City Opera was different. Ford's interest in new work dovetailed smartly with Rudel's. The young conductor was already intrigued by how America was putting its own stamp on the operatic form. He loved Broadway musicals—in 1956, he even conducted Cole Porter's *Kiss Me Kate* in Vienna, the first complete American musical ever done there—and was fascinated by how composers like Weill and Blitzstein could integrate purely American idioms like jazz and popular song into the structure of musical theater and opera, creating hybrids like *Street Scene* and *Regina*. He also saw the variety of work being created by more orthodox American composers like Floyd, Lee Hoiby, Moore, and Weisgall, who, he felt, were creating a new American operatic language that was not simply an imitation of their European predecessors. The Ford commissioning grants gave Rudel the resources to champion contemporary operas. He was constantly reviewing scores, looking for potential librettists, working with inexperienced opera composers to help them make their creations stage worthy, passionately speaking up for the value of performing contemporary works even in the face of audience apathy or critical dislike, and, of course, conducting them.

After the first three American seasons, Rudel pitched Lowry on a new idea: a five-week season of twentieth-century American works staged side by side with European ones, to see if the American product could hold its own next to Poulenc, Prokofiev, and Shostakovich. Ford would eventually come through with funds to support this initiative during the 1965 and 1966 spring seasons, but in the meantime, Rudel tried out the idea on the company's dime, devoting its spring weeks of 1962 and 1963 to the juxtaposition of American and European contemporary operas. These two seasons featured revivals and new productions including an operatically scaled *Porgy and Bess*, with recitatives and a full orchestra instead of the more familiar Broadway version; the world premiere of Abraham Ellstein's *The Golem*; and, since Rudel adored Britten, *The Turn of the Screw* and the New York premiere of *A Midsummer Night's Dream*, the latter starring the young mezzo Tatiana Troyanos in her company debut as Hippolyta. In 1963, Rudel proudly noted that his three-week spring season of contemporary opera reached more people than the impresario Rolf Liebermann's much-publicized week of new work in Hamburg, Germany—even though "he has the tradition, and we don't." (The company could not afford to do this every year: in 1961 and 1964, City Opera, as the City Center Gilbert and Sullivan Company, performed runs of Gilbert and Sullivan operettas instead of opera during the spring weeks.)

The Ford-funded 1965 and 1966 spring seasons of contemporary operas were longer and more ambitious than 1962 and 1963, and they introduced some important works. The 1965 season, for example, put a pair of female monsters on display with the world premiere of Jack Beeson's *Lizzie Borden* (one of the Ford commissions) in juxtaposition with the New York premiere of Shostakovich's *Katerina Ismailova* (a.k.a. *Lady Macbeth of Mtsensk*) in an English translation by Rudel. Not only were all seven of the company's spring opera seasons from 1958 through 1966 devoted exclusively to contemporary repertoire, but Rudel also mounted twentieth-century pieces in the fall seasons: world premieres of American operas commissioned by Ford and local premieres of works by European masters, such as Honegger's *Jeanne d'Arc au Bûcher* and Prokofiev's *The Fiery Angel* (billed by the company as *The Flaming Angel*). Through the combined efforts of Rudel and Ford, the New York City Opera became the only American house where twentieth-century work was regularly premiered, revived, and celebrated. It was a company of the present.

City Opera's sets and costumes had become more professional since the early days, but production values were still modest, given the cramped conditions of the City Center backstage, and the company's perpetually straitened finances. In 1963, the company had a budget of about $1 million, its top singer fee was still $150 a performance, and its top ticket cost $4.95. Rudel proved an adept balancer of funds and vision. In a twentieth-anniversary story in the *New York Times* that year, Martin Mayer quoted Lowry: "The miracle of Rudel is that he holds all the elements together with baling wire and chewing gum. He's the most single-minded man I've ever met: apart from his children and his wife, he never thinks about anything but music and his opera company."

By contrast, the Metropolitan Opera had a budget of $8 million, and its top ticket cost $11. There was another difference as well: despite the exciting work Rudel was producing, City Opera had no subscription program until 1964—and as a result, it rarely sold out. Morton Baum had always felt that subscription impeded flexibility but Ford, which was concerned about the sustainability of performing arts organizations, had begun working with Danny Newman, the guru of subscription, and pushed its grantees to adopt this method of guaranteeing a reservoir of cash up front. When City Opera did finally institute a small-scale sub-scription program in 1964, it was at Lowry's insistence. Meanwhile, the Met was selling out—indeed, it was difficult for nonsubscribers to get Met tickets at all. However, both companies depended, as always, on some kind of subsidy. Even with sold-out houses, the Met's box office covered only three-quarters of its expenses, and in 1964, it started a patron program—the company would soon be moving into its new house at Lincoln Center, and for a donation of $1,000, current subscrib-ers could be assured good seats.

Lincoln Center, the splendid new performing arts center, with its marble buildings and grand plaza, was the game changer for New York institutions. Started as a Robert Moses slum clearance program in the 1950s, its development was long and complicated, and the political wran-gling over its buildings and constituents seemed endless. On a sixteen-acre site on the Upper West Side, new theaters were being built for the Metropolitan Opera and the New York Philharmonic. A third theater, paid for by the state of New York, was to house the performing arts component of the 1964 New York World's Fair; it was then to be given over to the opera and ballet companies of City Center, who would pro-vide popular-priced entertainment at the new complex.

But Lincoln Center, dominated by the powerful Metropolitan Opera board, only wanted Balanchine's lively, cutting-edge New York City Bal-let. There was already an opera company in place at Lincoln Center—the Met—and its general director, Rudolf Bing, was not keen on having the cut-rate City Opera next door. And if City Opera had to be there, the Met expected to be able to control what it viewed as the "second" com-pany's artistic program, dictating what repertoire it could perform and insisting on scheduling priority in the event of any overlap. Further-more, Lincoln Center and its president, William Schuman, wanted con-trol of the New York State Theater, so that it could book outside attractions during the dark weeks and charge premium prices for them. But Morton Baum went to war with Schuman and his board and won control of the building for City Center and autonomy for City Opera.

City Center of Music and Drama (CCMD) would now wear two hats. It would run the New York State Theater and its two constituents based there, City Ballet and City Opera. (A new, short-lived company also had a share in the State Theater: Richard Rodgers's Music Theater of Lincoln Center, which mounted revivals of classic musicals like *Annie Get Your Gun* during the summer from 1964 through 1969.) CCMD, meanwhile, would continue to control the Fifty-Fifth Street Theater, where the New York City Center Light Opera Company, directed by Jean Dalrymple, presented musicals; the theater company's activities had become intermittent, and some outside attractions filled out the season. With City Ballet's departure for the State Theater in 1964, more dance companies were booked to fill Fifty-Fifth Street's weeks, and in 1966, the lively young Joffrey Ballet would become the City Center Joffrey Ballet. Other companies, including Alvin Ailey American Dance Theater and Dance Theatre of Harlem, would eventually take up regular residence at Fifty-Fifth Street as well.

At first, Rudel was not enthusiastic about the move. He did not want to be next door to the Met, either, where "poor relation" comparisons would be inevitable, and he feared that City Opera would lose its distinctive character. Most of all, he was concerned that operating the company at Lincoln Center would be unaffordable, given the higher running costs of the new theater. On Fifty-Fifth Street, the rent was $1 a year and the city paid for utilities; at Lincoln Center, the company would be expected to pay rent as well as a share of the costs for the theater and the complex. The move would also mean a bigger orchestra and chorus, more stagehands, and more elaborate (and expensive) productions. But the advantages were hard to deny: a fine new theater with a well-equipped backstage, to say nothing of modern air-conditioning, and the ability to draw audiences with the appeal of a brand-new arts center. Furthermore, if the City Opera did not move, there were fears that the Met might present its own lower-priced satellite company at the New York State Theater. The Met's fledgling National Company, intended predominantly for touring and to give opportunities to young singers, looked worryingly like the Met's version of City Opera. If the National Company, or something like it, was installed in the fancy new

State Theater, who would want to attend performances of City Opera, back in the seedy old Mecca Temple?

The benefits appeared to outweigh the disadvantages, and, many years later, Rudel would say that the move to Lincoln Center had been the making of City Opera. However, his initial misgivings would also turn out to be well-founded. The expense of the new neighborhood was indeed enormous. And although the Met had grudgingly agreed to City Opera's arrival, the company's status as the stepchild of Lincoln Center would never really go away.

One problem no one had foreseen was that of the acoustics in the New York State Theater. The hall had been built for the New York City Ballet, and its director, George Balanchine, told the architect, Philip Johnson, that he didn't want to hear the sound of the dancers' feet, so the house had been deliberately designed to deaden reverberations from the stage. Rudel brought in an acoustical consultant, Christopher Jaffe, to analyze the problems. He found that the proscenium walls were designed to throw sound back onto the stage and that the theater's many flat surfaces created echoes, sound focusing problems, and balances that were inconsistent even from seat to seat. To address these issues, some acoustical elements were added to the balconies to break up the flat surfaces and rugs were put on the floor. A temporary proscenium cover and cyclorama that would project sound into the audience were constructed, to be used during the opera seasons and removed for the ballet. Rudel felt that the resulting acoustics, while not ideal, were much improved. But the question of the theater's sound would persist for years.

City Opera moved into the New York State Theater for its final all-twentieth-century season in the spring of 1966, a run that was most notable for the US premiere of Ginastera's *Don Rodrigo*, starring a young, unknown Mexican tenor named Placido Domingo. But it was the fall 1966 season that changed everything. Rudel had decided to open with Handel's *Giulio Cesare*. Once again, he was thinking unconventionally about repertory—no one did Handel operas, which, if they were considered at all, were thought to be hopelessly static and dull, and this would be the New York stage premiere. He also wanted a vehicle for Norman Treigle, the giant-voiced bass-baritone who had been a City

Opera stalwart for more than a decade and had recently galvanized audiences with his performance as Boris Godunov. Rudel had planned to cast Phyllis Curtin, as Cleopatra (she and Treigle had paired well as antagonists in *Susannah* in 1956), although Curtin, who now had a busy career around the country and abroad (including a handful of appearances with the Met) was no longer performing regularly at City Opera. Negotiations were well advanced when one of City Opera's rising stars, Beverly Sills, got wind of them.

Sills—the red-haired coloratura soprano who had made her debut at the company in 1955 as Rosalinda in *Die Fledermaus*, and had since gone from strength to strength, including her touching performance in the title role in *The Ballad of Baby Doe*—insisted that as a current member of the company, Cleopatra should be hers by right. She confronted Rudel about it over an impromptu bagel breakfast at his apartment. In their respective memoirs, the two reported this showdown differently. Sills insisted that she threatened to quit City Opera if she didn't get the part and told Rudel that her wealthy husband would rent Carnegie Hall, where she would sing a concert of Cleopatra's arias and "you're going to look sick." Rudel contended that Sills made no threats and was joking about Carnegie Hall. However, he took her seriously enough to change his mind and give her Cleopatra, ostensibly because Curtin was unavailable for some of the performances. For Curtin, who was a City Opera stalwart and one of the artists who persuaded Newbold Morris to appoint Rudel in the wake of the Leinsdorf debacle, "A knife went into my back. . . . I simply couldn't believe that my [City Opera] family would do that to me." Apart from one performance as the Countess in *Figaro* in 1976, she never sang at the company again. And despite his insistence that Sills never issued an ultimatum, Rudel noted in his book that from that moment on, "the power dynamics of our personal relationship were changed."

The *Giulio Cesare* opening night on September 27, 1966, is one of those legendary events of opera history. Tito Capobianco, Sills's preferred collaborator, directed, with the singers using stylized, dance-like movements to evoke the baroque era. There was sculptural scenery by Ming Cho Lee and sparkly costumes (including grand headdresses) by Jose Varona. Sills inhabited the mercurial role of Cleopatra as both an actress and a singer. In her autobiography, *Beverly*, she looked back on that performance of the long lament in act 2 as "the single most extraordinary piece of singing I ever did." There were no coloratura fireworks—Sills displayed plenty of those during the evening, but in that aria, she held the stage through control and pianissimo singing. The audience had been completely silent throughout the aria and remained so even as the curtain slowly descended. Then the house erupted. The international press, which had flocked to New York for the inaugural performances of the Metropolitan Opera in its new house earlier in the month, was in attendance, the reviews were ecstatic, and news of Sills's triumph spread quickly. Overnight, with the help of the press agent Edgar Vincent, she became a star.

The story of Beverly Sills, America's girl-next-door diva, is its own legend. Suddenly, a Jewish girl from Brooklyn was big news in an art form that was all about European elitism and wealthy privilege. There were newspaper articles and television talk shows—in 1969, she was on the cover of *Newsweek* and made her first appearance on *The Tonight Show with Johnny Carson*—and the public couldn't get enough of her. Sills had the personality for that kind of fame—down-to-earth, approachable, and happy to demystify opera. Her celebrity spilled over into her opera company, where people came to the box office to buy tickets for the "Beverly Sills opera." The "People's Diva" for the "People's Opera"—it was a perfect pairing.

With *Giulio Cesare*, City Opera had bested its grand neighbor: the Met's opening night had been disastrous by comparison. Its world premiere of Samuel Barber's *Antony and Cleopatra*—another take on ancient Egypt—was starrily cast with Leontyne Price and Justino Díaz, but Franco Zeffirelli's production, designed to show off the new house's elaborate stage machinery, including a turntable, was gaudy, grandiose, and confusing, and the principal singers were overwhelmed by enormous costumes and phalanxes of supernumerary actors and choristers. Barber's music was also lambasted by the critics; one called the piece "a slick, chic, fashionable opening-night opera." City Opera, accustomed to putting together unusual works, had picked a winner, and its more modest stagecraft ambitions contrasted favorably with the Met's pomposity. The upstart "shoestring" company had proved that it could more than hold its own in this fancy new neighborhood.

And the audiences came. All the company's productions had to be reconfigured and upgraded for the State Theater, and that, along with the novelty of the theater and the Sills Effect, helped stimulate ticket sales. John White recalled that for the first three or four years in the State Theater, "the box office had nothing to do. You looked at the racks [of tickets in the box office]—there was nothing to sell."

City Opera gradually expanded into its new house. During the 1964–65 season, its last full year at Fifty-Fifth Street, the company had performed for just twelve weeks there. By the 1971–72 season, it was playing a full twenty-one weeks at the New York State Theater, still split between fall and spring, while maintaining the same breakneck schedule, which often meant eight performances a week, with minimal repeats, of two dozen different titles. Rudel took tremendous pride in the fact that the company could perform five operas in the fifty hours between Friday evening and Sunday evening, with ten hours to mount, perform, and dismantle each one.

Buoyed by Lincoln Center's prestige, the company also stepped up its efforts to expand beyond New York. City Opera had been taking its shows on the road since its earliest years, providing additional work for the artists and exposure and income for the company. Touring had its pitfalls—in one very early outing, the local high school students enlisted as supers for *Tosca* were told that in the last act, they were to follow the soprano wherever she went. And they did exactly as instructed, even as Tosca jumped to her death. There were happier moments as well. At the end of the monthlong Philadelphia-to-Cleveland tour in November 1955, Beverly Sills, who had just made her NYCO debut in New York, attended a party given for the company by the Press Club of Cleveland where she met Peter Greenough, the associate editor of the *Cleveland Plain Dealer*. A year later, they were married. Now, in 1967, NYCO began a major new endeavor: an annual visit to Los Angeles after the conclusion of the fall season. Los Angeles had no opera company

of its own. It did, however, have Lawrence Deutsch, a devoted opera fan
who had worked briefly for Halasz in the early City Opera years. Since
then, he and his partner, Lloyd Rigler, had hit the jackpot: in 1948,
they bought a seasoning recipe for $10,000 from a Santa Barbara res-
tauranteur, popularized it as Adolph's Meat Tenderizer, and made a fortune (they later sold Adolph's, in 1974, to Chesebrough-Pond's). Rudel
invited Deutsch back to New York to hear City Opera in its new theater, and so was born the annual "airlift": the company would take its
entire fall repertory to Los Angeles and perform for a month in the
Dorothy Chandler Pavilion at the recently opened Los Angeles Music
Center, subsidized by Deutsch and Rigler.

Another new performing arts center, this one in Washington, DC,
would also bolster City Opera's visibility and influence. The John F.
Kennedy Center for the Performing Arts opened in 1971, and Julius
Rudel took on the additional responsibility of serving as its music director while continuing to lead City Opera. The Kennedy Center did not yet
have its own opera company, so NYCO became a regular visitor. The
company also performed for the opening summer (1971) of the new
Wolf Trap National Park for the Performing Arts in Virginia, the land
for which had been donated by Catherine Shouse, a good friend of
Rudel's. Between its New York weeks and its various engagements on
the road, City Opera's annual performances nearly tripled in a decade:
in the 1974–75 season, the company gave over two hundred performances, a remarkable number.

However, the new, bigger City Opera also cost more. As Rudel had
foreseen, just running the theater—air-conditioning and heating costs,
stagehands, and the like—was significantly more expensive than it had
been at Fifty-Fifth Street. Productions had to look better in the new sur-
roundings, so they cost more, too. Low fees for the singers persisted,
but even they had to increase somewhat. "We went from Dickens to
Rockefeller," said John White.

Perhaps the greatest change from the scrappy, "we're all in it together"
old days at Fifty-Fifth Street was the attitude of the orchestra. Like every-

one else, the players had long worked for relatively low wages, but with the move to Lincoln Center, they began to look enviously at their more prosperous neighbors. The Metropolitan Opera orchestra had had numerous showdowns with its management over the years, and its union was savvy about timing, insisting on new demands just as the Met prepared to open its new Lincoln Center house. After a one-week strike that threatened the opening season, the new contract, ratified during the intermission of the opening night of *Antony and Cleopatra*, made the Met the highest-paid orchestra in the world.

The City Opera orchestra union's foray into saber rattling that same September was considerably more modest: its first-ever strike—on a rehearsal day—lasted only a few hours. However, it netted health and vacation benefits and a few extra dollars per performance. In the second year of their two-year contract, the musicians would be earning a base pay of $210 per week. It was a long way from the Met's $355, and for more performances each week, but it was a start.

The upward trend would continue. With its first strike, however minimal, City Opera's orchestra joined a wave of militancy that been growing among symphony and opera musicians over the previous decade. Pay increases for musicians in the postwar period had not kept pace with those of other industries, and symphonic musicians had begun to flex their muscles, forming aggressive orchestra committees and winning significant increases. Orchestras from Los Angeles to Philadelphia were walking out whenever their contracts came due. Philadelphia's 1966 strike lasted fifty-eight days, San Francisco's in 1967 lasted forty-nine days, and in 1969, Bing responded to stalled talks with the Metropolitan Opera's orchestra by canceling rehearsals. The house shut down for three months, only reopening on December 29, with a disastrous loss of box office income that would haunt the company for years to come. From 1966 on, the City Opera orchestra's contract negotiations would rarely be settled without a work stoppage. Issues of pay, benefits, performance numbers, and guaranteed weeks would be wrangled over endlessly, and a Byzantine structure of work rules also emerged, adding more costs.

For City Opera, new leaders would be needed to manage the changes. Within two years of its move into a more expensive house and its

subsequent expansion, City Opera lost, in rapid succession, its two
principal pillars. Newbold Morris, whose social connections had been a
financial lifeline for City Center, died on March 30, 1966. Morton
Baum, who had long been City Center's (and, thus, City Opera's) unofficial, unpaid managing director, was appointed to replace Morris as
chairman of the board of directors. The two had worked as a team;
Baum would now have to shoulder the burden alone. City Ballet and
City Opera were selling out at the State Theater, but even with higher
ticket revenues, the greater expenses meant that they were still losing
money—more than double what Baum had expected—and would have
to rely all the more on donations and grants. Baum felt the loss of Morris keenly, particularly in terms of fund-raising.

Then, in February 1968, Baum, just sixty-two, suffered a fatal heart
attack. It was a devastating loss; Baum had been the guiding force of
City Center from the beginning. As the critic Harold Schonberg pointed
out in an appreciation in the *New York Times*, "Baum could never dele-
gate authority. He did everything himself, down to the tiniest details,
and never trained anybody to take his place." And the buck, literally, had
always stopped with Baum. "Morton Baum was single-handedly responsible for keeping City Center going during its first quarter-century of
existence," Rudel wrote in his memoir. "These were words that I heard
more than once from Morton: 'Don't worry, I'll get you the money.' And
somehow, he always did."

Now, someone else would have to take on the task of sustaining City
Opera in this new era of growth. Like other performing arts organizations across the country, it would discover that expansion brought
new challenges. Symphony orchestras, for example, under pressure from
their musicians to provide more work, were steadily increasing the
amount of work guaranteed in their contracts. In 1960, no American
orchestra had a year-round, fifty-two-week contract; ten years later, six
did, and five other orchestras had contracts of forty-five weeks or more.
This meant more performances and, thus, more tickets sold, but the
increase in earned income could not continue to keep pace with the rise
in expenses. In 1966, two economists, William J. Baumol and William G. Bowen, published *Performing Arts—the Economic Dilemma*,

which examined the finances of orchestras and other institutions and demonstrated that the gap between expenses and box office income would only continue to grow, and exponentially. The performing arts, they noted, are a handicraft product and thus are not amenable to economies of scale or productivity: you always need the same number of violinists to play a Mahler symphony, working for the same amount of time, while improvements in automation and efficiency can, for example, bring down the number of person-hours required to build a car. On the income side, ticket prices could only be raised so far before the audience would resist and stop coming. The resulting "income gap" had to be filled by a subsidy of some kind, and as the gap increased, new types of subsidy would have to be found. The establishment of the National Endowment for the Arts in 1965 was an encouraging development, but it seemed highly unlikely that the United States would ever be willing to subsidize the arts to the extent that European governments did. It was thus up to private patronage—individuals, foundations, and even corporations—to make up the difference.

The Ford Foundation, which had been a leader in supporting the nonprofit performing arts with its backing of American composers and performers, expanded its US-wide arts investment considerably in the 1960s, funding regional theater and dance companies and committing several million dollars to help about twenty small "civic" opera companies increase the length of their short but regular seasons. Its largest commitment was a whopping $80.2 million matching grant program, designed to help sixty-one orchestras stabilize their finances and build endowments. Matching grants required the recipients to find new funders, expanding the universe of subsidizers. But that unearned income was not always easy to find. A Ford study in 1974 reported that of 166 organizations it had surveyed, half had failed to balance their budgets in 1970–71. Expansion—in principle a good thing because it enabled artists to make a more consistent living and institutions to improve their artistic quality by keeping ensembles together for longer periods of time—would also create institutional structures with built-in perils.

By the end of its first decade at Lincoln Center, City Opera had become a new animal. It was not simply bigger and more expensive, it had a different character. Its greatest strength had always been in its identity as an ensemble company, but the overnight recognition of Beverly Sills had given it star power for the first time. That change, while certainly welcome, threatened to diminish the character it had taken the company years to establish: the contract artists who sang big and small parts throughout the repertory; the debutant who was gradually promoted into bigger roles; the singers who worked tirelessly together to create operatic theater, with no one's name above the title. People had come for the operas; they didn't ask who was singing.

Now, Sills was its prima donna. And although she was very much in demand, other than at the Met, where Rudolf Bing did his best to pretend that she didn't exist, she remained a stalwart company member at City Opera, sometimes singing as many as three roles there during a single season and for much lower fees than she could command elsewhere. John White would organize the schedules so that each subscription had a Sills performance, ensuring that the subscriptions would sell out.

Sills also became a repertory driver, with new operas mounted to showcase roles she wanted to sing: *Manon* in 1968, and, as she became more interested in bel canto operas, works like *Lucia di Lammermoor*, Donizetti's three Queens (*Roberto Devereux, Maria Stuarda, Anna Bolena*) and *I Puritani*. Many of the productions were staged by Tito Capobianco, whom Sills trusted implicitly. Rudel was also keen to capitalize on the onstage chemistry of Sills and Norman Treigle, and did so in operas as different as Rimsky-Korsakov's *Le Coq d'Or* (in which Sills did a belly dance), *Faust*, and *Les Contes d'Hoffmann*. Rudel also worked to promote Treigle as a solo star, mounting Boito's *Mefistofele* for him in 1969, in a spectacular production by Capobianco that made the most of Treigle's lanky, spiderlike body, black-hued, hugely resonant voice and remarkable talents as a singing actor. In an elaborate costume and makeup that made him appear near naked, he leaped and twisted in a bravura display of demonic energy.

New singers continued to arrive, providing the City Opera audience with the potential discovery of a rising star. Some of the well-known artists who made their debuts between 1969 and 1978 include Carol Neblett, Johanna Meier, Richard Stillwell, José Carreras, Alan Titus,

Olivia Stapp, Justino Díaz, Diana Soviero, Pablo Elvira, Willard White, Catherine Malfitano, and Frederica von Stade. Most stayed for at least a few seasons, and many eventually moved on to the Met. In the years since City Opera's founding, the Met had gradually opened its doors to American singers, and the "second company" across the plaza became an excellent place for it to find them.

However, no singer other than Sills was able to reliably sell tickets. And in an interview years later, Rudel commented that, as a result of the Sills-and-Treigle phenomenon, "the ensemble idea began to lose its validity." Two singers identified as "superstars in our modest setting began to have a deleterious effect on the whole idea of ensemble. . . . Before, people had never asked who was singing; they were satisfied that what we would give them would be all right. Now, they were buying a Sills performance or a Treigle performance." And Treigle, an unhappy man, particularly when Sills's fame outstripped his, began to sing less frequently with the company; ironically, he said in an interview that he missed the old ensemble spirit. His last City Opera performances were in *Mefistofele* at the Kennedy Center in 1973. He died in 1975, an apparent suicide. City Opera was no longer truly an ensemble company, but with only two stars—or one—it wasn't a star company, either.

What's more, the move to Lincoln Center had diluted the company's identification with twentieth-century and American opera. Although City Opera would continue to present premieres, there were no more all-twentieth-century or all-American seasons. The company had nearly doubled the number of weeks it performed in New York each year, and, as a result, crowd-pleasers like *Carmen* and *Bohème* came to occupy a greater portion of the company's total performances, since contemporary works could not be counted on to sell more than two or three performances each. The repertory mix from season to season took on a new look: half standard repertory titles, half unusual or contemporary works, but with many more total performances of standards. Some of the nonstandard works were revived—particularly if they were Sills vehicles—but most of the twentieth-century titles vanished after one season.

Rudel, however, remained passionately committed to contemporary operas, noting in 1973 that he had produced fifty-six of them, thirty-two by Americans, since taking over the company. (In the next six years, he would produce half a dozen more.) And City Opera still boasted inventive theater, as well. Rudel, of course, cared deeply about the theatrical dimension of opera, and the two principal directors of his era were originals in different ways. Tito Capobianco's stylized stagings—balletic, and carefully planned down to the last gesture—were visually striking: *Opera News* praised his 1966 staging of *Don Rodrigo*, saying that "its unity and discipline made one think of Bayreuth," the home of Wieland Wagner's revolutionary minimalist productions. Capobianco often collaborated with the set designer Ming Cho Lee, whose abstract creations were an integral part of his staging concepts. Frank Corsaro, who had made his debut with City Opera's third production of *Susannah* in 1958, became well-known for his psychological insight into characters. His production of *Faust* in 1968 was a revelation: Corsaro turned a familiar war horse, usually staged as a static parade of favorite tunes, into a passionate human drama. With his production of Debussy's *Pelléas et Mélisande* two years later, a critic declared that he had restored the opera's "bloodedness." Corsaro was also imaginative in his use of media: in 1970, his production of Janáček's *The Makropulos Affair* ingeniously used projections and film to show the many incarnations of the 337-year-old Emilia Marty, all grippingly played by Maralin Niska; similar techniques made Korngold's haunting *Die Tote Stadt* in 1975 a surprise success.

Other aspects of the original People's Opera spirit remained as well. Though the top ticket price had crept up, at $8.95 in 1973 it was still only half what it cost to sit in a prime seat at the Met. (In today's dollars, $8.95 is $51, a steal when you consider that the top price for the New York City Ballet's regular repertory at Lincoln Center is now $175.) And for all the adventurousness of City Opera's repertory, the company also offered less-well-heeled New Yorkers—schoolteachers, civil servants, and the like—the opportunity to see *Carmen* and *La Bohème* for prices that they could afford.

But costs kept rising. In 1964, City Center's total budget had been $2.5 million. By 1972, both City Ballet and City Opera had dramatically expanded their seasons, driving up costs significantly—including inflation, the budget had multiplied to $11.5 million. With Baum gone, Rudel and John White had to assume the arduous work of fund-raising themselves. They proved capable at it and developed a number of connections: the Mary Flagler Cary Charitable Trust paid for *The Makropulos Affair* and continued as a City Opera supporter for many years; individuals like Ralph and Patricia Corbett also sponsored productions. Lawrence Deutsch and Lloyd Rigler, in addition to paying for the Los Angeles tour, gave the company $10,000 to record *Giulio Cesare*, and Sills had devoted patrons who paid for productions to be built around her. But while contributions—from foundations, government, and a patrons group, the Friends of City Center—made up some of the income gap, by the early 1970s, it had grown too large. City Center and, thus, City Opera were badly in the red once again.

Labor continued to play a role in the company's rising costs, as the players and singers tried to push toward economic parity with performers at the Met and some of the wealthier orchestras around the country. In addition to wage and benefit improvements, a constant issue for the orchestra was the number of workweeks they were guaranteed every year. Since the 1960s, the contract had included eleven additional guaranteed weeks beyond the regular New York opera season. In the past, those eleven required weeks of work were fulfilled when the orchestra played with the City Center Light Opera Company back at the Fifty-Fifth Street Theater during the spring and summer light opera and musical seasons. But the City Center Light Opera was folded in 1968, so City Opera essentially became a booking agent for the orchestra and often found itself obliged to pay the players anyway when no work could be found. The company wanted to cut back on the guarantee to help reduce its deficit. The orchestra, determined to win as close to a year-round income as possible, was not sympathetic.

In September 1973, when negotiations over a three-year contract renewal reached an impasse, the orchestra went on strike, forcing the cancellation of a sold-out weekend. In an interview, Beverly Sills stressed that this put the entire company in a precarious situation—a prolonged strike, she said, would mean the company's death. The strike lasted twenty-four days. When it was settled, the players had kept the extra eleven weeks, albeit with reduced payments for them in the second and third years of the contract.

City Opera's orchestra was not the only union to flex its muscles that fall: the New York Philharmonic and the dancers of the New York City Ballet also went on strike at around the same time. The labor strife was just one indication of the fiscal crisis among the arts organizations at Lincoln Center: the Metropolitan Opera, which was operating in the red, was forced to cancel both its new production of *Don Giovanni* and its annual series of summer parks concerts to make ends meet. The fragility of nonprofit arts institutions was becoming so pronounced that the public could hardly ignore it: the settlement of the City Opera strike was reported on page 1 of the *New York Times*. The paper editorialized about it as well, applauding the musicians for compromising and suggesting that it would have been "suicidal, as well as socially irresponsible for the musicians to have pressed their demand for an assured year-round income to a point that would have brought only total unemployment." But still, no one seemed to have a real answer to the problem, other than to call on government to fill in the gap. The *Times* editorial about the settlement concluded that "it is unfair for the community to expect musicians, soloists and other artists to go on indefinitely making economic sacrifices to hold down the heavy deficit of the New York City Opera and other centers of culture. More federal, state and city support is clearly in order for these civic adornments."

One voice came out of left field: Laszlo Halasz, in a letter to the editor of the *Times*, suggested that City Opera's bloated budget was a sign that it had lost touch with its roots. The misguided move to Lincoln Center, he contended, had put the company into competition with the Met, thereby upsetting the "healthful balance between musical and visual values" and running up a large deficit as a result of "unwarranted high expenditures for scenic effects." Halasz also noted that $9 was not a "popular price" for a ticket.

Halasz was not the only person to question whether City Opera's identity had been irrevocably compromised by the move uptown. With a more star-focused repertory, bigger productions, and forays into more grandly scaled, "Met-like" operas demanding larger forces, as well as works that required a deep bench of strong singers, had it become merely a cheaper version of the Met rather than something distinctive, a real artistic alternative house? In a Sunday *New York Times* Arts and Leisure column in 1975, the critic Dale Harris suggested that City Opera had done just that, citing its undercast productions of *Turandot* and *Die Meistersinger*, and pointing out that *Puritani* needed a quartet of great singers, not just Beverly Sills.

Rudel fired back in the *Times* against Harris, defending his productions and pointing out that City Opera continued to present the new and unusual works, which the Met did not. He also argued that, even if there was now some repertory overlap with the Met, "there was little or no audience overlap—City Opera had its own dedicated patrons who deserved the opportunity to see 'Turandot' or 'Meistersinger.'" The number of people who attended both companies was, as he put it, "insignificantly small." He further insisted that City Opera's work was done not for critics, but for its audience and singers, and for the advancement of the art of opera.

> This notion alone does not allow the indulgence of nostalgia for our youth, when everyone loved us because we were little and cute and ever so humble, when we constituted a challenge to no one and even our stars went unnoticed. Identities change and we can't go home again, nor do we want to.

City Opera had become a big operation, with a substantial, months-long presence in New York. It was next door to the Met and, by virtue of proximity and level of activity, invited comparison with the older, more traditional company. Rudel resented the implication that City Opera was still an upstart that could be dismissed and told to stay in its place; he felt that his artistic program could hold its own and that there was no reason for the company to curtail its ambitions. However, with the longer season and more performances of standard repertory, perhaps City Opera *was* starting to look a bit like a cut-rate Met.

One of the interesting details of Rudel's salvo is the idea that the two companies' audiences were distinct, and yet the two large houses were both selling well. However they perceived the company's identity, and whether they were drawn by price, loyalty, affinity for a particular way of producing opera, or Beverly Sills—in the 1970s, City Opera was still attracting its own audience. Artistically, it seemed, the company could have it both ways, ambitiously producing standard "grand opera" favorites while maintaining its artistic credibility and its status as a champion of unusual repertory and unknown singers. The only pressing issue was how to keep paying for it all.

Once again, the Ford Foundation, whose giving policies now included helping struggling arts institutions around the country build stability, stepped in to help City Center with its financial problems, first with a $1 million loan to help City Opera and City Ballet cover their deficits for 1972 and 1973, and then, in 1974, with a $5.3 million grant, to be distributed to the two companies over seven years. Much of the grant would have to be matched two-to-one with new funds from other donors, and if the original $1 million loan were matched, it would not have to be repaid. This would be the end of the line for Ford and City Opera, however. In the late 1970s, the foundation changed its focus and ceased its large-scale funding of arts.

Another stipulation of the grant was that City Center of Music and Drama would separate the assets of the opera and the ballet and create fund-raising boards for each of them. The structure that had worked when the enterprise was small was no longer tenable, now that the whole City Center budget (all constituents and both theaters) was approaching $17 million, with 80 percent of that going to the opera and the ballet. So, in 1975, City Center reorganized its structure, creating a board of governors, which would in turn create three separate boards: one each for the opera, the ballet, and the Fifty-Fifth Street operation. To the surprise of many, John S. Samuels, forty-one, a Texas businessman who had recently moved to New York after making a fortune in the coal industry, was elected chairman of the new City Center board—and subsequently, chair of the boards of both the opera and the ballet.

New sources of ample private money were what the City Opera and City Ballet needed, and Samuels, though he was not widely known, was thought to be in a position to help. A *Times* article announcing his appointment as chairman of the City Center board mentioned that his coal conglomerate, ICM/Carbonim, was said to have grossed more than $360 million in sales the previous year. Certainly his elaborate Manhattan town house and mansion on Long Island, lovingly pictured in the press, suggested that he had significant means. But Samuels was no Morton Baum, singularly devoted to the company and the art form; it seemed he was more interested in buying legitimacy for himself in his new town. He quickly began to shake things up at City Opera, calling for administrative changes—including doubling the staff—and clashing with Rudel.

In 1976, three years after the strike over its last contract, the orchestra walked out again; and again, the extra eleven weeks of guaranteed work beyond the New York season were raised as a key issue. This time, changes at City Center meant that the weeks were even less likely to be used. Earlier that year, CCMD, wanting to focus its attention on running the New York State Theater, had subcontracted out the management of the Fifty-Fifth Street Theater. When CCMD was still in charge of that theater, the City Opera musicians had been guaranteed employment playing for the dance companies that performed at Fifty-Fifth Street, but with the new arrangement, the dance companies could make their own choices about musical accompaniment. City Opera management was determined to trim back the cost of services that it didn't need, and this time, the company won: the settlement, after an eighteen-day walkout, converted the extra eleven weeks to a guaranteed payment that amounted to slightly less than it would have been under the old terms.

Yet money was still short: in the fall season of 1977, artists were making curtain speeches and passing the hat to the audience. The company, though still playing to a healthy 85 percent capacity, declared that it did not have the funds to put on the spring season for the first time since 1964. The spring season was eventually saved, though only after some cost-saving modifications were implemented and ticket prices were substantially raised.

But in the meantime, with the spring season in doubt, critics went out of their way to praise the company that fall: reviews lauded, among other productions, a *Figaro* that returned to "the true tragicomic spirit of Mozart," and a revival of Tito Capobianco's *Manon* production deemed to be as spectacular as it had been in its City Opera premiere in 1968, when "Mr. Rudel showed the world how to conduct the work even if your name wasn't Pierre Monteux [the gold standard for French opera]." There was also excitement in the press over a young Romanian soprano named Mariana Niculescu, "whose debut performance stood up to the rigorous measure of a soprano's technique, versatility and stamina"— Violetta in *La Traviata*. Other reports praised Catherine Malfitano as "the hit of the evening" singing the role of Liù in *Turandot*, and a "galvanizing" performance by the young bass Samuel Ramey in the title role of *Mefistofele*.

For Rudel, however, it was the beginning of the end. Samuels had already made an administrative move toward getting rid of him by trying to fire John White, who had been Rudel's right-hand man from the beginning of his tenure, in an effort to transform the company from what he saw as a mom-and-pop operation to something more corporate. Sills helped to block that action, but the writing was on the wall. Samuels, as it turned out, accelerated an idea that Rudel and Sills had discussed some years earlier: the possibility of the two of them sharing the general director post, with Sills eventually retiring from singing and taking over, while Rudel would be free to more actively pursue other conducting work. In January 1978, the two announced their plan to do just that, beginning in 1980.

The announcement, together with the known financial fragility of the company, provoked yet another think piece on City Opera's supposed identity crisis in the *New York Times*, this time by music critic Donal Henahan, who wrote, "Both financially and artistically, the City Opera is in such a disturbed and confused state that for the first time in many years, one can hear an ominous old question being asked in musical circles: Does New York really need more than one major opera company?"

Henahan concluded that the answer was yes, given City Opera's history of "enterprise and innovation," as opposed to the sclerotic Met, but he went on to point out that the company's much-celebrated focus on ensemble performance was no longer universally evident, a casualty of low fees and slim budgets. "Too often, one is left with the impression that getting the performance on and off the stage is the major concern of everybody involved. There sometimes seems to be no enforceable standard for vocal quality. Conducting has regularly been left in the hands of mediocrities or tired routiners." And so on—Henahan's implication was that no one was minding the store.

That artistic complaint would resurface over and over in the years to come. At City Opera, it had become almost a point of pride that the company could get a show up without a full stage rehearsal. Rudel had made his conducting debut, back in 1944 (a production of Johann Strauss's *The Gypsy Baron*) without any rehearsal at all; and a young conductor named Christopher Keene had done the same in 1970 with his debut conducting *Don Rodrigo*. In 1975, Rudel insisted, "Unless you really have adequate rehearsals, you are much better off without them. Of course, people have to be prepared before they go on, but you can work spontaneously this way." Many opening nights at City Opera, it turns out, were actually dress rehearsals.

The flip side of presenting exciting, unknown young singers is that those singers have less experience and need more rehearsal. And rehearsal time, particularly with an orchestra, is expensive. City Opera's practice of paying singers such low fees, furthermore, made it difficult to keep a cast together for the full run of an opera. Hastily implemented cast changes, in turn, could wreak havoc on an ensemble, rendering all of that expensive rehearsal time irrelevant. A repertory system with many titles in rotation can work inexpensively when members of the company are able to sing both small and large roles in different productions— but for City Opera, that was no longer the status quo. The ensemble structure that the company had built on Fifty-Fifth Street—when everyone was young and poor and eager, and the seasons were shorter—was harder to maintain on a grander stage, where the expectations were now exponentially higher. Audiences and critics had been tolerant of certain shortcomings during the days "when everyone loved us because we were little and cute and ever so humble," as Rudel had sarcastically described the company's past. No longer.

La Guardia, Baum, Morris, and Halasz had launched a People's Opera; Rudel, with help from the Ford Foundation, and with the move to Lincoln Center, had built it into a major institution. City Opera's distinctive repertory profile and its championship of young singers were both consequences of its poverty: it had made enormous virtues out of necessities. But that poverty—albeit less obviously grinding than it had been in the earliest years—was still central to its existence. And with the board unable to raise the money to make up its deficits, the company's year-to-year survival was a matter of continual speculation.

In December 1978, Rudel resigned, effective at the end of the spring 1979 season. The co-directorship idea was quietly scrapped; Sills would accelerate her retirement from singing and assume the helm alone. She, too, would inherit the wind.

CHAPTER 3

Beverly Sills Takes Over

IN JULY 1979, Beverly Sills became the fifth general director of the New York City Opera, succeeding Julius Rudel. It was an uncomfortable transition. When Rudel heroically assumed the leadership of the company in 1957, it was a young operation, on the margins of the American cultural scene and teetering on the verge of collapse. Over twenty-two years, he had built it into a large, nationally significant opera company, second only to the Met in activity, and his ideas and artistic vision were inextricably linked with it. Now housed at Lincoln Center, where it played for twenty-one weeks each year, and with an annual presence in Los Angeles, City Opera was a major force. It was also the biggest employer of young American singers anywhere, and especially valuable as a showcase for them, given its New York location.

Beverly Sills was the most famous American opera singer in the world. She was neither a conductor nor a man, which led some observers to question whether she would be up to the general director job. An American company had been led by a female opera singer only once before, and the precedent wasn't a good one: in 1921–22, Mary Garden's one-year directorship of the Chicago Opera lost $1 million and bankrupted the company. The circumstances of Rudel's departure, with the board chair, John Samuels, pushing to oust him, had sowed some ill will between the outgoing and incoming general directors. Rudel stayed on briefly, serving as principal conductor through the fall 1980 season, but his once-friendly relationship with Sills was blighted. Furthermore, as Sills would discover, City Opera's rocky finances required a perpetual balancing act. Would her celebrity be enough to set it on course for a stable future? And was she tough enough to deal with the inevitable difficulties that would arise?

Sills, like Rudel, was inextricably linked to City Opera: she was its most famous product. Tall, red-haired, and ebullient, she was a diva accustomed to getting her way and a populist who had happily appeared on television with Johnny Carson, Carol Burnett, and the Muppets. She had turned fifty in May and was winding up her singing career. Eager for her next act and ready to unleash her boundless energy in a new direction, she began her new job with plenty of ideas about how the company should move forward, and many of them involved change. Sills told the *New York Times*, "I sense now that our company needs to have its own face. Once, we did. I want to put it back on, that special face. Yes, American singers, American repertory, opera in English, but I'd also like to have a more adventurous repertory than we've had in the recent past."

The company appeared poised for a reset. Sills was determined to bring the fizz back to the City Opera by reviving its all-American roots. To achieve this, she laid out a bold agenda. First, she planned to build up a new generation of American star singers who might one day be able to draw audiences as she had. Second, she wanted to juice up the box office sales numbers with American operettas like Victor Herbert's *Naughty Marietta*—which had sold well during a two-week run the previous season—and musicals like *Sweeney Todd*, which had just premiered on Broadway. Sills's planned overhaul was also a canny branding move: by more explicitly characterizing itself as the "American" company, with red, white, and blue on its subscription brochures, City Opera could position itself for a national audience and draw even more fundraising support. Sills pointed out that City Opera was unique: the Met was an international house, San Francisco was the "Met West," and Chicago skewed Italian. With her grander aspirations, Sills contemplated changing the company's name to American National Opera.

But the world of American opera had undergone an enormous transformation since the founding of the New York City Opera in 1943. Dozens of opera companies had sprung up across the country. The 1950s had seen the birth of such powerhouses-to-be as the Lyric Opera of Chicago, the Dallas Opera, and John Crosby's innovative summer festival, the Santa Fe Opera, along with numerous smaller operations in cities from Louisville (the Kentucky Opera) to Toledo, Memphis, and Kansas City. In the 1960s, new companies were born in Seattle and the Twin Cities. Seattle specialized in Wagner's complete *Ring* cycle, presented over the space of a week, which no other company in the United States did, while the Minnesota Opera was launched with a mission of producing contemporary work. The San Diego Opera, originally founded as a means of importing the San Francisco Opera's productions, began presenting its own. In the 1970s, Virginia, Arizona, and Michigan all started companies; in Tennessee, after several years of preparation, the Nashville Opera was launched with a production of *Madama Butterfly* in 1981.

With the 1970s oil boom, a number of fledgling opera companies had appeared in Texas. Indeed, Texas had become an opera center, and the Ford grants of the 1960s and '70s helped expand smaller companies like the Fort Worth Opera. Most critically, the Houston Grand Opera, under the visionary leadership of David Gockley since 1972, was beginning to challenge NYCO's status as the leading champion of American works. Gockley, a Columbia Business School graduate and former aspiring opera singer who had taken over the company at the age of twenty-nine, had persuaded his board and audience early on that Houston should build and rehearse its own productions and cultivate its own singers rather than following the old-fashioned model in which an expensive Met star flew in for a few days to sing a performance or two. He also believed that living composers would excite audiences and keep the art form new, and he cultivated them as well. Gockley's ability to talk both money and civic pride with his backers would continue to pay off: in 1987, HGO would open a grand, expensive new home, the Wortham Center, with a large opera house and a smaller theater under one roof.

In many respects, these companies were the children of the New York City Opera. Some of the biggest ones, like Chicago and San Diego, still imported European stars, but City Opera's influence was unmistakable: the company had demonstrated that American singers, now emerging in increasing numbers from conservatories, could excel in major operatic roles, not just minor ones. And with so many new opera companies finding success, there were now a multitude of opportunities for American singers all around the country. For many of these young Americans, City Opera's coaching staff and ensemble system had helped to bridge the gap between conservatory training and professional work.

Here, too, City Opera's model had a profound influence on the world of American opera. By demonstrating the importance of supporting young artists during this intermediate stage in their careers, City Opera helped spur the creation of a new structure in American opera companies. Companies like Santa Fe, Houston, and San Francisco had all founded resident training programs for young Americans. These apprentice programs offered the singers stipends, coaching, and the opportunity to sing supporting roles and serve as covers for the stars. (Even the Metropolitan Opera would soon recognize the value of nurturing a stable of young singers; it launched its own young artist program in 1980.) In companies such as the Santa Fe Opera, apprentices also sang in the chorus, a neat and economical solution for singers and companies alike. San Francisco and Houston had also launched touring arms for their young artists, which gave them experience and widened the mother company's reach.

The regional companies operated on a far smaller scale than City Opera, usually offering only a few performances of each opera, and only one at a time. However, they paid well, which soon began to put great pressure on City Opera. Having gone for so long without any real competition for the young American singers it employed, the company still paid notoriously low fees. The lure of performing in New York City remained, but even so, singers who might otherwise have been inclined to stick around for the whole season now saw that they could earn a living elsewhere, making the prospect of building and maintaining an ensemble company all the more difficult.

Years later, Sills would say that she had no idea what she had gotten herself into. She was confident that she understood the fundamentals of producing opera, and as a member of the company for a quarter of a century, she was sure that she understood City Opera itself. "I knew the theater and the company backwards and forwards. Opera has no terror for me. I can light a show—I knew every special in the house." But as she would quickly discover, the balancing act of actually running a company was something entirely different from singing on its stage.

The challenges began immediately. For her very first season, she was faced with contract negotiations that were just as contentious as those of the two previous cycles, which had resulted in debilitating strikes. Despite the ongoing negotiations, the fall 1979 season began on schedule—but five weeks into it, the company called a lockout, concerned that if no deal could be reached with the orchestra and there was a strike, City Opera would be liable for the costs of the upcoming Los Angeles visit, which, as usual, was slated to begin as soon as the season in New York concluded. After a week, the two sides compromised, and the company went back to work.

Fund-raising would also present unexpected challenges for the new general director. Sills had expected Samuels, who had launched his tenure on the City Opera board with a substantial gift, to be a "sugar daddy" for the company. But by the spring of 1979, Samuels had experienced financial setbacks, causing him to scale back his philanthropy, and he would not have been likely to fill the gap single-handedly in any case. The 1978–79 season had run a deficit of nearly $900,000; the following year, Sills's first season, it would more than double. Sills herself would have to find the money to keep the company going.

In her autobiography, Sills wrote, "From the moment I took over, I found myself constantly in a life or death pursuit of money." The company owed vendors everywhere: at the height of the fall 1979 season, its advertising agency demanded immediate payment or it would stop placing ads. Sills became a one-woman hustler, hitting up all her friends and her husband's friends for funds. "Everyone I ever did a favor for—I called in all my chips." The connection with the company's longtime Los Angeles patrons was still strong: Lawrence Deutsch had died in 1977, but Lloyd Rigler remained Sills's devoted supporter and gave the company a $1 million challenge grant. (Rigler, apparently, still talked regularly to his deceased partner and reported that Larry wanted him to keep funding the opera.) Susan Woelzl, who had joined the company in 1975 and become its press director under Sills, remembers how Sills would leave on Tuesday mornings to fly around the country and return to the office on Friday morning, where she would open her handbag and dump a pile of checks on her desk. It was a grueling change for the once-pampered diva, and it kept her from being as hands-on as she needed to be in overseeing the company's artistic product. But it was up to her to produce the funds. In October 1980, the company put on a gala for Sills's farewell performance as a singer. The evening, with dinner and dancing, was built around act 2 of *Die Fledermaus*, with Sills singing Rosalinda and a cast of luminaries joining the fun—and balloons and confetti falling from the ceiling at the end. It raised a whopping $1 million.

But it wasn't enough. The company's operating expenses continued to climb—they would jump from $11 million in 1979–80 to over $15 million in 1981–82—and its deficit accumulated. "Finally, it dawned on me that moving out of City Center was a horrible mistake," Sills wrote. "At City Center, we were building one new production a year for $8,000. When we moved to Lincoln Center, we were immediately building two new ones a year for $65,000 each. Now, we were doing three a year, for $200,000 each." In the early 1980s, furthermore, inflation was driving up basic production costs significantly: three square feet of balsa wood, once $5, was now $40; men's high leather boots had gone from $30 to $300 (the company switched to rubber boots for the soldiers in *Carmen*). Keeping the State Theater clean, air-conditioned in the summer, and heated in the winter cost $40,000 per week on average, or about $2 million a year. Sills went to Mayor Ed Koch's office and persuaded Deputy Mayor Nat Leventhal, an opera fan himself, to authorize a $1 million budget line to help defray the costs of running the theater.

In the spring of 1981, Samuels resigned as chairman of the board. His financial misfortunes had been public knowledge for some time, and he had recently sold his East Side town house for $4 million to settle debts. Samuels had given up the chairmanship of the City Ballet board the previous summer but stayed on at City Opera, he said, to help with the leadership transition from Rudel to Sills. He was succeeded by Robert W. Wilson, an eccentric financier and opera lover who declared City Opera's financial situation "extremely grave but not without hope."

That spring season was the first Sills had planned in its entirety, and it offered a look at her artistic priorities. Perhaps the most striking new production was Janáček's *The Cunning Little Vixen*, in its New York stage premiere. This enchanting, bittersweet work, which celebrates the renewal of life in the animal world, even as humans grow old and die, was beautifully served by Maurice Sendak's storybook designs, directed with wit and pathos by Frank Corsaro and conducted by Michael Tilson Thomas, making his company debut. It starred Gianna Rolandi as the irrepressible Vixen, who torments chickens, falls in love (producing many more little foxes), and finally is killed by a poacher, all in an idiomatic English translation.

Sills also showcased Samuel Ramey that season in Verdi's early blood-and-thunder opera *Attila*. The powerful, handsome bass had been with the company for eight years, taking on the mantle of Norman Treigle and reinterpreting some of Treigle's signature roles in operas like *Mefistofele*, *Faust*, and *Les Contes d'Hoffmann*. Ramey's gifts had already taken him to major houses in the United States and Europe; his uncanny coloratura flexibility made him a natural for baroque and bel canto repertory, and in 1984, he would make his Metropolitan Opera debut as the Saracen king Argante in Handel's *Rinaldo*. In addition to promoting her current stars (the luminous soprano June Anderson sang *I Puritani* and *Lucia*, while the agile-voiced Diana Soviero got a new *Traviata*), Sills invited the renowned soprano Grace Bumbry to make her debut in *Nabucco*, another Verdi rarity.

But ticket sales were not encouraging for that spring season or the subsequent fall one, so at the end of the fall season, the company slashed its subscription prices by 20 percent for spring 1982, dropping the top ticket on weekends from $25 to $20. At the end of the Rudel years, Samuels had insisted on hiking ticket prices considerably, and Sills had done so again in order to raise operating capital. But she now declared what many both inside the company and out had come to feel: the prices were becoming too high for the People's Opera.

Furthermore, NYCO's subscription rate, the lifeblood of any performing arts company, had tumbled by more than half in the last ten years, to 30 percent. With that drop, the company had gone from filling 90 percent of its seats in 1973 to a projected 77 percent for 1981–82. What was different? One obvious change was that there was no Beverly Sills to drive the box office. When the star soprano sang 30 performances a year at City Opera, it was easy for the company to include one of those on every subscription series, ensuring healthy advance sales. Now there was no singer on the roster who could accomplish that feat, making it far more difficult for the company to sell its 160 performances in the State Theater. The Met, by contrast, had double that subscription rate and was still selling 90 percent of its capacity—even though, like City Opera, its top ticket price had more than tripled over the ten-year period, arriving at $60.

City Opera's price cut boosted both subscriptions and overall sales in the spring 1982 season, though revenue was still down. It also had the effect of building goodwill for the company's populist mission: a music publisher announced, for instance, that it would cut its rental fees to City Opera, and the songwriting duo Betty Comden and Adolph Green wrote a playful radio jingle for the company, advertising "High C's and low prices!" True to her Johnny Carson and Muppets persona, Sills excelled at making an informal, approachable sales pitch for the company: she even contributed some brochure copy puns such as "Feel like hell? Come to *Faust!*"—defying the stuffy, tuxedoed stereotype of opera.

But the artistic success of the 1981–82 season was more mixed: in May, the *New York Times* called the year's performances "ragged and unpredictable" and judged half of the eight new productions failures. One particular disaster was a production of Verdi's *I Lombardi* that Sills

had imported, sight unseen, from San Diego: it featured a drab collection of staircases, revolving dispiritedly on a kind of lazy Susan. On a more
positive note, the *Times* went on to say that the overall level of singing
at the company had risen, and it boasted a wealth of exciting sopranos,
including June Anderson, Faith Esham, Ashley Putnam, Gianna Rolandi,
Diana Soviero, and Carol Vaness, to say nothing of the luminaries of
other voice types, like Jerry Hadley, John Aler, and Chris Merritt.

The company's finances remained its most pressing problem, and
Sills was now beginning to realize that her constant begging trips and
fund-raising appeals were not going to be able to solve it anytime soon.
She was going to have to cut expenses. In March 1982, Sills called a
company meeting and made an emotional speech, laying out the company's cash flow problems, asking everyone to accept a wage freeze for
the following fiscal year, 1982–83. There was not enough income to cover
the $15 million budget, and Sills's fund-raising efforts could only do so
much. "I'm dancing as fast as I can," she told them.

A few years later, she would recall, "the people we owed money to
were coming out of holes in the walls. I took the books home and spread
them out on the dining room table, and my husband and I looked at them.
He immediately saw a $4 million deficit. We didn't have any money for
payrolls. He recommended that we put the company in Chapter 11."

Sills did not want to go down in history as the person who killed
the New York City Opera. She called on every source she had, including Lloyd Rigler, who agreed to cover the payrolls for seven weeks. Over
the next two years, Rigler would lend the company $3 million to keep
it solvent, eventually forgiving all the loans. But looking ahead that
spring, Sills knew that she did not have enough money to put on both
a fall and a spring season for 1982–83. She came up with a plan: beginning with the 1983 calendar year, she would combine the ten spring
season weeks (normally February through April) and the eleven fall
weeks (normally September through mid-November) into one long
stretch of twenty or twenty-one weeks, which would now run from July
through mid-November.

The number of performances would be only slightly reduced, but the
company would save on marketing and start-up costs. And by starting

the season in July, the plan offered a potential period of exclusivity when the company wouldn't have to compete with the Met. There were, after all, plenty of opera lovers who remained in the city during the summer—the People's Opera attendees, in theory, did not decamp for summer estates as the Met's patrons did. And the idea was not totally untested; the success of Lincoln Center's Mostly Mozart Festival, launched in 1966, had shown that there was plenty of appetite for summer classical programming. But the most immediate advantage was that shifting the company's first performances on the 1983 calendar from February to July would give Sills an extra few months of breathing room to raise more money.

The orchestra and chorus, however, were not pleased by Sills's plan. Their three-year contracts, signed after the 1979 strike, were coming to an end, and the orchestra in particular was aware that the Met's players had reached a favorable deal after a lengthy strike in 1980—not only were their wages increased dramatically, but each player's workload was reduced from five to four performances a week. Met players were now making a base rate of $624; City Opera players were at $535—for six performances a week. Parity with the Met seemed more unlikely than ever, and now City Opera was asking the orchestra to accept a one-year wage freeze and a new season configuration.

City Opera's musicians were particularly upset that this consolidation of seasons had been implemented without consulting their unions. The change meant a loss of (paid) rehearsal weeks and created a conflict with the regular summer employment that some players had been depending on for years to supplement their City Opera jobs. The orchestra union adopted a bellicose posture at first, refusing the wage freeze: "We've been subsidizing these arts organizations for too long," declared Lou Russo of the American Federation of Musicians. With tensions rising, the fall 1982 season—the company's last before the restructuring—looked to be in jeopardy. However, at the end of August, the orchestra decided to accept the freeze, given the company's precarious economic state. Len Leibowitz, its lawyer, said, "We don't want to take the blame for closing the opera house." The chorus, represented by the American Guild of Musical Artists (AGMA), said flat out that they needed the work. "We've got to have the fall, or we're dead," said Don Yule, a City Opera bass and the president of the Guild. The acceptance of the freeze, however, merely put the inevitable confrontation off for a year.

The fall 1982 season opened on a more positive note. One of Sills's priorities on becoming general director had been to tackle the State Theater's acoustics, which she called "just plain lousy compared to any of the world's great opera houses," even with the fixes that Rudel had secured when the building first opened. With a combination of foundation and City funds, a yearlong $5.3 million acoustical renovation, supervised by the acoustician Cyril M. Harris, had been completed over the summer. The porous ceiling had been filled in with a two-inch layer of plaster to help with sound leakage; the side walls of the theater and the proscenium had been rebuilt as convex rather than concave to scatter sound equally in the house, rather than focusing it and creating dead spots and echoes; and a large overhead reflector made of curved plaster was placed above the stage to help beam sound back down. New seating, made of acoustically friendly materials, was also installed.

Another positive development was that Sills had finally taken steps to get assistance with some of her responsibilities. She named conductor Christopher Keene to a newly created post of artistic supervisor, responsible for advising on repertory, productions, and casting, with a special emphasis on contemporary opera. In addition to supporting Sills in artistic planning and execution, Keene would also conduct a significant number of performances. (His title was subsequently changed to music director.) Sills had also begun upgrading and expanding the development department, with help from Rigler and an outside consulting firm, C. W. Shaver, so that the responsibility for fund-raising would no longer fall entirely on her shoulders.

The flagship new production that season was Hal Prince's "opera house" version of Leonard Bernstein's *Candide*, a smash hit that introduced soprano Erie Mills as the winsome Cunegonde and featured David Eisler as the earnest wanderer Candide along with the veteran John Lankston in the double role of Voltaire and the philosopher Dr. Pangloss.

Candide had premiered on Broadway in 1956, starring the young Barbara Cook, and Bernstein's sparkling score had turned this eighteenth-century satire by Voltaire into a thoroughly modern creation. But it received mixed reviews, with most of the criticism directed at Lillian Hellman's book, and closed quickly. In 1974, Prince directed a new, shortened version, also on Broadway, with a new book by Hugh Wheeler—and this time it was a hit, running for nearly two years.

For City Opera, the 1974 Broadway *Candide* was expanded into a two-act "opera house" version. Bernstein and conductor John Mauceri reinstated much of the music that had been cut, Wheeler wrote some new scenes, and a full orchestra was in the pit. Prince also restaged the production as a circus sideshow, with Voltaire as a carnival barker and the hapless characters dashing across continents and oceans while enduring war, earthquakes, prostitution, shipwreck, and innumerable other horrors, while nevertheless professing that "All is for the best in this best of all possible worlds." Erie Mills, tossing off the roulades of "Glitter and Be Gay," was a new City Opera star, and *Candide*, a hybrid American musical/operetta, had found a welcoming home in the opera house.

Like Rudel, Sills believed strongly that musical theater was a significant American art form, and she was even more eager than he had been to integrate pieces that had originally been written for Broadway into the opera house. She also had an eye on the box office: these more "popular" works were likely to sell tickets, and the success of *Candide* was a sign that she was on the right track. Even though it was a quarter of a century old, *Candide* remained a fresh, contemporary take on the operetta form, but Sills's other repertory-expanding venture, featuring more old-fashioned operettas like the 1920s-era pieces of Sigmund Romberg, was a blatant appeal to nostalgia. During her tenure, each of the fall seasons had opened with a week or two of operetta, with new productions of chestnuts like Romberg's *The Student Prince* and Robert Wright and George Forrest's *Song of Norway*, which adapted music by Edvard Grieg, and her own beloved showcase, the Viennese model of the form, *The Merry Widow*. The operettas, which were funded by the patron Leslie Samuels, did well at the box office and gave the company a chance to rehearse the fall repertory. However, they also had the effect of branding Sills as a purveyor of lowbrow entertainment, a label that would stick to her like a burr throughout her tenure and beyond.

The fall 1982 season also showed off a great deal of vocal talent. One event in particular demonstrated the company's deep bench of singers, especially sopranos. Carol Vaness, who had made her debut in 1979 and quickly became a company star, was onstage singing her first Violetta in *La Traviata*. She was running a fever, and when she got to the first "Gioire!" in "Sempre libera," the virtuoso showpiece that concludes the first act, she stopped the performance and announced she couldn't go on. "The whole orchestra gasped, and they brought the curtain down, and I went to my dressing room," Vaness recalls. "The cover was crying, she had never memorized the last act." Fortunately, Ashley Putnam, another young soprano and a regular performer with the company (she was scheduled to sing Ophelia in *Hamlet* the following night), was in the audience and had come backstage. "Beverly turned to her and said, 'Well, kid, you want to be a star?' Ashley said, 'Not if I have to sing "Sempre libera."' So Beverly said, 'OK guys, go get her a dress.'" After a brief intermission, the opera resumed with act 2, and Putnam, who had sung Violetta for her own City Opera debut in 1978, received enthusiastic ovations. When Vaness returned to sing the role a few weeks later, Sills sent her flowers. "She said, 'One word of advice—don't try to prove you can do this role, just go do it.' And I did."

In February 1983, NYCO announced the repertoire of its first combined season; it was to begin in July with a Puccini festival, headlined by the company's first-ever production of *La Rondine*. (The tagline was "Opera for a Song All Summer Long.") But all was not well. An attempt to use NYCO's now-empty spring weeks at the State Theater for a run of *Candide* in cooperation with the Broadway producer James Nederlander, a board member, had foundered when the orchestra would not agree to Broadway work rules, which mandate eight performances a week instead of the opera's usual six, and the use of only forty players instead of the full orchestra of sixty-nine. Even worse, the monthlong Los Angeles residency, which had been a staple of the company's schedule since 1966, was history. Lloyd Rigler had been the force behind the annual visit, but the new leadership of the board at the Dorothy Chandler Pavilion in Los Angeles had overruled him and decided that the 1982 visit would be City Opera's last: it wanted either to import a starrier ensemble or create an opera company of its own. (The board's ambitions eventually led to the founding of the LA Opera in 1986.)

Adding to City Opera's troubles, the one-year wage freeze that the unions had accepted the previous year was set to expire right at the beginning of the new season. The company started rehearsing on schedule in June, but the day before the opening night, the orchestra went on strike. Patrons who had not gotten the word that the opening night was canceled arrived on July 7 for a gala performance of *Turandot* only to find the players, in concert black tie and gowns, on a picket line instead of in the pit and notices posted on the doors of the New York State Theater.

Local 802 had decided to play hardball. Of particular concern was how much work the players would be guaranteed going forward, since the company's overall schedule appeared to be shrinking with the consolidation of the fall and spring seasons. Previous contracts had established how many weeks the orchestra would be paid for the regular New York seasons, a number that had risen as City Opera expanded its presence after the move into the New York State Theater. The most recent contract stipulated twenty-one weeks of regular season performances. In addition, the company still guaranteed an extra four "supplemental benefit" weeks, meaning that additional work would be found for the orchestra, or the company would pay the players $350 per week to supplement their unemployment benefits. These extra weeks were left over from the 1960s, when the orchestra regularly played for the light opera company for eleven weeks in the old City Center Theater. The light opera group had been defunct since 1968, and those weeks had been whittled down under successive contracts, but the union, determined to get its members as close to full-time work as possible, was unwilling to let them go altogether.

However, the company was now undergoing dramatic schedule changes, some of which were beyond its control. For its last full season, 1981–82, the orchestra had had a robust thirty weeks of work, including both performances and rehearsals, with twenty-two weeks of opera performances in New York and four in Los Angeles. But for 1983–84, the new July–November combined season would be just twenty weeks long. The Los Angeles residency was gone. The company had also made an annual visit to the Kennedy Center in Washington, DC, during the Rudel years, which Sills had replaced, starting in 1980, with tour dates at the Wolf Trap theater in Virginia, but that theater had burned down in 1982 and was still being rebuilt. The company thus had no tour commitments at all for the 1983–84 fiscal year, leaving only the twenty weeks of New York State Theater performances. Already in dire financial straits, the company's management now wanted to eliminate the extra "supplemental benefit" weeks from the contract, reasoning that it made no sense to pay for work that City Opera didn't have.

The orchestra wanted all the guarantees to stay in place and even fought for an increase. It also asked for much higher wage hikes than the $35 per week that City Opera's management said it could afford to pay. Aggressive labor tactics had worked for the Met Orchestra in 1980— among other things, they won a 35 percent wage increase over four years, and Len Leibowitz had represented the dancers of American Ballet Theater in 1982, winning substantial wage and benefit increases. In Leibowitz's view, holding firm in negotiations would push arts groups to expand their operations, leading eventually to year-round contracts. "If companies are mandated to pay," he told the *New York Times*, "they will find work and ways to pay for it."

The bitterness continued throughout the summer. The company canceled performances through mid-September and each side accused the other of using the impasse to scuttle the idea of the combined season. But the other unions did not fall into line with the orchestra's aggressive tactics: AGMA agreed to a new one-year contract and, along with the other unions, publically urged the orchestra to accept binding arbitration and make a deal so that the rest of the season could go on. Rigler was said to be a key factor in making sure that the company did not yield to the orchestra's demand for a large wage increase but held firm on its offer of 6.5 percent. "We have an unreasonable group of musicians," Rigler told the *Times*. "They just present their demands and then say, 'Go out and get another $3 million from Lloyd Rigler.' You have to work in relationship with what you can spend." As the People's Opera, he added, it was impossible have a $25 top ticket and pay what the Met does.

Finally, on August 29, 1983, the orchestra narrowly approved a settlement. The company won on wages, with the same 6.5 percent increase in each of the three years of the contract that AGMA had gotten for the chorus. The union held on to the guarantees, with the regular New York schedule weeks increasing from twenty to twenty-two and then twenty-three weeks, as well as additional "supplemental unemployment" weeks. However, under the new agreement, recordings, tours, and telecasts, which had not previously counted toward the guarantee, now would, and the company would be granted flexibility in using a reduced orchestra for commercial runs. The strike, which lasted a grueling fifty-four days, twice as long as the one in 1973, lost the company seventy-four performances and postponed several new productions and major revivals.

On September 21, 1983, City Opera finally opened its season with a charming new production of Massenet's *Cendrillon*, a company first. This enchanting fairy tale boasted not only Faith Esham, Erie Mills, and Delia Wallis, but also the first major US appearance of supertitles, which Lotfi Mansouri, the head of the Canadian Opera Company, had introduced earlier that year at his own company. Mansouri, who was frustrated that audiences missed much of the detailed direction that he put into a text-centric piece like *L'Incoronazione di Poppea*, had had a revelation while watching the subtitled *Ring* on television. "My wife, who is not a Wagner fan, said, 'Now I understand what's going on because of titles.' I said, 'Why can't we have the same thing in the theater?'"

Surtitles, as they were then known, were a natural fit for Sills's populist vision, since they could break the barrier of language that kept opera novices at bay. "Some critics accused me of turning opera into 'a lowbrow art form that anybody could enjoy,'" Sills noted proudly in her autobiography. Indeed, the titles were an enormous hit with the City Opera audience. The company immediately installed the system for all its non-English operas, and eventually for English ones as well. Titles were quickly adopted by other opera companies around the United States. The only holdout was the Metropolitan Opera, where James Levine famously said that titles would be introduced over his dead body. (It did not come to that: Met Titles debuted in a special seat-back configuration in 1995. When the Santa Fe Opera rebuilt its outdoor theater in 1998, it also installed seat-back titles.)

Another major event was the New York premiere of Handel's *Alcina* conducted by the historical performance expert Raymond Leppard and starring Carol Vaness, who had been singing for the company for several years at that point. A decade and a half earlier, Handel's *Giulio Cesare* had made Sills a star at City Opera; here was just such an opportunity for the company to showcase Vaness, and perhaps create another star. She excelled in the title role of the lovesick sorceress, and her costars also shone: Erie Mills in the high-flying coloratura role of Morgana, and D'Anna Fortunato, making her debut as the enchanted knight Ruggiero. But things had changed since Sills's day, when City Opera was the only game in town for an American singer. Within a year, Vaness was swept up by the Metropolitan and would never return to City Opera.

The company also introduced another new American opera into its repertory, presenting the New York premiere of Carlisle Floyd's *Of Mice and Men*, which was directed by Frank Corsaro and conducted by Christopher Keene. This opera, based on the tragic Steinbeck novella about a pair of migrant ranch hands—the stalwart George and the mentally disabled Lennie—marked another success for the company. Like Floyd's earlier *Susannah*, *Of Mice and Men*, with its poignant characters, would turn out to be one of the rare American operas of the 1950s, '60s, and '70s that had a life beyond their premieres.

There were low points as well. In September, Gilbert V. Helmsley, who had designed the lighting for dozens of City Opera productions and had been named production supervisor for the company in 1981, died of cancer at forty-seven. And it must have galled the City Opera orchestra when the Met, on the eve of its October 22 Centennial Gala, announced an early and peaceful settlement to its orchestra labor negotiations, including significant pension increases. After the bitter battle, the City

Opera contract settlement had been widely considered a loss for the orchestra and a win for management. On top of that, both the company and the audience seemed to harbor lingering resentment over the orchestra's aggressive tactics, which had led to many lost performances—on opening night, the orchestra was booed. And now, without having to strike, the Met orchestra had secured a guarantee of forty-four weeks of employment, including five weeks of vacation, and eight weeks of supplemental employment benefits, effectively a year-round contract. The Met, presumably, could afford it: to celebrate its significant birthday, it had raised $100 million.

Still, labor peace meant that the 1984 season, which, since 1983 had been curtailed by the strike, would be the first complete one in the new July–November configuration, could go on as planned, albeit with a few changes from the original repertory. New productions of Puccini's *La Rondine* and *The Mikado*, which had been planned for the previous season but were canceled because of the strike, were reinstated. This meant the company had to mount eight new productions in twenty weeks, jamming more stage rehearsals into the already packed schedule. With a nod to the company's fortieth anniversary, every seat in the house for the July 6 opening-night performance of *The Barber of Seville* cost $2.40—the 1944 price. Single tickets for the rest of the season were more conservatively discounted, ranging from $5.50 to a top price of $35.

And the audiences came. When the dust cleared, the season had significantly outperformed expectations, selling at 86.5 percent of capacity overall, closer to the highs of the halcyon early 1970s. Half of the 136 performances sold out. *La Rondine* was a surprise hit; *Lakmé*, starring Gianna Rolandi, sold out; and a new *Carmen* directed by Frank Corsaro and grittily updated to the period of the Spanish Civil War, with Carmen as a Loyalist peasant and Don José as a Fascist soldier, also did well. Sills's commitment to American musical theater, which had been so successful with *Candide* two years earlier, continued to pay off: a new production of Sondheim's *Sweeney Todd*, directed by Hal Prince, with Timothy Nolen in his company debut, was a huge hit, selling out thirteen performances. (*Candide* was also back, packing the houses for a one-week run of performances in July.) Perhaps most surprising was the success of the New York premiere of Philip Glass's *Akhnaten*, a "portrait opera" about the Egyptian pharaoh, which sold out all four of its performances in advance. Every opera not sung in English was titled, and surveys reported that 96 percent of the audience was in favor.

The combined season, originally planned as a desperate tactic to stave off disaster, had actually turned out to be a winner. And then, still riding high on the much-needed success, City Opera announced in November that Lawrence A. Wien would give the company $5 million to mount multi-week runs of Broadway musicals in the State Theater during the February–April slot that had once been City Opera's spring season period. The first would happen in 1986, with one in each of the four subsequent years. This would significantly increase the company's activity, filling more of the weeks guaranteed in the orchestra contract. Furthermore, Sills planned to cast the musicals with opera singers rather than music theater performers, which meant that the Wien grant would provide additional work for the company's singers as well. On the whole, with other fund-raising efforts also picking up and robust ticket sales holding steady, City Opera was not only operating in the black—it was steadily reducing its accumulated deficit, which had reached $5 million in 1982 but was now closer to $1 million. For the first time since Sills had taken over, the year-end audit of 1984–85 did not include the auditor's reservations about City Opera's future ability to operate as a "going concern."

Sills was delighted to have contradicted the naysayers who expected her to fail. She had successfully translated her charisma into fund-raising acumen and her Jewish mother persona into an effective management style, which many of her staff members would later recall with enormous affection.

Mark Weinstein, a twenty-eight-year-old Harvard Business School graduate, had spent several years working in corporate marketing and management consulting when he took a finance job at City Opera in 1983. "I had studied organizational design at Harvard, and this organization was exactly what you would never design," he says.

It was a wheel with Beverly Sills in the center, and spokes going out to almost every single person in the organization. Ordinarily, it wouldn't work, but it worked with Beverly. She was in there at 7 AM every morning, before everybody else. She made a pot of coffee. We'd all float in at 8:00 or 8:15 and we would all end up in her office, getting coffee, talking together. It was a kaffeeklatsch.

Sills's office was a homey oasis in the bunker-like State Theater basement, filled with chintz-covered love seats, mementos, and knick-knacks, and, as a bit of trompe l'oeil, a big picture of the ocean view from the window of her house on Martha's Vineyard. "We all loved Beverly," Weinstein recalls. "She was inspiring. It was not only her personality, but her dedication. She always put the company first."

Weinstein was also impressed with Sills's business acumen. One example was her ability to estimate the cost of a new production instantly, which she often did in meetings.

She'd say, okay, how many choristers? And someone would say, thirty-six. She'd turn to the wig person and ask how many changes for the chorus? He'd say four for men, three for women. Then, what size orchestra? Seventy-one but four doublers. We would go through this, and I would be adding up what each one of these things would cost. I had my HP12C, a sophisticated little calculator, and I would be pounding away as everyone was calling out numbers and changes back and forth. Then at the end, Beverly would turn to me and say "So, about $1.2 million." I would say—"Wait, Beverly, I'm not done," and I would keep cranking for another three minutes and come up with $1,194,018. She knew every dollar. She would have been an amazing businesswoman. If she hadn't had a great voice, she would have been the CEO of Macy's.

Sills later said that she took the job because she thought that the company needed her. She and Rudel were its public faces, and if Rudel was going to step back, she had to step forward, or there would be no one to fill the void. In addition to bringing the company back from the brink with her fund-raising and business abilities, she was determined to change the public image of City Opera. While many had come to see it as a struggling competitor to the Met, Sills hoped to recast this unfavorable comparison as a strength by encouraging the perception of City Opera as a "feeder" company, building on its reputation for championing young American singers. "Our singers went on to other great companies and that's what we were training them for. That was my point—as opposed to giving the public the impression that we were losers; that every time we developed a great talent we lost it." In her view, City Opera was incubating talent and she was the "mother hen."

Even if many of the singers who came up at City Opera ultimately departed, Sills recognized that recruiting and developing them could still be enormously beneficial. Despite the company's limitations, she hoped that at least some of the singers would stick around long enough to help build the company—a few, perhaps, would even attain fame and become the kind of box office draws that she had been. Competing for singers with the Met and the regional companies, both of which paid considerably better fees, was difficult—but Sills, having been a singer herself, was well-situated to figure out how to identify, support, and thereby retain talented singers. Often, she drew on her own experiences. For example, in her early years, the chance to sing dozens of performances of a role in a concentrated period with a traveling opera company had been formative for her. Thus, one of her first initiatives upon taking over as general director was to found the National Company, a bus-and-truck tour of fledgling artists that took a single opera on the road. Sills continued the company's open audition policy, and singers found her to be an enormously supportive champion, skilled at spotting talent and ready to promote young artists.

Gianna Rolandi, a coloratura soprano who bloomed at City Opera during Sills's tenure, considered her "my teacher, my coach, my psychiatrist and finally my friend. She brought back some of her greatest and most successful productions for me, and was my biggest cheerleader and fiercest critic." Rolandi's later decision to take a job overseeing the young artist program at Lyric Opera of Chicago was, she says, a way to honor what Sills had done for her.

Carol Vaness was a Sills discovery—Sills had actually recruited Vaness even before she took over the company. In 1978, Vaness, then twenty-six, was covering the role of Amelia in *Un Ballo in Maschera* at the San Francisco Opera, and Sills, who was singing *Puritani*, heard her in a cover rehearsal. "She came up to talk to me, and asked if I sang Mozart, and if I would like to sing for Mr. Rudel, because City Opera was doing a new production of *La Clemenza di Tito.*" Sills got the money to send Vaness to Los Angeles, where the company was performing its annual residency, to audition for Rudel, who immediately tried to hire her to sing the Countess in *Figaro* the following day—the scheduled soprano was sick. Vaness passed on the Countess but took the offer of Vitellia in *La Clemenza di Tito* for the following fall, even though she did not know the whole role, only the character's big aria, "Non più di fiore."

By the time Vaness made her debut with three performances of *Clemenza*, Sills was in charge. "She started to put me in a lot of things—she took somebody out of Donna Anna because she thought it would be a good role for me." Over the next four years, Vaness became a City Opera fixture, singing nearly a dozen roles, from Antonia in *Les Contes d'Hoffmann* and Leila in *Pearl Fishers* to standards like Violetta in *La Traviata*, Gilda in *Rigoletto*, Mimi in *La Bohème*, and the Countess in *The Marriage of Figaro*. "She kind of took me under her wing, and she would tell me things like, 'If a tenor comes over to you, and he's too short, just bend your knees.' It sounds funny, but it's really good advice. No one ever said that to me before." Sills was a consistent, supportive presence for Vaness, and would continue to be until she left for the Met in 1984. "She came to every performance, and sat in first ring, in the first seat on right hand side. If anything was wrong, she'd ask, 'Is something wrong?' But she also knew how to leave you alone."

While Sills was especially comfortable helping young singers of her own voice type, she also mentored non-sopranos. Mezzo Joyce Castle auditioned for Sills in 1982 and was hired on the spot to sing Katisha in *The Mikado* the following season. *The Mikado* was lost to the strike that year, so Castle made her debut in a small speaking role in *The Merry Widow.* "I didn't care, I was thrilled to be there," Castle said. She was on a weekly contract (at $260.10 a week), responsible for eleven roles, of which she performed only *Merry Widow* (the others were covers and roles lost to the strike). But the following year, she was very busy, singing forty-four performances of roles like Mrs. Lovett in *Sweeney Todd* and the Old Lady in *Candide* and covering numerous others. And there were more opportunities every year, many of them in unconventional operas, like Baba the Turk in *The Rake's Progress*, and Fata Morgana in *Love for Three Oranges*. Experiences like these helped Castle develop a specialty in modern and unusual repertoire. "Beverly gave me every good mezzo role for my type that came across her desk," she says. In the 1985 season, Castle sang six different roles, and her pay rose to $600 a performance.

While Sills would work to distinguish City Opera from the Met, comparisons were inevitable. She had, after all, inherited a repertory company structure, with daily performances and multiple operas being performed in rotation. Across the plaza, the Met operated under the same basic system but with about four times the budget. Over the years, City Opera had become adept at doing more with less—lower fees, fewer rehearsals, cheaper sets and costumes. The orchestra's regular agitation for a better living wage—particularly in the light of successful campaigns by symphony orchestras elsewhere in the country—always ran up against the fact that City Opera was, for all its activity, by design a shoestring operation.

To be successful with this model, City Opera's employees needed to go all out—and under Sills, they did. The sheer level of activity—136 performances of eighteen operas over twenty consecutive weeks in the New York State Theater in 1984—demanded a breakneck pace and split-second timing. Unlike the Met, Sills knew, City Opera could not rely on star power to sell out performances, so she continued her strategy of spreading runs of operas over multiple weeks rather than concentrating them in a short period of time. This allowed for word of mouth to build sales. For the most part, no opera would be repeated within any given week under this system (musicals and operettas were the exception—because they were much easier to sell, they were scheduled in continuous one-week runs). In most weeks, there were eight performances of eight different operas, with matinee and evening shows on both Saturday and Sunday. Frequently, there was a new opera opening every week.

This required a tight schedule for the stage crews, particularly since they did not work overnight. Chuck Giles, who served as the company's technical director for two decades, describes what it was like under Sills:

> We did twenty operas in twenty weeks. It was an endurance strug-
> gle. We came in at 8 in the morning, and had four hours to work;
> there would be a show onstage when we came in, so the first thing
> was removing that show, and loading in a brand new production or
> a revival. The meal break was at 12 (union rates meant the cost was
> double if we worked through a meal, so we rarely did), and then we
> were back at 1 pm for a rehearsal. Rehearsal would last three or three
> and a half hours, depending on the opera. Then we would do the
> changeover for the evening performance: our goal was one and a half
> hours to change everything—thirty drops [hanging scenery], ground
> cloth, deck [set floor], and focusing over a hundred lights. Dinner was
> from 6 to 7, and maybe an additional half hour of work if it was a
> really big show. Half hour call was at 7:30, the performance was at
> 8. We'd finish between 11 and 12 and come back the next morning
> at 8 and do it all over again.

Giles and the crew regularly worked ninety-hour weeks during the season; by 1985, the one official dark day was Monday. The runs of musicals or operettas, which became a regular feature under Sills, meant that
the evening performance show was always the same, making for fewer
changeovers. This gave the company a chance to hang six or seven other
opera productions without expensive extra calls and more stage time to
prepare the upcoming repertory.

The repertory system meant intensive work for the artists as well.
Joseph Colaneri, who was twenty-seven when he joined the company as
chorus master in 1983, was thrown directly into preparation for what
was supposed to be the first combined July–November season and had
to learn a pile of scores. New productions got time; revivals did not.
"We were not working with a luxurious amount of rehearsal," Colaneri
says. For a standard repertory revival, like *La Bohème*, he would get just
an hour of music rehearsal before the staging. Sometimes, there was only

a piano dress rehearsal and an orchestra sitzprobe (an unstaged run-through of the whole opera) in the pit and no final dress rehearsal. "So the first time you put the opera together was opening night," he says. "It taught everybody a lot—you had to know your stuff. You had to hit the ground running. For a young person starting out, having to be at the top of your game in that kind of quickie professional environment is [instructive]. Either you are going to survive, or you are not. You need energy, you need enthusiasm, you just need to do it. I loved it."

Conductors, too, had to deal with the breakneck pace and time constraints—orchestra rehearsal time was expensive and strictly regulated under the contract. Colaneri remembers a conductor who was given three hours for a *Butterfly* sitzprobe. "I was his assistant, and he turned to me, and said, 'You realize that if I stop for anything, I won't finish it? Including the orchestra's break, I have exactly the time to play it.'" Furthermore, the company's contracts with its various unions sometimes had conflicting or incompatible provisions—there was, for example, a mandatory break for the orchestra that came at a different point in the rehearsal than the chorus's mandatory break, further complicating rehearsal scheduling.

As it had from the beginning, the company continued to maintain a cadre of weekly artists, some right out of school, who would sing covers and small roles in different operas for a weekly fee. Some would move up in the ranks and become per performance singers, as Joyce Castle did, combining their work at City Opera with featured or starring roles at other companies. Others would remain on weekly contracts long term. One notable group of singers, including James Billings, William Ledbetter, and Don Yule, stayed put at the company for many years, singing all the low-voice comprimario and featured parts—and covering others. Such singers, along with the resident stage directors, stage managers, and backstage staff, became the company's institutional memory, making it easier to revive productions quickly and with less rehearsal. Beth Greenberg, who joined the company as resident stage director in 1989, explains:

There's a collective memory that develops in a repertory company, where people tend to come back, from season to season, from the makeup artists, to hairstylists, costume people, running crew, stage managers, directors, conductors, singers, who know the shows. As much as a repertory company tries to document a show with films, blocking guides, production guides, and stage management paperwork, there is just stuff that lives in someone's memory about a show. And if it's a good show, it sticks.

Physical conditions were also challenging. Rehearsals took place in the lower concourse of the State Theater. Orchestra readings were in a room that musicians knew to be "totally dead"—with unresonant acoustics. Vaness remembers musical rehearsals in tiny storage rooms, with a piano squeezed in and boxes piled on top of it, and for staging, two big cinder-block rooms that were always freezing. New productions might eventually move up to the big rehearsal room on the fifth floor, the so-called Balanchine room, but revivals stayed below. For her first Antonia in *Les Contes d'Hoffmann*, Vaness recalls that she was shown key parts of the staging in advance, but she never walked on the set before the opening night.

The lack of stage rehearsal sometimes had hilariously calamitous results: when Jerry Hadley made his 1979 debut in *Lucia di Lammermoor*, he managed to get his scabbard stuck in the rungs of a chair, which he then dragged behind him. He then inadvertently set the plume of his hat on fire and suffered painful jabs from some unexpected swords—all during a single scene. (When the curtain went down, Hadley got a round of guffaws from the company, as well as from Sills, who said, "Don't worry! We'll talk!")

Sills's plan for the 1985 season was a celebration of bel canto—her own specialty—making the point that her young singers, like Gianna Rolandi, Erie Mills, Faith Esham, and Judith Forst, were perfect for the repertory and, most critically, that she at last had a sufficient number of appropriate tenors—John Fowler, Barry McCauley, Richard Leech, Gran Wilson—to put on and cover five such operas at the same time (bel canto tenors are a much rarer species than bel canto sopranos). Verdi's *Attila* was revived to showcase Samuel Ramey. Also on the schedule were a new production of the musical *Kismet*, another Wright and Forrest adaptation, this one with music by Borodin, and a Maurice Sendak–designed production of Prokofiev's *Love for Three Oranges* from Glyndebourne. A highlight was the New York premiere of Dominick Argento's comedy *Casanova* (originally titled *Casanova's Homecoming*), a witty piece about the eighteenth-century libertine whose story featured a female singer disguised as a castrato and Casanova's plot to swindle a rich, deranged old lady that required a gondola ride on a Venetian lagoon in the middle of a hurricane.

And then, on Monday, September 2, Labor Day, the company suffered a blow that was as unexpected as it was devastating. Several boys playing with matches in Passaic, New Jersey, started a fire that engulfed an industrial complex—among the destroyed buildings was the warehouse where New York City Opera stored its costumes. The costumes for the current season's repertory were at the State Theater, but everything else was gone: over ten thousand costumes for seventy-eight operas, all the "stock"—shoes, gloves, corsets, hoops, petticoats, armor, uniforms, and the like—plus bins for storage and transport, sewing machines, washing machines, and other essential items. The losses included costumes for recent company hits: the Sendak animal outfits for *The Cunning Little Vixen* and Judith Dolan's cartoon-inspired ones for *Candide*. Famous City Opera classics, like the Donizetti *Queen* operas, were also gone. Many were irreplaceable, given the rising costs of labor and materials. The costumes for *Mefistofele*, which was on the schedule for 1986, featured intricate embroidery and other special effects. They had cost $75,000 when they were made in 1969; an initial estimate to re-create them after the fire came to $400,000.

The total loss was first estimated at $10 million and later adjusted upward to $14 million. The company was underinsured and thus received only $1.5 million. Sills immediately launched a $5 million Fire Emergency Fund drive. The need was urgent: seven of the destroyed shows were scheduled for the following season. Sills and her deputies began to reconsider the 1986 repertoire and ultimately canceled two planned new productions, Philip Glass's *Satyagraha* and Puccini's *Il Trittico*. They were able to rent costumes for two of the revivals, leaving a total of nine productions for which costumes had to be created. Other opera companies offered help. The Metropolitan donated several productions that it was discarding, and once the season ended, Joseph Citarella, the head of City Opera's wardrobe department, traveled to the Netherlands Opera and the Royal Opera in London to collect more costume donations. In London, Citarella was shocked by the stark differences between a state-subsidized company and his own. City Opera always cannibalized its own productions, taking pieces from one to use in others; the Royal Opera built every production's costumes from scratch—shoes, underpinnings, and all—and never touched any of it until the show went back onstage.

Back at City Opera, Citarella and the costume shops figured out how to use less expensive materials to re-create iconic costumes from the company's past while repurposing the donated costumes as creatively as possible. For example, Citarella made slight changes to the chorus costumes for Amsterdam's *Manon Lescaut* and put them into Romberg's *The New Moon*, which is set in eighteenth-century New Orleans, along with some *Traviata* skirts from the Met. Much of Amsterdam's "rag clothes"— that is, clothing for the poor, which conveniently looks the same in any period—were used for *Don Quichotte*.

Mark Weinstein, the company's chief financial officer, took a more optimistic view of the fire. "It was devastating—and the best thing that ever happened. Some of the costumes were 40 years old, used once and pristine, from an opera that no one wanted to revive; others had been used nearly every year for 20 years, and were threadbare." Between the insurance settlement and the fund drive, which exceeded its $5 million goal, thanks in part to Sills's idea to have donors sponsor individual *Vixen* costumes, the company was able to "replace an aging inventory with cash." The Costume Replacement fund became an asset that remained on the books for years.

Indeed, despite the fire, New York City Opera's fortunes were still on an upward trajectory in 1986. Sills had developed an artistic formula that seemed to be working for audiences and critics, and the single-season format had proven efficient. The company's public image was no longer overshadowed by financial peril; instead, it was again becoming known for its lively repertory mix, its innovations (such as surtitles), and its American singers. With its quick response to the fire, that calamity, rather than one more trial of Job, became a demonstration of the company's pluck, resilience, and can-do spirit.

City Opera was also beginning to expand its presence. In February, the company mounted the first of the series of musicals presented outside the regular season with funding from Lawrence Wien, *Brigadoon*. (Sills had hoped for *Carousel* but was unable to secure the rights). Not only was the five-week run successful at the box office; it added valuable workweeks for the orchestra and chorus. Furthermore, the company had acquired two weeks of touring work in June, before the opening of the summer season: one each at the rebuilt Wolf Trap theater, which had reopened in 1985, and a new venue—the Saratoga Performing Arts Center. The Metropolitan Opera had announced that it would no longer tour after 1986—the expense was too great—and City Opera hoped to step into the vacuum. Already, a visit to the new performing arts center in Orange County was set for January 1987, as was a week in Tampa Bay. All of this would increase the company's activity to thirty weeks in 1986–87, up from a low of just twenty-one weeks a few years earlier in 1984–85.

More national exposure came through the New World Records recording of the company's *Candide*, which won a Grammy in 1986, and the November telecast of the production. The company's singers were handsomely showcased that season in a festival of French repertory— Jerry Hadley in *Werther* and *Faust*; Faith Esham in *Pearl Fishers* and *Cendrillon*, Samuel Ramey and Victoria Vergara in *Don Quichotte*. The company also continued its focus on new works with its twentieth world premiere: *X: The Life and Times of Malcolm X* by Anthony Davis—the subject generated some controversy but the opera sold out all four of its performances. Best of all, in June, the orchestra ratified a new three-year contract without a work stoppage. And, providing some help with the bottom line, the company received a financial windfall: the air rights above the City Center Theater on Fifty-Fifth Street, now used primarily for dance, had been sold, and City Opera's share was $3 million. The sum became a working capital reserve fund, which could be used to provide unrestricted cash for operations, but had to be replaced by the end of the fiscal year.

The company seemed to have found its equilibrium. Through the next two years, Sills maintained the repertory mix that she had established. There were new productions of American operettas, like *The Desert Song*, and revivals of the Viennese ones. Classic City Opera shows were brought back: *The Ballad of Baby Doe*, not seen for twelve years, returned with Faith Esham in the role made memorable by Sills many years earlier, and *Mefistofele* again worked its devilish magic, this time with John Cheek writhing in the title role.

Contemporary opera remained in the mix, though not always as successfully as *Akhnaten* and *X*. After the company commissioned composer Jay Reise's first opera, *Rasputin*, the turgid piece fell flat at its 1988 premiere, despite Frank Corsaro's nudity-laced staging. The previous year had seen the better-received New York stage premiere of Oliver Knussen's lively *Where the Wild Things Are*, with designs by Sendak that brought his famous children's book playfully to life. Chuck Giles remembers the orchestra dress rehearsal of *Wild Things* as being a little livelier than he might have wished: after the fire-breathing dragon shot a much longer flame than it was supposed to, a prop person pedaling a boat swerved frighteningly toward the orchestra pit to avoid the flame; one of the twice-life-size Wild Things tripped over its giant feet and fell through a drop; and a cascade of mistakes left the singer playing Max, who was supposed to be flying onto the shoulders of a Wild Thing, hanging instead, "like a paratrooper in a tree," and swearing at the stagehands. The rehearsal was open, with public school students and Guild members in attendance, and, says Giles, "They had the best day of their lives."

By contrast, the Metropolitan Opera was withdrawing from contemporary work. While it had never been a particularly noted champion of the new, the company had commissioned some operas in honor of its centennial in 1983. But in 1987, it canceled one and postponed another indefinitely. The latter opera, John Corigliano's *The Ghosts of*

Versailles, would not see the stage until 1991, when it would become the Met's first world premiere in a quarter century. (Philip Glass's *The Voyage* followed in 1992.) Bruce Crawford, who had become general manager of the Met in 1985, was moving the company toward operas that could fill the house, pointing out that the Met's large theater was financially and artistically unsuitable for anything but popular, large-scale spectacles and that influential donors were unexcited about contemporary opera.

In addition to its restored financial health, City Opera began to see the critical response to its productions improve as well in the late '80s, with positive words for many of the singers and stagings and less carping about productions looking and sounding slapdash and under-rehearsed. Such complaints did not go away altogether, of course—and Christopher Keene, who had gotten his share of unfavorable notices, left the music director/principal conductor post after the 1986 season. He was succeeded by Sergiu Comissiona, known as an orchestra builder from his time at the Houston Symphony.

Work outside the regular season also continued. The annual spring musicals played even longer runs, with eight weeks of *South Pacific* in 1987 and six of *The Music Man* in 1988. The preseason visits to Wolf Trap and the Saratoga Performing Arts Center went on as well, and in 1987, City Opera was named a "resident company" at SPAC, along with the New York City Ballet and Philadelphia Orchestra. A special endowment was established with a donation from the H. Schaffer Foundation (whose trustees included Lawrence Wien) to help cover the cost of paying the company. In December 1987, City Opera—225 strong—went to Taipei, Taiwan, to open the new performing arts center there. The musicals and tour fees helped to keep the company's income stream from performances steady at about $12.5 million.

Fund-raising was also steadily increasing, keeping pace with the rise in operating expenses. The development department had been expanded and professionalized, but much of the fund-raising was still attributable to the indefatigable efforts of Sills and her enduring celebrity appeal. At a board meeting in April 1987, Lloyd Rigler inquired how much of the fund-raising Sills was personally responsible for. The answer was about half of it. And while the operating budget continued to climb, reaching $23.5 million in 1988–89, the company was still managing to run a modest surplus every year. Although the board occasionally floated the idea of an endowment campaign, none was ever undertaken, but thanks to the costume replacement fund and the air rights windfall, City Opera had eliminated its accumulated debt of $5 million and had some money in the bank. The one remaining worry was audience: after the success of the first combined season, numbers had fallen off, to the point where seasons were averaging below 80 percent capacity, which, in Robert Wilson's view, was 10 percent too low.

In May 1988, Sills announced that she would retire as general director of the company, effective January 1, 1989. She would turn fifty-nine that month and wanted to retire at sixty. She also felt that her successor should have a free hand in planning important upcoming events, like City Opera's fiftieth anniversary in 1993–94. "I don't think this young, vital company should be run by a 65-year-old woman," she told the *New York Times*. City Opera was stable and operating in the black. The plan was for Sills to take a leading role in the choice of her successor ("I always said that the ideal person for the job was a 40-year-old orphan who was insane," she said later). She would become president of the board, with Robert Wilson remaining as chairman; her plan was to "wean" the company from her fund-raising celebrity.

Four months later, the new general director was announced: it was Christopher Keene who, Sills said, had always been her first choice. The search committee had interviewed a number of impresarios, including Houston's David Gockley and Washington's Martin Feinstein, but again, City Opera chose from within its artistic ranks. Although Keene had left the music director post in January 1987, amid rumors of artistic disagreement between himself and Sills, he was nonetheless one of the family. He had been the first winner of the Julius Rudel Award, which had been set up to train conductors and artistic directors, and had made his company debut in 1970. He was known for his interest in contemporary music (his debut performance was Ginastera's *Don Rodrigo*), but most of all, he was young—forty-one—and energetic.

Still, in a "Whither City Opera Now?" piece after the announcement of Keene's appointment, Donal Henahan, the chief music critic of the *New York Times*, who had never been a fan of Keene's often "incomprehensibly graceless, hard-driven" conducting, wondered about the choice, especially given the conductor's "reputation for arrogance and lack of tact in dealing with orchestras." Perhaps, he wondered, the board hoped that Keene would know how to attract a younger audience to the company? Whatever the reservations that outside observers might have had, Keene's familiarity with the complex workings of City Opera appeared to be a plus; certainly he could hit the ground running.

For the moment, the company seemed stable, even flourishing—poised to enter the next phase of its life. But Beverly Sills would be sorely missed. When Martin J. Oppenheimer, an attorney and longtime board member, was asked in 1984 what he would wish for the company's fortieth birthday, he said, "A package of $100 million in endowment funds and a clone of Beverly Sills onstage." It was a prescient desire, more so than Oppenheimer knew at the time, and one that would never be granted.

CHAPTER 4

The Inside Choice:
Christopher Keene

AS CHRISTOPHER KEENE assumed the general director role in March 1989, the company appeared to be financially stable, with money in the bank. But Keene immediately faced the same challenge that Sills had when she took over a decade earlier. The orchestra's three-year contract would expire in May, and the existential question of guaranteed weeks once again came to the fore. The five-year Wien grant—$1 million a year to put on a multi-week run of a Broadway musical in the spring—was ending. The 1990 run of *The Sound of Music* would be its final year and the last time those additional weeks of work would be in the schedule. With nothing on the horizon to replace the musicals, the company predictably wanted to eliminate the supplemental employment weeks from the new contract. Also predictably, the orchestra balked. David Titcomb, a trombonist with the company since 1986, who was on the orchestra committee at the time, says, "The orchestra felt that City Ballet was managing with twenty-six guaranteed weeks, and the Opera should be able to do so as well. They thought that if management started down the road of reducing weeks, it would continue."

In the 1983 negotiations, the company had begun by arguing against paying for any guaranteed weeks beyond the regular New York season. It had lost that battle and had ultimately come up with work to fill the weeks—adding the Wien musicals and the tour dates to Saratoga, Wolf Trap, and a handful of other one-off visits—setting a precedent that was not lost on the musicians. And the orchestra's envy was again fired by the Metropolitan Opera orchestra's continuing sweet deals (it once again signed a generous new contract in July, thirteen months before the previous one was set to expire). The City Opera orchestra committee also pointed out that the orchestras of Lyric Opera of Chicago and the San Francisco Opera made 20 percent more money for the same amount of work.

The 1989 season began on schedule on July 7 with a new production of *Don Giovanni*, directed by Hal Prince, but the planned production of Schoenberg's *Moses und Aron*, which required a great deal of extra rehearsal time for its enormously complex choral parts, was postponed to a future season since the orchestra would not rule out a strike. (Company leaders did not want to pay for the expensive rehearsals if the *Moses* performances would not take place.) And indeed, their fears were not unwarranted: a strike began on September 13, causing performances to be canceled. On October 12, with no deal on the horizon, the remainder of the season, which was scheduled to run through November 19, was canceled, and the company threatened to cancel the spring musical as well if an agreement was not reached soon. Amid claims and counterclaims, the company's weaknesses—its uneven artistic product, inadequate rehearsal time, and difficulty competing with better-paying regional companies for singers—surfaced regularly in the press. John Palanchian, vice president of Local 802, a City Opera violinist for twenty-two years and the orchestra's chief negotiator, told the *New York Times*, "I think the company needs a rethinking. The most glaring thing that has been lacking is every kind of long-range planning—artistic, financial, logistical. They just go on from year to year."

After a sixty-six-day strike and the cancellation of seventy performances, the orchestra finally ratified a five-year deal that increased the number of guaranteed weeks from twenty-three to twenty-six in the second year of the contract but eliminated the supplemental employment weeks. It also increased wages, though the increases were still less than what the union wanted. The union leadership was not pleased with the signing of a five-year agreement rather than the usual three, but Frank Morelli, the orchestra's principal bassoonist and chairman of its negotiating committee, said that the deal was the best possible outcome under the circumstances.

> We were faced with the choice of coming to terms with this board or taking them at their word that they would go out of business [if they were forced to pay at the level of the Chicago and San Francisco opera companies]. I personally couldn't assume the responsibility of trying to force this thing to a cataclysm and hoping something better would emerge from the ashes.

Morelli also pointed out, threateningly, that a quarter of the orchestra would reach retirement age before the end of the new contract. Since those players would be replaced by younger musicians, who were more accustomed to freelance work, the orchestra would be better able to sustain a strike the next time around.

With the strike settled and a five-year window of labor peace ahead, Keene revealed more about his artistic plans. Hoping to raise performance standards, he developed a strategy of presenting fewer operas (fourteen rather than twenty per season) in more consolidated time periods and eliminating Sunday night performances, which would bring the maximum number of performances per week down to seven. With fewer operas competing for stage time at any one point, the new schedule would permit more stage rehearsal and cut down on technical expenses. The schedule would still be hectic, but not as hectic. On the other hand, as Chuck Giles, the technical director, explained, "A fish grows to the size of its bowl. I advised Christopher that this schedule would allow him more time to do bigger things. But that would mean that things would get bigger, and it would not get easier or less expensive."

Sills had often complained about how difficult it was to attract and keep singers when the regional opera companies paid them far more than City Opera could afford. By scheduling performances in shorter, more compressed periods, Keene would, in theory, have an easier time attracting better singers, since the shorter runs conveniently fit in with lucrative engagements elsewhere. The shorter time frame also made it easier to keep casts together, which in turn would keep quality consistent throughout the run.

Keene's artistic interests were very different from Sills's popularizing aesthetic. While she had sought to distinguish the company from the traditionalism of the Met with musicals and other popular works, Keene's strategy was to make an aesthetic statement with knotty, important contemporary operas. The first of these was the New York stage premiere of *Moses und Aron*, on September 22, 1990, postponed from the previous season, which Keene and Sills had actually planned years earlier, when he was music director of the company. (The Metropolitan Opera's music director, James Levine, had also hoped to stage the austere, twelve-tone Schoenberg work, a longtime dream project of his. But the Met had withdrawn upon learning of City Opera's plans; it wouldn't present its own production until 1999.) City Opera's version, an abstract, all-yellow 1978 Cologne production by Hans Neugebauer, complete with eight naked dancers for the orgy scene, was deemed an artistic triumph and even sold well. The enormously complex choral parts required expensive additional rehearsal time, but it paid off. "No one had seen anything like that in New York before," says Beth Greenberg, who had recently joined the company as a stage director. Keene had numerous other challenging twentieth-century European works on his wish list, including Zimmermann's brutal *Die Soldaten*, and Busoni's *Doktor Faust*. Ultimately, he hoped to institute a commissioning program at City Opera that would result in a new opera every year. The 1993 season, celebrating the company's fiftieth anniversary, was to be "all-American," in a nod to one of its most significant achievements. Over the years, City Opera had presented more than fifty American works, a remarkable number, far surpassing what other American opera companies had done.

Keene had little interest in Sills's beloved candy-floss operettas, but he liked the sophisticated scores of Stephen Sondheim, Kurt Weill, and Marc Blitzstein: a new production of Sondheim's *A Little Night Music* would debut in the 1990 season. "We want to give the impression of more gravitas than we did in Beverly's day," board chairman Robert Wilson told *New York* magazine. "Opera is not fun and games." Wilson's model for City Opera was London's English National Opera, which, with its stimulating, often daring artistic sensibility, acted as a foil for the more conservative Royal Opera at Covent Garden. Keene concurred, commenting for the same *New York* magazine story, "I'd like to see us become a real part of the intellectual life of the city, which has not been the case for some years."

Keene's first complete season in 1990 provided some bracingly distinctive fare. In addition to *Moses und Aron*, the company's US stage premiere of Janáček's grim prison opera, *From the House of the Dead*, won much praise, with one critic declaring that Keene's conducting was better than that of the Czech opera expert Charles Mackerras. A new production of Ravel's *L'Enfant et les sortilèges* and *L'Heure espagnole* got more mixed reviews. However, these innovative ventures made some of the standard repertory revival productions look ordinary by comparison: as one critic noted, the company "advertises high quality and innovation [like *Moses und Aron*] yet spends much of its time purveying generic productions of old favorites, where artistic value usually corresponds to the relatively low cost of tickets."

Keene, concerned about the acoustics of the State Theater, which, despite the changes made in 1982, were still imperfect, flirted briefly with the idea of moving the company to the derelict New Amsterdam Theatre on Forty-Second Street, which was to be renovated. The possibility went nowhere: one reason to stay put was the fact that the company received a share of Lincoln Center's corporate funding, which it would lose should it depart. The staff also wondered if the audience, used to Lincoln Center, would be willing to venture into a different neighborhood, though it was a mere twenty blocks away. Keene also considered a sound enhancement system, as well as video screens to make the stage more immediate for the upper tiers; neither of these initiatives came to pass. Still, Keene's effort to find a new theater for City Opera was the first suggestion since the company's arrival at Lincoln Center in 1966 that it might be better off somewhere else. (Keene also fantasized about an uninterrupted season in a theater that did not also house the New York

City Ballet, and its Christmas cash cow, *The Nutcracker.*) The smaller
(seventeen-hundred-seat) New Amsterdam might well have been a better venue than the large, grand opera–scaled New York State Theater,
but City Opera did not have sufficiently deep pockets to be a pioneer in
the then-seedy precincts of Midtown Manhattan. Others did: the New
Amsterdam was eventually taken over by Disney. It opened in 1997
and became a centerpiece of the revival of Forty-Second Street.

Keene's honeymoon period was short-lived. The first blow came just
weeks after the success of *Moses und Aron*, in 1990, when Beverly Sills
left the City Opera board, ostensibly because she felt that Keene needed
a free hand. But when she joined the Metropolitan Opera board the following spring, it was clear that her loyalties and interests had shifted.
Worse, her fund-raising prowess was gone with her, and Keene, who had
little interest or skill in fund-raising, could not fill her shoes. (Sills clearly
missed being in the administrative limelight; she would go on to become
chairman of Lincoln Center in 1994.) Keene's adventurous choices in the
1991 season did not receive the universal praise that his 1990 ones did
and sold much worse than expected. Though *Die Soldaten* was deemed
"a triumph," the US premiere of Bill T. Jones and Leroy Jenkins's *The
Mother of the Three Sons*, a mixed-genre piece, was called "unsavory" and
"confused." By the spring of 1992, ten years after Sills had confronted
her own financial catastrophe, the City Opera was once again in serious
trouble. The operating budget had grown by an additional $3 million
over the previous year, and without Sills, fund-raising efforts had not
kept up. In fact, the company was facing a deficit of $2.9 million.

Belt-tightening efforts included a freeze on administrative salaries
and some repertory revision. One of the five new productions for the
upcoming 1992 season, the New York premiere of Janáček's *The Excur-
sions of Mr. Brouček*, was canceled, its four dates filled by additional performances of *Carmen*. (The *Carmen* that season was a new production by
Jonathan Eaton, a more traditional staging that replaced the controversial Spanish Civil War version by Frank Corsaro.) The other novelties of
the season stayed in place—the New York premiere of Busoni's *Doktor*

Faust as well as *Regina*, Blitzstein's verismo take on Lillian Hellman's savage play, *The Little Foxes*. But ticket sales were lower than projected. Keene suggested that the problem was timing—the novelty of a single, consolidated season beginning in July had worn off, and perhaps it was time for the company to return to the old fall–spring season configuration.

Along with the financial worries, dysfunction and suspicion began to take their toll. Robert Wilson offered to donate $1 million if the unions would accept a one-year wage freeze. The unions, who felt he was pushing an antilabor agenda, declined the offer; Florence Nelson, a spokesperson for the orchestra, said that it was unfair to ask for a freeze in the final year of a back-loaded contract—one of the reasons for the five-year term had been to give the company a chance to improve its financial situation. Wilson, not for the first time, suggested that the company be shut down. (Wilson's tussles with the orchestra did not end there—in 1995, he would send a colleague to a Kentucky Opera performance featuring a digitized orchestra—a move that suggested he wanted to find a way to replace the live orchestra altogether.)

Keene, never an enthusiastic or skilled administrator, was not up to the double task of handling the financial and artistic affairs of the company, and he was drinking to excess. Mark Weinstein, then the managing director of business and finance, recalls, "There was going to be an intervention to help him, with four or five board members, at Bob Wilson's beautiful apartment on Central Park West. It was supposed to start at 1 p.m. I showed up at 12:45; Bob and Christopher had been drinking together since 10 a.m. No one said anything; we all just looked at each other. At that point, I decided there was no hope. No one was going to intervene. So I quit." In April 1993, Wilson stepped down as chairman but remained on the board. He was replaced by a team of cochairs: Irwin Schneiderman, an attorney, who had joined the board in 1986, and Lloyd Rigler, even though Rigler, who had once been a major donor and had bailed City Opera out in the Sills years, had pulled back on his support since Keene took over. He was now devoting his funds and attention to Classic Arts Showcase, a nonprofit, twenty-four-hour satellite programming service for television of high-culture video clips, which would launch in May 1994.

The 1993 season, which was supposed to celebrate the company's fiftieth anniversary, was a low-key affair. It opened in July with *Carmen*, followed by a few weeks of standard repertory and operettas. The idea of putting on an all-American season to mark the occasion had been scrapped; instead, in October, there was to be a weeklong festival of three world premieres: Ezra Laderman's *Marilyn*, Lukas Foss's *Griffelkin*, and Hugo Weisgall's *Esther*. Company leaders tried to put a good face on this modest showing, but few were persuaded. Robert Wilson, still the voice of doom, declared that Keene's efforts to raise performance standards had been expensive and had not translated into better ticket sales. The board had been wanting to hire an executive director to manage the company's financial responsibilities, leaving Keene free to concentrate on artistic matters. It was a division of labor that had not been attempted in the company before, and it seemed likely to encroach on the general director's authority, so Keene had been opposed. But now, even he could see that it was clearly necessary.

Then, just as the fall part of the season was getting under way in September, Keene abruptly left New York and went to the Betty Ford Center in California to be treated for alcoholism. His statement to the company referred to the past year, with its "load of personal tragedy" and the economic pressures threatening the survival of the company, saying, "I have finally had to acknowledge to myself that I have developed an alcohol problem which is beyond my own control."

The "load of personal tragedy" referred to the loss of friends and colleagues from AIDS. This scourge, which had first come to the public's attention a decade earlier, seemed to have hit the New York City Opera particularly hard, killing its artists, backstage personnel, and administrators. David Eisler, who had been City Opera's first Candide; Glenn Rowen, a chorus member for seventeen years; James Festa, the company manager; and Mark Jollie, the company's financial administrator were among those who had recently died, and the ongoing presence of the terminal illness cast a pall over the company. Joseph Colaneri, the chorus master, recalls, "There were men in the chorus—all of a sudden, he's not coming in, he's out sick. Then you'd see him, and you'd know right away." Joyce Castle remembers standing backstage, watching David Eisler perform in *Briga-*

doon just a few months before he died. "He sang so beautifully. But we knew. Those were dreadful times, with a lot of frightened people."

While Keene was away, Schneiderman moved to finally bring on an executive director. He approached Mark Weinstein, now the president of Pierre Deux, who had remained in touch with the company since his wife, mezzo Susanne Marsee, was still performing there, and Weinstein agreed to take the job. When Keene returned from Betty Ford, he found a fait accompli. He hadn't been consulted on the terms of the arrangement and objected to Weinstein being given equal authority with him in nonartistic matters as well as hiring and firing authority over non-artistic staff members. After an acrimonious dispute, which was aired in the press, Keene capitulated, renewing his contract through 1997 and acquiescing in the coequal arrangement so as not to "hurt the company."

Even without any expensive anniversary hoopla, the company again ran a deficit for the 1993–94 season. Another strike would likely spell the end, and Weinstein decided that it was time to take a new approach to the upcoming union negotiations in 1994.

> I asked that the players and management representatives meet and talk several times a week, starting in January. There were no lawyers in the room, and no one would give any proposals for the first two months. There was no table, no circle—we sat in between each other. We talked about how hard it is to be a musician in NYC, how expensive the rent is, how your fingers hurt after six performances, how hard it is to cobble together jobs. And we talked about how hard it is to fundraise and sell tickets. After two and a half months, I asked the union to go into a room and bring back a management proposal, and the management brought the union's proposal. If that didn't work, there was plenty of time to call in the lawyers. The proposals came back, and they were within inches of each other.

The three-year contract, signed two months before the previous contract was set to expire, included modest salary increases in the second two years but none in the first, to give the company time to get its finances in order.

The 1994–95 season returned to the old format, split into fall and spring weeks. The fall was heavy on traditional repertoire, with highs like Elizabeth Futral's performance of the title role in *Lakmé* and lows like a chaotic *Butterfly*, in which the singers didn't seem to know the blocking. The corners cut to save money were most evident in the revivals of standard repertory; even the singers were dispirited, aware of the unflattering reputation the company had developed as "Shitty Opera"—a label that it could never entirely escape.

The soprano Amy Burton, who had made her company debut as Pamina in *The Magic Flute* in 1992, repeated the role that season. She had been working, first in American regional companies and then in Europe, for ten years before she started at City Opera, and she found the contrast startling. In Europe, singers prepared productions under "white glove conditions," with generous fees and plenty of rehearsal time; even at the American regional companies, she had been earning $3,000 or more per performance for leading roles. At City Opera, there was no rehearsal pay, and she earned $750 per performance for Pamina. "There was this feeling of exhaustion," she recalls. "Everyone brought a lot of energy and spirit to it, but there was a feeling that even if you did your best, maybe the final artistic product wasn't going to be that great."

The famous camaraderie of the City Opera "family" was a plus, of course. "The people were always wonderful," Burton says.

> Everybody was incredibly warm and friendly and there was always this unpretentious, welcoming feeling there. I loved the people in the chorus, the stage managers, the crew, the assistant stage directors. . . . My dresser, Susan Harris, was the salt of the earth—for my debut, the alterations hadn't been done on my costume, and she got me out onstage with safety pins holding the back of my dress together. But it was a very underfunded company trying to be a busy repertory house without the resources to do it. I had sung a lot of Paminas so I was pretty confident, and that was a good thing, because we didn't have a lot of musical rehearsal. We may not even have had a

sitzprobe—that was pretty common. The artistic product suffered because there just wasn't the time, money or space.

That season's novelty opera was Borodin's *Prince Igor*—Russian operas were not regular fare, though City Opera had done this one once before, in 1969, and the audience knew some of the tunes, which were used in *Kismet*. The company had continued to present runs of musicals during the regular season, and this season's was a campily directed new production of Bernstein's *Wonderful Town*, which had two weeks of performances in November. In the spring '95 season, a new, traditional *Traviata*, directed by the retired soprano Renata Scotto, replaced the 1991 Nicholas Muni staging that had Violetta expiring in an AIDS ward. The company imported a lavish production of *The Merry Widow* from the Paper Mill Playhouse in New Jersey. A new work, Stewart Wallace's *Harvey Milk*, about the assassination of the gay San Francisco city official, co-commissioned by the Houston Grand Opera and the San Francisco Opera, came in for some brickbats. Hagiography, said its critics, did not necessarily make for good opera.

But Keene was determined to carry on with his signature contemporary works. The next year's program was to include one of his favorites, Hindemith's dour *Mathis der Maler*, about the sixteenth-century artist Matthias Grünewald's struggle for artistic freedom, as well as a new Japanese piece, *Kinkakuji*, which was entirely paid for by the organization Music from Japan. (It was a devil's bargain—the opera, based on a novel by Yukio Mishima about a monk who burns down a temple, was terrible.) *Harvey Milk* was supposed to be the first entry in what Keene hoped would be a new program for the company—a "Freedom Cycle," underwritten by Philip Morris. The cycle, which would feature "operas about victims and victors in the struggle for freedom from oppression," was to continue the following season with Jost Meier and George Whyte's *The Dreyfus Affair*. Future projects included Charles Wuorinen's *Celia, a Slave*, for which Keene wrote the libretto, and operas by Hugo Weisgall and Anthony Davis.

But Keene's vision was not to be realized. HIV-positive for more than a decade, he had been intermittently ill, and in February, he was diagnosed with AIDS-related cancers. He continued to work as much as he could, but he was weakened; Joseph Colaneri took over many of the *Harvey Milk* rehearsals, while Keene did the performances. In the summer, the board, with Keene's knowledge, began a search for his successor. He managed to conduct the opening performances of *Mathis der Maler* in September, but he was visibly shaky and frail.

Colaneri remembers his last meeting with Keene.

It was the opening night of *Mathis der Maler*. He used to use his office as a dressing room, but that season, it was too far for him to walk, so he was using the conductor's room, which was right near the pit. I went to the dressing room to wish him well. He was by himself, trying to button his vest. He looked at me, wan and weak— he had lost his hair and he was taking a lot of meds—and he said, "Can you help me?" He couldn't use the buttons anymore because he was so thin, and he had to use pins. I drew the vest around him; he was all bones, and Christopher had been a very fit guy. He turned around and he said, "Joe, how am I going to get through this?"

I said to him, "Christopher, the chorus and orchestra know this piece. You've got a really good cast, and everyone wants to make it a success, not just for the premiere of the piece, but for you, because we know how much you love it, how much it means to you." He went out and did it.

To add to the stress of the evening, the leading baritone, William Stone, was ill and unable to sing; he walked through the role of Mathis on the stage while the cover, Stephen Powell, who was not entirely well, either, sang it from the pit. (Unlike Ashley Putnam's quick substitution as Violetta when Carol Vaness fell ill a decade earlier, replacement singers for a rarity like *Mathis der Maler* are not readily available.) It would be one of Keene's final appearances. Colaneri says, "I remember after the second performance, as he was leaving the pit, he went around the orchestra shaking hands with the principal players. Usually he would just shake the concertmaster's hand. The players were exiting the pit, weeping, and I remember one player said to me, 'Oh my god, I know he was saying goodbye to us.'"

Keene died on October 8 at age forty-eight. His obituaries saluted his adventurous spirit and his determination to bring challenging repertoire and stimulating production styles to the New York City Opera, but concluded that he had been dealt a difficult hand.

Some of Keene's strategies for grappling with City Opera's intractable issues had been prescient. He eased the grind of the repertory system by doing fewer operas. He invited creative new stage artists, like Jerome Sirlin, brilliant in the use of films and projections, to work at the company. He staged "difficult" operas that he thought New York should hear—works that were challenging for the audience in both subject and musical language—and spent the company's limited funds on their musical preparation rather than their physical productions. The production for *Moses und Aron*, for example, cost a mere $35,000; *Die Soldaten*, $65,000. Bigger budgets were allowed for physical productions of more popular, longer-running pieces, like *The Merry Widow*, that would pay off at the box office. Still, the inexpensive stagings sometimes backfired. Tippett's *The Midsummer Marriage* appeared particularly undernourished: a raked stage, a few curtains with stencils on them, and earth-toned costumes that seemed to come from J.Crew didn't help the audience make sense of this strange Jungian fantasy.

Furthermore, critics' reactions to the contemporary pieces were often tolerantly appreciative rather than ecstatic: they seemed like "good try" efforts, not the kind of events that were essential to the cultural conversation Keene had dreamed of. New York audiences remained fundamentally conservative, and Keene's attempts to push the limits of their taste faltered, in part as a result of the low-budget execution. He may also have been ahead of his time. In 2008, seventeen years after its New York premiere at City Opera, *Die Soldaten* played the Park Avenue Armory in a spectacular production from the Ruhrtriennale festival. With the audience seated on bleachers that slowly moved on rails along a central

runway where the heroine, Marie, was serially degraded by a succession
of soldiers, and the huge orchestra positioned on platforms around the
vast space, it became the talk of the town. The following year, Janáček's
From the House of the Dead, which Keene had done in 1990, was a highlight of the Metropolitan Opera season in a chilling production by Patrice
Chéreau.

And if the Met of the 1990s was still mired in bloated spectacle and
unadventurous repertory, New York operagoers with a taste for something different had new venues available to them. In 1989, audiences
had flocked to the PepsiCo Summerfare festival at SUNY Purchase for
Peter Sellars's groundbreaking productions of the three Mozart/Da Ponte
operas, with Don Giovanni as a drug dealer and *Figaro* set in Trump
Tower. The same year, the Brooklyn Academy of Music launched its own
opera project, with the lovingly staged *Falstaff* of Peter Stein from the
Welsh National Opera, and the astonishing *Atys* of William Christie
and Les Arts Florissants, which introduced New Yorkers to a contemporary yet musically authentic realization of French baroque opera.
Both BAM productions had come from Europe and were beneficiaries
of a generous state-backed funding system that allowed for careful preparation and lavish production values. City Opera's cut-rate standard
repertory operas and feints at contemporary relevance seemed wan and
earnest by comparison.

Whatever the reason, City Opera's audience was dwindling. The
twenty-seven-hundred-seat State Theater was becoming increasingly
hard to fill; Mark Weinstein noticed that even repertory staples like *Carmen*, which could once be relied on to sell a dozen performances, were
not drawing as well as before. The company's budget, over $24 million
in 1994–95, required vigorous fund-raising to close the gap of nearly
$10 million beyond ticket sales, tour fees, and other income. Corporate
and government support was becoming less reliable. Beverly Sills's celebrity had opened many pockets, appealing to donors who saw City
Opera as an extension of her; but Sills was now on the Met board—and
Keene had never been much of a fund-raiser. He said at the outset of
his regime that fund-raising would now have to be the job of the board,

but no one had managed to translate his vision into contributed income, and the gaps had appeared quickly. Slashing budgets had stemmed some of the hemorrhaging, and after a rise in ticket sales, the 1994–95 season had ended modestly in the black. But City Opera's past rescuers—Robert Wilson and Lloyd Rigler—were no longer to be depended on, and its current board chair, an opera-loving lawyer, was not in their league when it came to wealth.

Was there still a vital role for a second company to play? Keene's contemporary opera focus was not enough, and his illness and premature death left open the question of whether his vision for the company could have succeeded in the long run. Certainly his lack of interest in fundraising and administration, and the board's failure to deal with those inadequacies until it was nearly too late, did not help matters.

Now City Opera's board had to find someone who could reinvigorate the institution. Keene's appointment had followed the company pattern of choosing insider candidates, but given City Opera's troubles, a fresh perspective seemed to be in order. The robust regional opera world presented some possibilities. Summer festivals, in particular, offered an intriguing model, one that had been extremely successful and differed distinctly from the repertory grind at the New York State Theater. Interesting work was happening at the Santa Fe Opera, founded in 1956 by John Crosby, the eccentric scion of a wealthy New York family, and at Opera Theatre of Saint Louis, a force to be reckoned with under its founder, Richard Gaddes, a Crosby protégé, and then under Charles MacKay. The compact festival setup proved to be more conducive to creativity than the year-round repertory model. Artists stayed in place for the whole time, creating an ensemble spirit. Out-of-town visitors could take in all four or five of the festival's annual offerings during a single stay if they wished, and the productions were always new. Festival directors could mix up their offerings with unusual titles and did not have to pad out a long season with many performances of standard repertory works. The summer festivals also had smaller theaters, making for a more intimate experience than the grand opera–scaled auditoriums of the urban repertory houses.

The third significant American summer festival began modestly in 1975 with *La Bohème* in a high school auditorium in upstate New York. In 1979, the Glimmerglass Opera was taken over by Paul Kellogg, a former high school French teacher, who had moved to bucolic Coopers-town a few years earlier to write a novel. Kellogg was a visionary, with a taste for offbeat repertory and unconventional stagecraft. He was also a persuasive fund-raiser, and in 1987, the Glimmerglass Opera moved into the brand-new Alice Busch Opera Theater next to Otsego Lake. Designed by Hugh Hardy, it was a simple but elegant structure—a weathered barn exterior with a comfortable, nine-hundred-seat auditorium inside. One of Kellogg's first endeavors for the new theater was to commission a new opera from William Schuman to be presented on a double bill with his 1953 opera, *The Mighty Casey*, based on Ernest Thayer's poem, "Casey at the Bat," about a legendary strikeout, and an appropriate choice for an opera company sharing its home with the Baseball Hall of Fame. He invited exciting directors like Jonathan Miller, Martha Clarke, and Mark Lamos. And he recognized that his theater was the perfect size for a whole swath of neglected repertory—the baroque—mounting Monteverdi's *L'Incoronazione di Poppea* in 1994 and Handel's *Tamerlano* in 1995.

People noticed. The Glimmerglass *Poppea* was coming to BAM in 1996. James Marlas, who had been on the City Opera board since 1980, was one of the many visitors from New York City who had made the summer trip up to Glimmerglass and been greatly impressed. In January 1996, City Opera announced that Paul Kellogg would be its new general and artistic director.

CHAPTER 5

The Man from Upstate:
Paul Kellogg

PAUL KELLOGG ARRIVED at the New York City Opera in January 1996 to find the company profoundly demoralized after the death of Christopher Keene. Kellogg was a courtly figure, always dapper in a bow tie. His first goal was to bring a sense of calm and leadership back to the company because, as Joseph Colaneri recalls, "it had been chaotic."

Kellogg was a new phenomenon for City Opera. For the first time since the brief, catastrophic regime of Erich Leinsdorf in 1956, the company had looked outside for a leader. And for the first time, instead of an artist, it had hired an impresario, one with a significant history of accomplishment in institution building. In seventeen years, Kellogg had transformed the Glimmerglass Opera from a semiprofessional, local operation into a prestigious destination summer festival, known for its aesthetic risk-taking and repertory innovation, with a purpose-built nine-hundred-seat jewel box of a theater set amid rolling lawns and woods next to sparkling Otsego Lake.

Could the Glimmerglass magic be transferred to the New York City Opera?

The scale was certainly different. With operating expenses of about

$28 million and 110 performances of more than a dozen operas over eighteen weeks every year in New York City, plus its tour dates, City Opera was considerably larger than Glimmerglass, which put on just forty-two performances of four operas each summer on a $3.5 million budget. Furthermore, Glimmerglass was a nonunion theater, with much of its labor supplied by interns, both backstage and onstage. And while Glimmerglass controlled its theater, City Opera shared the New York State Theater with the New York City Ballet.

However, under Kellogg's acute artistic eye, Glimmerglass had developed a distinctive and appealing aesthetic, attracting curious opera lovers from far away. In a single long weekend, a visitor could enjoy a stimulating range of operatic experiences available nowhere else. The 1995 summer season had included a touching production of Gilbert and Sullivan's *The Yeomen of the Guard* and a malevolent *Don Giovanni* with the title character (sung by James Maddalena) in a wheelchair. Even more exotic was a buoyant staging, by the theater director Mark Lamos, of Britten and Auden's obscure *Paul Bunyan*; the production's iconic red rocking chairs epitomized the opera's folksy charm. Kellogg also found that his house was ideally sized for putting on long-forgotten early operas, written for smaller instrumental ensembles and subtler voices than the grand spectacles of the nineteenth century, and that year, the audience at Handel's virtuosic *Tamerlano* was galvanized by the astonishing young countertenor, David Daniels, in the title role. Daniels would soon become an international star, and his voice would help put baroque opera onto the stages of major opera houses.

Kellogg believed that he could woo audiences to City Opera with the kind of work that had been successful at Glimmerglass: "alternative repertoire and alternative production styles," as he put it. With the Met offering major singers in traditional operas next door, he felt that standard repertory was not "the way to lead the company into a new life." As had always been the case, City Opera needed to differentiate itself strongly from the Met and make its differences read as strengths.

Keene had also championed alternative repertoire, but the kind of alternative repertoire that he preferred—dark, knotty, twentieth-century operas by European composers—had not pleased the company's audience. "Beverly had built up the company on traditional productions," Kellogg said, productions that appealed to operagoers who were not necessarily connoisseurs. But that group, he went on, "didn't necessarily like pieces called *From the House of the Dead*. The audience had gone down seriously under Christopher, and we had to try to build it again."

Kellogg planned to program twentieth-century work that the audience would actually like. "I don't think there's much to be gained from treating opera like medicine," he said.

> It's not something that's "good for you," and you've got to swallow your cod-liver oil. It's got to be something accessible to experience, so people give something to it but receive something at the same time. If it's all giving on the part of the audience, they're eventually going to get tired of it.

Pre-Mozart operas, by composers like Handel, Gluck, and Monteverdi, would represent another important category of alternative programming. Not only had Kellogg been successful with both contemporary and baroque repertory at Glimmerglass, he also had a New York City model in Harvey Lichtenstein, who had built a strong audience at the Brooklyn Academy of Music with his Next Wave Festival and baroque operas performed by William Christie's Les Arts Florissants. And while City Opera would have to continue to perform standard works, Kellogg felt they could be made distinctive through new and imaginative production styles.

Kellogg quickly recruited a team to aid him in his quest to refresh the artistic complexion of the New York City Opera. His right-hand man would be Sherwin Goldman, a board member at Glimmerglass, who was best known for producing the first opera house staging of Gershwin's *Porgy and Bess* at the Houston Grand Opera in 1976, which went on to Broadway. In 1982, he mounted a second production of *Porgy* for Radio City Music Hall, which later toured seventeen American opera companies. Goldman, a tough, Yale-trained lawyer from a wealthy Texas family and a fervent opera lover, signed on with the title of executive producer. Kellogg also enlisted the aid of John Conklin, another key player at Glimmerglass and a revered stage designer, to be City Opera's director of productions. Through Conklin, he heard about Robin Thompson, a young stage director and administrator who was then working for the Los Angeles Opera, and brought him east as director of artistic administration. Finally, he engaged George Manahan, a conductor with excellent orchestra-building credentials, as music director, to raise standards for the orchestra. This brain trust, dubbed the "Gang of Five," met weekly to discuss strategy in a conference room next to an enormous through-the-wall fish tank that Kellogg had installed to cheer up the subterranean offices.

Kellogg's plan was to establish a close relationship between City Opera and Glimmerglass, where he would remain artistic director. Operas built and rehearsed at Glimmerglass would be restaged in New York, giving City Opera a steady stream of all-important new productions, created at a far lower cost, because they would be built under nonunion conditions and shared. "A new production at City Opera cost $700,000 to $800,000," Goldman recalls. "It had gotten to the point where City Opera couldn't produce things that they could run in repertory"—that is, shows that were durable enough to be brought back as revivals year after year. "They could do special, one-off items, but they hadn't built a new *Carmen* for years. At Glimmerglass, we could do a new production for as little as $50,000. With a few extra bucks from City Opera, we would make the Glimmerglass productions more professional, moveable, and playable in repertory."

The joint shows would be teched and rehearsed at leisure at Glimmerglass—a nonunion house—so they could go into the State Theater already polished and basically ready to play. The productions would, of course, still have to be rehearsed when they arrived at the State Theater, but all major decision-making about production and staging would already have been done under less expensive conditions. Goldman noted that the arrangement was also advantageous for Glimmerglass: it gave the rural, upstate company a "river to the sea": exposure to new audiences, critics, and, perhaps most important, donors. "Our idea was that if we could join the advantages of Glimmerglass and City Opera, we could create a new model."

At the same time, Kellogg was determined to raise the artistic standards of City Opera. He was concerned about the quality issues that had plagued the company for its entire life, and in conversations with current artistic personnel, including Colaneri, he heard the same complaints repeated. "Many [revival] productions opened with no stage rehearsal, or only one," Kellogg said. "Even if an opera had been done the year before, it needed time on the stage. This was one of the criticisms we heard everywhere, and the press was full of the orchestra's bumps, and how it was not in synch with the stage." If the company's quality were better, Kellogg believed, the audience would follow.

Robin Thompson arrived at City Opera on April 1, 1996. He had been an intern at the company in 1977–78, and now he dreamed of making it a contemporary version of what it had been during its heyday under Julius Rudel: as Thompson put it, "an important place to go, with a repertory of interesting pieces that you couldn't see anywhere else, performed by people of import."

One of Thompson's primary jobs was hiring singers, and he was eager to cast a wide net. But there were many obstacles. First of all, there was the task of figuring out his predecessor's opaque methods. "There was no detailed budget for singers," Thompson recalled. "There was a lump sum of money. I seem to remember it being about $880,000. But there was no piece of paper that I could look at and see if, say, someone were to come and sing Violetta here, what would we have to pay her?"

Most American opera companies, including Los Angeles, where Thompson came from, did not run in repertory and built their casts by the opera. In City Opera's system, many singers were still hired on a weekly basis, and these weekly singers made up the backbone of the casts. Weekly salaries might be divided up to include a leading role, or several smaller roles, each of which had its price. To make matters even more complex, the weekly singers were compensated based on their seniority within the company. There were no per diems, and covering singers were only paid if they actually performed the parts they were covering. In the old days of the company, City Opera singers either lived in New York or would sleep on someone's couch—the opportunity to sing at the New York City Opera was worth the hardship back then, but the opera world had changed. "The fees were out of synch with the marketplace," Thompson said.

> Houston, Los Angeles, San Francisco, Chicago, Pittsburgh—all those companies had singers who didn't make a lot of money, but they weren't making as little money as the City Opera had been getting away with for a long time. It contributed to the talent drain at City Opera. It was not competitive for hiring the kind of singers that I thought we needed to raise the level of the company, and Paul [Kellogg] agreed.

But additional rehearsal time and a more generous pay structure for singers would require plenty of money. To meet the need, Kellogg launched a new Fund for Artistic Excellence, raising several million dollars from a group of donors including the chairman of the board, Irwin Schneiderman, board member Mark Newhouse, and several others. The Andrew W. Mellon Foundation, which had funded the company in the past but had not done so for a decade, also put in $1 million. The idea was to take the company, as Thompson put it, "from the Flintstones era to the modern era." With the additional funds, Kellogg hoped, would come higher artistic standards—and, as a result, better ticket sales.

The operating expenses for Kellogg's first season with the company were about $28 million. By the 1997–98 season two years later (the first planned entirely by Kellogg and his team), expenses had jumped by $3.5 million, an increase made possible by the new Fund for Artistic Excellence. But not everyone was convinced that pursuing a new path with increased spending was the right choice. John White, the veteran manager of the Rudel and early Sills years, had come out of retirement to help the new team and told Kellogg that the plan was misguided. The extra rehearsal time, White said, was "inappropriate for City Opera and was going to cost the company more than it should." Kellogg was unconcerned, but perhaps he should have been; his strategy fit into a worrisome pattern established by his two immediate predecessors. Both had significantly raised the company's budget in their first years and had run into trouble as a result.

With the pumped-up budget, Kellogg intended to make his mark on the 1997–98 season—it was his declaration of artistic intent. There were fifteen operas, including eight new productions (as opposed to the four or five of recent years), for a total of 115 performances. Seven of the eight new shows had originated elsewhere—a canny, cost-saving strategy not only to supply new material but also to position City Opera as the New York showcase for the important work that was increasingly happening in other US cities.

Four of the new productions came, as planned, from Glimmerglass, including Leon Major's clever *Don Pasquale* and an antic, updated *L'Italiana in Algeri* directed by Christopher Alden, with Phyllis Pancella as the Italian girl of the buffo Middle Eastern dictator Mustafa's movie star pinup dreams. Glimmerglass also supplied two of the more exotic titles: the Mark Lamos *Paul Bunyan*, one of Kellogg's favorite productions, and Francesca Zambello's production of Gluck's *Iphigénie en Tauride*, with the gifted young soprano Christine Goerke as the imprisoned Greek princess forced to perform human sacrifices as a priestess of Diana, and the early music specialist Jane Glover in the pit. Word of the Gluck opera spread quickly—though not necessarily because of the production's musical merits. Talk focused mostly on the deliberately homoerotic spectacle of the two buff, loincloth-clad male leads, Andrew Schroeder and William Burden, playing the captives Oreste and Pylade, who spent much of the opera roped together and drenched from the continual onstage rain. *Iphigénie* became a hot ticket for gay men.

The biggest hit of the season was Handel's *Xerxes*, meticulously directed by Stephen Wadsworth, in a production that had originally been staged for the Santa Fe Opera but also played in Seattle and Boston. This remarkable production, sung in Wadsworth's own lyrical English translation and set in an eighteenth-century country house, demonstrated how powerfully a Handel opera could resonate for modern audiences. Many directors were flummoxed by the form's static dramaturgy and its many da capo arias, but Wadsworth made *Xerxes* into a wrenchingly contemporary personal drama about the nature of love and the sufferings that people inflict upon each other in its name. There was much excitement about the two rising baroque opera stars who would be making their City Opera debuts in leading roles. The first, Lorraine Hunt, a protean, plangent-voiced mezzo, proved every bit as mesmerizing in the role of Xerxes as she had been a few years earlier in Charpentier's *Médée* with Les Arts Florissants at BAM. The other was countertenor David Daniels, whose singing in the role of the love-lorn Arsamene demonstrated that he could be as expressive in despair as he was in virtuosic fury. They were joined by Amy Burton, stepping out of her old City Opera round of Pamina, Micaela, and Susanna to exquisitely embody Romilda, the unwilling object of Xerxes's desire.

With only five performances scheduled, the shows sold out, and scalpers hawked tickets on the Lincoln Center plaza. Years earlier, the company had been a pioneer in baroque opera, with a few isolated but important offerings like *Giulio Cesare* and *Alcina*, but with *Xerxes*, City Opera became the place where baroque repertoire was being reborn. Nearly every subsequent season of the Kellogg years offered another baroque opera title. And this time, other companies would follow its lead. Times had changed: in the last decade, the historical performance movement (including groups like Les Arts Florissants) had exhumed and celebrated this earlier repertory on a much broader scale—and there were now singers and conductors who specialized in it. City Opera's successes demonstrated how a traditional opera house could integrate these works and invigorate its own artistic program. Daniels made his Metropolitan Opera debut as Sesto in *Giulio Cesare* the following spring; Wadsworth would make his Met bow in 2004 with an elaborate production of Handel's *Rodelinda*, created for Renée Fleming and Daniels, a project that would have been unthinkable without City Opera's successful series of productions.

The new regime's taste in contemporary repertoire was markedly different from that of Christopher Keene. Tobias Picker's poignant *Emmeline* had thrilled Robin Thompson when he saw its world premiere at Santa Fe in 1996. A tale of a nineteenth-century mill girl who unwittingly marries a man who turns out to be her own son, *Emmeline* starred a heartbreaking Patricia Racette and exemplified a new direction in contemporary opera with its tautly dramatic, approachable score, as opposed to Keene's grim, twelve-tone favorites, the kind of operas that Kellogg thought of as "cod-liver oil." This was indeed an opera that "gave back." Not every choice was successful, of course: the Chinese-born composer Tan Dun's *The Voyage of Marco Polo*, staged with dancers and tableaux by Martha Clarke, was inscrutable.

City Opera mounted only one newly built production that season: a twentieth-century "Russian constructivist" *Macbeth*, with the men in black trench coats rather than kilts, which the company could not afford, and the witches as black-shawled battlefield scavengers. The stark production—featuring neon, metal catwalks, staircases, and a crane—was designed by John Conklin, who had already demonstrated his genius at repurposing elements from the company's vast warehouse of scenery for the previous season's *Les Contes d'Hoffmann*. Baritone Mark Delavan and soprano Lauren Flanigan starred as the murderous Macbeths. Flanigan, a dramatic soprano, had made her debut at the company in 1990 as Musetta and had sung a number of major roles, particularly in contemporary repertoire. In the years to come, City Opera would try to position both singers, especially the fiercely theatrical Flanigan, as company stars.

The rest of the 1997–98 season's operas were revivals of standard repertory titles—including fourteen performances of *La Bohème*. Tellingly, there were no musicals or operettas, the popular, ticket-selling genres that had become fixed elements of the company under Beverly Sills and continued under Keene. The previous season, for example, which had been largely planned by the Keene regime, included both a fourteen-performance run of *Brigadoon*, and productions of two Gilbert and Sullivan operettas, *HMS Pinafore* and *The Mikado*. Now, with complete freedom to choose, Kellogg was charting a new path.

The critical response was encouraging; reviewers remarked upon both the many unusual operas and the improvement in musical preparation. In his review of *Xerxes*, Bernard Holland remarked, "The City Opera orchestra, sounding so disconsolate in recent years, seemed enthusiastic and energetic." Kellogg was counting on these dramatic artistic changes to boost the box office, even without the easier-to-sell operettas and musicals, but the total number of tickets sold for the season did not increase—indeed, it was slightly lower than the previous year. Kellogg knew that his innovations would likely face some resistance from the company's old guard, who preferred opera titles that they recognized. Kellogg recalled a focus group the company commissioned to gauge the appeal of their proposed programming. "I'll never forget," he said, "one woman sat in the focus group, very glum, and said 'EX-er-exis [Xerxes]. If I can't pronounce it, I'm not going to see it!' There were so many operas that the focus group didn't know, or hadn't heard of, and they were a little suspicious, but we went ahead with it anyway." It was exciting for the company's leaders to see people on the plaza holding up money to buy *Xerxes* tickets, but at the same time, titles like *Paul Bunyan* did not sell out.

Building the audience was a key goal, and Kellogg and Goldman soon began to realize what they were up against. "City Opera had this very strong, quite old, constituency," Goldman said. "It was primarily first- and second-generation, European, and Jewish, based on the Upper West Side of Manhattan. It was a delicious, loyal, wonderful audience. But it was disappearing. We still had a large audience of teachers, university officials, and intellectuals, who liked the affordable tickets in the second balcony and the orchestra," Goldman continued. "They couldn't get seats like that at the Met. But that audience was smaller [than the first group] and less intense."However, the continuing decline in City Opera's audience—which Kellogg had attributed to his predecessor's "cod-liver oil" operas and the company's often threadbare artistic level—would turn out to be more systemic and intractable than he and Goldman suspected. Kellogg would later acknowledge that some of his own programming initiatives had not done enough to build the audience. "Some of the repertory we were bringing in appealed to a different group," he said, "but there were not as many of them."

For the time being, the team pressed forward on the artistic path it had mapped out that first season. The fifteen operas of 1998–99 were about half twentieth century and baroque, and half standard repertory—

eight were new productions. Again, five of the new productions came from Glimmerglass, including two twentieth-century works: Jack Beeson's searing *Lizzie Borden*, with Phyllis Pancella as Lizzie and Lauren Flanigan in an electrifying performance as her stepmother, which was broadcast on PBS's *Live from Lincoln Center*; and Floyd's *Of Mice and Men*, with the arresting young tenor Anthony Dean Griffey as the hulking, pathetic Lennie. A playful production of Handel's *Partenope*, featuring Lisa Saffer as the nymphomaniacal title character, had also premiered upstate. For the first time, Glimmerglass also supplied new productions of standard repertoire works: Mark Lamos's *Madama Butterfly*, a starkly beautiful interpretation that used Japanese shapes and colors in a wholly modern fashion, and his gritty *Tosca*, set in Fascist Italy of the 1930s, and a bracing contrast to the gargantuan 1985 Zeffirelli spectacular at the Met. City Opera's own new productions included a lively take on Richard Strauss's domestic comedy, *Intermezzo*, again featuring Flanigan, who roller-skated onstage; Monteverdi's *Orfeo*, a coproduction with the English National Opera, directed by Martha Clarke and featuring ten naked dancers as the Blessed Spirits; and an intriguing new *Hansel and Gretel*, set in 1890s New York City, where the children, now impoverished immigrant tenement dwellers, run away to Central Park and happen upon a frightening East Side mansion.

This coproduction with Los Angeles Opera was director James Robinson's company debut, and it wasn't easy. "One of the things that struck me immediately about the place was that there was a great deal of enthusiasm to do new things," Robinson recalled. "They had Paul Kellogg, George Manahan, and John Conklin, but my impression was they didn't really work together. I could never figure out who was really the person to make things happen. From a production standpoint it was one of the most dysfunctional places I ever worked. You never knew how much money you had to spend. Everything was enormously expensive."

One incident just before the opening of *Hansel and Gretel* crystallized the difficulties that Robinson encountered. "I needed a specialty prop that anyone should have been able to manufacture. Gretel makes a little snowman in Central Park, and Hansel needed to kick it over. They kept saying, there's no way we can make anything like that, we can't afford it." Robinson ended up doing it himself. "I made sushi rice at home, and brought in the snowman, made out of sushi rice—you could pack it like snow, it looked like snow, then you could kick it over and it would clean up fairly easily."

This kind of difficulty was almost invariably a result of Sherwin Goldman's supervision—as the administrator in charge of the company's finances, he was determined to keep the budget under control. Kellogg and Goldman operated on a good cop/bad cop system: Kellogg was the approving face; Goldman wielded the knife.

Still, in the new regime, things were better than they had been. Amy Burton recalls, "One of the first things Paul did was to raise the fees of the soloists. It was a gesture of acknowledgment, and very much appreciated." (The fees were still low, of course: a cover contract at the Met paid about the same as a leading role at City Opera.) In addition, by placing Robin Thompson in charge of artistic administration, Kellogg sent a strong signal that directing would be a priority—Thompson had previously worked as an opera stage director, so theater mattered to him, just as it did to Kellogg. And under Kellogg, the company's old-fashioned opera stagings were increasingly replaced by fresher designs. "The aesthetic began to be much more Paul's theatrical aesthetic," says Burton. "There was a beautiful design element coming in that spilled over in the costumes, makeup, everything. And suddenly, with *Xerxes*, it felt like an important place to work."

The company stage director Beth Greenberg remembers a distinct change in the work environment following Kellogg's arrival.

> There was a big expansion in rehearsal time, which we were all grateful for. Stage time, with lots of union crews hanging around, is expensive, and a good director will map out every minute of that rehearsal to get through the piece, including a grid of when people take breaks, so you can coordinate everything and not waste any time. Paul Kellogg and Robin Thompson made it happen that we got more rehearsal time onstage in the first few years, which was really great. I think part of

the reason was that Paul had come from Glimmerglass, where they don't have union crews, so that was his standard of rehearsal. Also, in Paul's regime, we started to get more of the actual set furniture and real costume pieces in the rehearsal room, which made the transfer to stage that much easier, because the experience was much more consistent.

Another notable change was the improvement of the orchestra. When George Manahan joined the company as music director in 1996, one of his foremost tasks was to sustain and improve the orchestra, which had become dispirited in the years of Keene's illness. Manahan had a history with City Opera: he had been music director of the National Company, City Opera's touring ensemble for young singers, for several seasons in the early 1980s and had stepped in to conduct performances for the main company in 1991. Keene had served as both the company's music director and its general director, and since he was ill for much of his tenure, the orchestra had been without a consistent music director for some time. When Manahan arrived, he found an orchestra of "fine players, but uneven in a lot of sections." He also knew a lot of the musicians—he had studied at the Manhattan School of Music with quite a few of them—which helped him win their confidence.

Part of Manahan's strategy was to conduct revivals and standard repertory operas himself. Music directors often leave these works to guest conductors, reserving only the splashy new productions of unusual works for themselves, but Manahan believed in building a connection with the orchestra through the standards. "You improve the orchestra by doing the repertory they know," he says. He was certainly not planning to "clean house" and for the most part was committed to working with the people he had—or in some cases, working around them. He found, for example, that he was able to avoid using some problem players by loosening up on the rules governing when players were allowed to send substitutes. "Christopher used to have ongoing battles with the orchestra committee because he was trying to keep everybody there. I loosened up on that, because I found that some first-call substitutes were better than the tenured players."

It was not an ideal solution, however, and union rules made it complicated to fire veteran players who were no longer up to the job. But after
winning a difficult legal fight during his second season that allowed him
to force a problematic player out, Manahan had an easier time. "Some of
the other players realized that if we had to, we would go to the mat." At
times, Manahan would also approach individual musicians and pay them
not to play in an opera with a particularly exposed obbligato, for example. "Some retired on their own, or we'd come to an understanding—'if
in a couple of years, you're going to resign, then I'll leave you alone, and
we'll just work around you.'" Critics noticed the improvement.

Manahan loved the repertory and the orchestra building and was having the time of his life. One of his most thrilling recollections of his early
tenure was working with Lorraine Hunt in *Xerxes*. Hunt was an electrifying stage presence and operated on split-second theatrical timing.

> There was a mad scene, with a lot of coloratura, and she was right in
> the other character's face, about to start the second verse. She was so
> specific about how she wanted to rip right into this person without
> any warning. I had to wear my glasses so I could see her start to form
> the word and pull the trigger [with the orchestra]!

The singers noticed the change in the orchestra as well. "George
didn't clean house, he just rearranged the furniture," soprano Amy Burton recalls.

> Little by little, new players were brought in. When we did *Xerxes*
> in 1997, for many of them, it was the first time they had played
> Handel—and some hadn't played any since *Giulio Cesare* decades
> before! But by the time the Handel revival really got started, and we
> did *Ariodante* in 1999, there was a core of younger players that really
> understood the style. In my early years, there were a lot of sour faces
> in the orchestra, but I remember looking out into the orchestra at an
> *Ariodante* rehearsal, and seeing all these beaming young faces. I
> remember noticing that and thinking, the culture is really seeping
> through now, and we have orchestra people who are so jazzed to be

playing this, and really getting it. George is such a fantastic conductor, and Paul reinvigorated everything, bringing in people like [conductors] Jane Glover and Harry Bicket. By my last full year there, in 2005, it felt like a different orchestra.

The 1999–2000 season featured nine new productions, including the New York premiere of *Central Park*, a trilogy of operas by three different composers, linked by their setting, that had been commissioned and performed at Glimmerglass the previous summer. Also imported from Glimmerglass was Christopher Alden's lively production of Virgil Thomson and Gertrude Stein's *The Mother of Us All*, starring Lauren Flanigan as a fervent Susan B. Anthony. The baroque wing offered Rameau's *Platée*, a hilarious show directed by the choreographer Mark Morris, with costumes by Isaac Mizrahi and featuring Jean-Paul Fouchécourt as the deluded swamp creature who imagines herself adored by everyone, as well as John Copley's aforementioned staging of Handel's *Ariodante*, a coproduction with the Dallas Opera. *Ariodante* was beautifully performed but is unfortunately best remembered for a theatrical absurdity: a giant sculpture of a horse's head, originally created to be used as part of the act 2 ballet, which had been cut to save time, was bewilderingly and risibly lowered into the heroine's mad scene, since the director didn't want it to go to waste. City Opera also brought back director Stephen Wadsworth and mezzo Lorraine Hunt (now Lieberson, since her marriage to the composer Peter Lieberson) for a wrenching production of *La Clemenza di Tito*, with Harry Bicket, a rising British early music specialist, conducting.

Ticket sales had remained obstinately flat through the 1998–99 season, but in March 2000, City Opera began its spring performances with *Porgy and Bess*, in a refurbished version of Sherwin Goldman's 1982 Radio City production. The run—four previews and ten regular performances—sold out before it opened, and the production was telecast on *Live from Lincoln Center*. With the success of *Porgy*, the 1999–2000 season's total box office spiked, with a jump of nearly $2.5 million in ticket sales and over twenty-seven thousand more tickets sold. The number of subscriptions, which had also been falling, had jumped as well, with over twenty-five thousand sold for that season.

Kellogg and his team now recognized that runs of musical theater and operetta titles, which had formerly been an important facet of City Opera's repertory, should be brought back. *Porgy* was revived in 2001–02, and in each of the subsequent six seasons, the company presented a musical or a Gilbert and Sullivan operetta during the spring, in long performance runs; on occasion, they mounted one in the fall as well. All the musicals were revivals of productions from previous eras, including some City Opera classics like the famous 1982 Hal Prince *Candide*. Rather than casting them entirely with opera singers, the company would often use theater performers, such as Jeremy Irons and Claire Bloom, who headlined Stephen Sondheim's *A Little Night Music* in 2003. However, none of the musicals had as significant an effect on the box office as *Porgy* did.

The new productions of the 2000–01 season continued to push Kellogg's aesthetic vision. The opening-night *Roberto Devereux* starred Lauren Flanigan, singing a role that had been associated with City Opera's most famous star, Beverly Sills, in a bid to position Flanigan as the company's current diva. Other City Opera stars were showcased: David Daniels and Christine Goerke in Handel's *Rinaldo*, and Elizabeth Futral, poignant in another Sills vehicle, the title role of *The Ballad of Baby Doe*, paired with Mark Delavan as a forceful Horace Tabor. Fresh new versions of standard repertory works came from Glimmerglass, including a handsome *La Bohème*, directed by James Robinson, updated to just before World War I and featuring Maria Kanyova and Rolando Villazón in his New York debut (he was quickly snapped up by the Met) as heartbreakingly young lovers. And Kellogg doubled up on the baroque: also from Glimmerglass was another Handel work, Mark Lamos's charming *Acis and Galatea*, with its playful picnic setting featuring lawn chairs and balloons.

For a few years, the company was able to keep pace financially with Kellogg's artistic plans. The budget expansion for the 1997–98 season had been covered by the fund-raising increase, even though the total box office revenue was lower than that of the previous year. The company also got an unexpected windfall in 1998 when a class action suit concerning the 1985 warehouse fire was finally settled. The suit involved over one hundred parties and several defendants, including the warehouse owner, Ashland Oil, and Texaco—City Opera netted $6.296 million after legal costs, wiping out the company's accumulated deficit of over $5 million, which it had been carrying since before Kellogg took over. And the good news continued: contributed income rose steadily for the next two years, reaching a high of nearly $18 million in the 1999–2000 season, and City Opera was able to balance its budget.

An even larger sum was still to come. For nearly two decades, City Opera had received an annual contribution from a foundation built on the DeWitt Wallace *Reader's Digest* fortune. But in 1998, the New York State attorney general's office began to investigate allegations of improper asset management by seven supporting organizations that had been set up to handle the nearly $2 billion in charitable funds stemming from the Wallace fortune.

In 2001, the Wallace funds' managers and the attorney general's office came to an agreement: the supporting organizations would distribute their $1.7 billion to the thirteen individual groups that had been the annual beneficiaries of their grants, to be used as endowments. The largest single gift, $424 million, went to the Metropolitan Museum. The six constituent organizations of Lincoln Center would receive approximately $300 million—City Opera's share, $51.5 million, established a new, permanently restricted Wallace endowment. The Wallace money represented a monumental expansion of the company's assets— previously, its endowment had never been more than a few million dollars. But the impact on City Opera's annual budgets would remain about the same, since the interest from the new endowment would be about the same as the annual Wallace gifts had been. However, the company would now be able to decide for itself how to invest the endowment money—and possibly get a better return. And, of course, this enormous infusion of funds had the additional benefit of giving City Opera the appearance of fiscal security.

Other changes were under way. The company's annual visit to the Saratoga Performing Arts Center had become problematic. "The acoustics were awful, and it was expensive," Kellogg recalled.

The management at Saratoga had apparently long wanted to get rid of the opera because it didn't draw the audience that they wanted, and they wanted to use the weeks for other things. We met with their trustees and told them that we couldn't do the tour for any less than they were already paying us. So we cut that bond.

City Opera's educational touring arm, the National Company, which for nearly two decades had traveled to smaller cities with a single opera performed by young singers, was also reevaluated. "As our orchestra budget increased, the presenters in the municipalities that we visited were not willing to pay what it cost us, and we couldn't get any national funding from anyone [to subsidize it]," said Kellogg. "The National Company was a terrible draw on the budget, and we had constant union problems with it. So it was better to drop it." The last National Company tour was in 1999. City Opera was not the only US company to rethink its educational touring arm. Houston Grand Opera had shuttered its Texas Opera Theater, and in 2003, San Francisco Opera's Western Opera Theater would also be terminated. Like City Opera's decision to end the National Company, San Francisco's decision was budget-related; however, in explaining the closure, its Opera Center director, Sheri Greenawald, called the operation a "dinosaur." Western Opera Theater's initial mission, when it was founded in 1967, was to take opera to the hinterlands, she said, but "as far as opera is concerned, there are very few hinterlands left. There are very few communities that don't have access to some kind of lyric theater." In Kellogg's assessment, neither the Saratoga visit nor the National Company made economic sense for the company in the current era—so much had changed since the 1980s, when they had begun. However, Kellogg believed that Beverly Sills was angry about the elimination of these two outreach activities, particularly the National Company, which was "her baby," and that their termination further strained relations between City Opera and its most famous diva.

The end of the Saratoga relationship was the end of City Opera's regular touring activity. Touring had once been a valuable source of income, both earned and contributed, and a way to provide more weeks of work for the orchestra and the chorus. But as the Metropolitan Opera had discovered more than a decade earlier, the cost of importing an opera company had gradually increased beyond what sponsors were willing to pay. Instead, cities and communities that wanted opera came up with other means of producing it. Los Angeles, City Opera's most significant tour destination until 1983, had created its own opera company in 1986, and the founding or expansion of many regional opera companies around the country followed the end of the Met's tour visits to their cities. Smaller-scale enterprises also sprang up: Saratoga briefly mounted its own productions with the much less expensive Lake George Opera following the break with City Opera, and after City Opera's annual visit to Wolf Trap came to an end in 1995, that summer festival would rely on its own homegrown company, Wolf Trap Opera, a professional training operation for young singers.

With the elimination of the Saratoga tour, the company was left with more unused weeks of guaranteed work. Some of these could be used by hiring the orchestra out for other presenters, such as the Lincoln Center Festival, which had begun in 1996. And another idea surfaced in 1999. David Titcomb, the orchestra manager, recalled that Deborah Drattell, who became composer in residence at the company that year, asked if the company could use an unused week of the guarantee to do readings of orchestra pieces. The orchestra was glad to agree rather than face the loss of guaranteed paid time in a subsequent contract. "We wanted to do whatever we could to facilitate the working off of the weeks because we wanted to hold on to them," Titcomb says.

The idea morphed from orchestra readings to opera readings. In May 1999, following the regular season, City Opera presented Showcasing American Composers for the first time. Coordinated by Drattell, it presented forty-five-minute excerpts of six contemporary operas, including Mark Adamo's *Little Women* and pieces by John Musto and Jonathan Sheffer, at Columbia's Miller Theatre. Over the next several years, the program expanded, featuring excerpts from as many as twelve operas, as well as panel discussions about the artistic and production challenges posed by the new works. Soon, the event was scheduled on multiple days over a two-week period. In 2002, now coordinated by

Mark Adamo, who had succeeded Drattell as composer in residence, it was renamed Vox: Showcasing American Composers.

An itinerant adventure that moved from Miller Theatre to Cooper Union, to Symphony Space, and various churches before finding a home at the Skirball Center for the Performing Arts at New York University, the free Vox events became a popular destination for audiences curious about the new, as well as representatives from other opera companies on the hunt for new compositional voices. Vox included experienced composers as well: unproduced works by veterans like David Del Tredici and Bernard Rands were among those featured.

Some of the operas got professional performances as a result of their Vox exposure. A scene from Scott Wheeler's *Democracy* was showcased in 2000 with Lauren Flanigan as one of the soloists, bringing the work to the attention of Placido Domingo, who commissioned the full opera and produced it in 2005 at the Washington National Opera, where he was general director. Works like Bright Sheng's *Madame Mao*, Richard Danielpour's *Margaret Garner*, and Thomas Pasatieri's *Frau Margot* got Vox readings before moving on to major companies like Santa Fe, Michigan, and Fort Worth. The Vox performances proved helpful to the composers as well, who had the opportunity to hear exactly what their orchestrations sounded like and how they fit with the voices, albeit with minimal rehearsal. In the early years, critics were asked not to review the showcases, since the pieces were considered unfinished, but that policy later changed to increase the event's visibility. Before long, City Opera was able to raise foundation funds, particularly from the Andrew W. Mellon Foundation and ASCAP (American Society of Composers, Authors, and Publishers), to underwrite the costs of the event. What started as a modest plan to use up a week of guaranteed services had soon taken on a life of its own: this annual offering of new operatic voices played a role in the burgeoning national interest in contemporary work, which would take off dramatically in the early 2000s. Two Vox directors, Yuval Sharon and Beth Morrison, would also later become forces in their own right in the championship of new works.

One thorny issue that would take on huge proportions was that of the acoustics in the New York State Theater. The house, built to the acoustical specifications of the New York City Ballet, had been designed to muffle sound from the stage (like footfalls) rather than project it. Various acoustic fixes had been tried over the years, including a major one overseen by Sills in 1982, but Kellogg felt that the problem had never been fully corrected. "You could sit on the right side of the auditorium, and you could not hear the brass, but if you sat on the left side of the auditorium, the brass was blindingly noisy," Kellogg said. "You heard only parts of the orchestra, and the orchestra couldn't hear itself. And unless a singer stood in Miss Sills's sweet spot, which is where she always stood for her arias, you couldn't hear them."

The house took a toll on the performers as well. "It was not just a dead hall, it was a weird dead hall," says Amy Burton.

There were acoustical pockets. If you sat on house left, and you moved ten seats over, suddenly, the person that you thought was louder than everyone else, you couldn't hear anymore, while the person who seemed to have no voice at all, you could hear perfectly well. It was the same onstage. You'd be singing, and you would hear your own voice twelve feet behind you. Then you'd move somewhere else onstage, and it would be very live—the famous "Beverly" spot (which she later claimed didn't exist). Then there were places that were just as dry as a bone, like singing into a closet full of sweaters. It was horrible. At the Met, you could feel your voice ping off the back wall. The hall is the rest of your instrument, and when you are in a hall that loves you back, you just sing better. You feel better.

Joseph Colaneri recalled the stark contrast between the State Theater's "horrendous" acoustics and those of the Met.

Look at the proscenium of the Met, all of that plasterwork, like faux pillars, built in. There's a spiral going up, and the sound rolls up those things. It's an amazing acoustic, the way that orchestra flows up and out, and the way the stage projects, even from the back.

Colaneri was particularly attentive to how the acoustics affected the players.

> The orchestra takes on a warmth; it's like a cloud in the house. The players hear that and they think, oh my god, listen to that sound, and as a player, you don't get tired. You think, fantastic, let's do more. The State Theater was the other way. The orchestra felt dull in that pit, because the sound was getting trapped.

The company invited acoustical consultants to propose changes, but their solutions were, for the most part, rejected by the New York City Ballet through City Center of Music and Drama, which controlled the theater. It was one of many ways in which Kellogg found that the company's second-class status in the theater made operating difficult. "The ballet had always had, and continued to insist on having, primacy about rehearsal spaces and scheduling," he said. As Keene had before him, he found the ballet's permanent lock on the theater in December for *The Nutcracker* limiting. "If we wanted to increase our time in the theater, it had to be late summer, a very bad sales time. If we wanted the big rehearsal room, they wouldn't give it to us. In later years, I wanted to set up a café in the lobby that would serve full meals, and the Ballet said, 'Mr. Balanchine [who had died in 1983] would not tolerate the smell of garlic in the theater!'"

City Opera tried a few inexpensive and unobtrusive solutions to the acoustical problems, such as padding on the rear wall of the house, but City Ballet's director, Peter Martins, was not enthusiastic about these, and, in any case, they did not come close to solving the problem. So Kellogg made the controversial decision to install an electronic sound enhancement system that he had heard in Denmark—a system of tiny microphones and speakers placed throughout the theater that distributed sound differently. It was not amplification, he insisted, and did not change the actual character of the voices. The system went live in September 1999, and Kellogg claimed that the singers and orchestra members liked the results. Burton recalls that the enhancement system solved the problem in a way—although whereas there had previously been no reverberation, it was now too fast. "The system gave you feedback instantly, in a nanosecond," she said. The audiences, for the most part, did not complain, though Mark Delavan's thunderous Falstaff did produce cries of "Turn off the mikes!" Some critics, on the other hand, objected vociferously, particularly *New York Times* chief music critic Anthony Tommasini, who was appalled by the idea of any kind of amplification in the opera house.

At the end of the first season with the system, Kellogg told Tommasini that the solution was an interim one. The ultimate goal was a full renovation of the theater, or, failing that—given that the Ballet was unlikely to approve an expensive acoustical change that was not in its interests—an entirely new theater. By the fall of 2000, the City Opera board had taken steps to move ahead with this plan, forming a task force to investigate the possibility of a new theater. Lincoln Center had embarked on a multibillion-dollar redevelopment plan in 1999, and City Opera hoped that it could include a new theater on the campus, one that would be purpose-built for its needs. Kellogg had built the Alice Busch Opera Theater at Glimmerglass, and he felt that a new building would not only address the acoustical issues, it would give the company control over its space and an escape from the inflexibility of the Ballet.

Building fever was in the air. Robert Wilson, the company's former board chairman, was outspoken about his dislike of the State Theater and his enthusiasm for a new one, and he dangled the possibility of a $50 million gift as seed money for it. Mayor Rudy Giuliani had already promised a quarter of a billion from the city's capital budget for the Lincoln Center redevelopment. In subsequent months, various proposals for locations of a new theater were floated. On the campus, there was the underutilized Damrosch Park. Also considered were two sites on Amsterdam Avenue, adjacent to the complex: the Red Cross building and the Martin Luther King High School. Nat Leventhal, who had been a deputy mayor under Ed Koch and served as president of Lincoln Center from 1984 to 2000, recalls that in those days, much of Amsterdam Avenue from Sixty-Fifth to Seventy-Second Street consisted of potential development sites.

However, the prospect of a new theater for City Opera quickly acquired some implacable enemies. The Ballet was unenthusiastic, because it would then become solely responsible for the facility expenses of State Theater. Joseph Volpe, the outspoken and combative general manager of the Metropolitan Opera, insisted that City Opera, given its history of perilous finances, could not possibly build or maintain its own theater, and that such a building would become a drain on the other constituents. Volpe had at first refused to participate in discussions of the Lincoln Center master plan at all, and he only joined the effort with the understanding that a new theater for City Opera was off the table.

Perhaps the most damaging opponent, however, was Beverly Sills, who was both a board member of the Metropolitan Opera and chairman of Lincoln Center, and seemed to have turned decisively against her old company. Leventhal, who became close to Sills when they worked together, recalled:

> She's not necessarily the biggest fan of any place she leaves. I think she felt the company had degraded, both artistically and in a business sense—she was always telling me what great financial shape she left the place in—since the time she was there. She was an artist, and could be pretty critical about things. And her loyalties shifted fairly quickly to the Met.

Sills was particularly upset that Kellogg had publicly complained about the theater's acoustics and put in the sound enhancement system. Certainly no one ever had trouble hearing *her* at the New York State Theater. She seemed to have forgotten that she had recognized the need for, and overseen, a major acoustical overhaul of the theater in 1982.

Concerns about the theater and its acoustics aside, the first several years of the Kellogg administration saw the company on an upswing. The budget was balanced. The artistic plans had met with critical enthusiasm, and the general impression of the company was that it was fresh and lively, particularly compared to the more staid offerings of the Metropolitan Opera across the plaza. The City Opera formula—exciting young singers; offbeat, enticing repertory; less expensive tickets—had been rebooted and seemed relevant once again, along with improved standards of production and performance. With many new productions that showcased inventive directors, as well as the baroque and contemporary operas, City Opera was filling an artistic niche for New York fans. Morale was high. All the indicators looked promising for the company's continued success and prosperity. But it was not to be.

CHAPTER 6

A Turn for the Worse

ON TUESDAY, SEPTEMBER 11, 2001, New York City Opera was set to open its sixth full season under the leadership of Paul Kellogg with a new production of Wagner's *The Flying Dutchman*, starring Mark Delavan. It was a huge artistic leap. The company had briefly taken up *Dutchman* and *Die Meistersinger* in the late 1970s, with Julius Rudel, but otherwise City Opera had left Wagner operas, with their large orchestras and choruses and strenuous vocal parts, to the Met. But now, with the newly strengthened orchestra, Kellogg was confident of the company's ability to pull it off.

Jane Gullong, the director of development since 1994, was at the theater early that morning, putting the finishing touches on the evening's gala, which, she recalls, was on track to be the most successful ever: many tickets had been sold; there was an enthusiastic new gala chair; and the involvement of George Trescher, a major society figure and fundraiser, promised a glittering audience. Gullong was meeting in the conference room with Hamish Bowles, the flamboyant British fashion journalist and writer for *Vogue*, who was going to cochair another event for the company. "Paul was in his office. Someone had a radio on. We heard that the tower had gone down."

The attack on the World Trade Center, a devastating shock for New York City and the whole country, would also prove to be a turning point in the fortunes of the New York City Opera. On that day, as the smoke hung over downtown, the city's residents were frantic to find out if their families and friends were safe and afraid of what would come next. The opening night of an opera company was the least of anyone's worries. The performance and the gala were quickly canceled, and everyone went home.

Four days later, on Saturday afternoon, Kellogg led the entire company—costumed singers, staff members, and stagehands—onto the stage and told the audience that at the request of Mayor Giuliani, the matinee of *Dutchman* and the rest of the season would go on. Like Greek drama, he said in his speech, such performances can fulfill a community's need for catharsis in a time of tragedy. "It was hard for people to come, but they did," Kellogg recalled later. City Opera was always the first New York City performing arts institution to open after Labor Day, and now, in a difficult time, it was the first to try to find a way back to normal life. For the audience, it felt strange and frightening to sit in the vaulted State Theater auditorium, wondering if that ceiling would be the next one to come crashing down, but the communal experience and the chance to focus on something other than the disaster downtown proved healing. The surreal production by Stephen Lawless was absorbing, and Delavan gave a breakout performance of the agonized Dutchman. The evening performance, of Jonathan Miller's Marx Brothers–esque production of *The Mikado*, offered consolation of a different kind: it felt good to laugh.

That show of New York resilience was a high point for City Opera. "I thought we would live through it," Sherwin Goldman, the company's executive producer, recalls. "I remember standing on the stage, and Paul telling the audience that the season would go on, it was all going to come back, everything was going to be rosy again." But the seismic effects of 9/11 rocked the cultural world. Behavioral patterns—about things as basic as what people planned to do in the evening—changed.

As the director Stephen Wadsworth put it, "There was a huge reassessment of what urban life was going to be, and all the performing arts took a hit, at least for a while."

City Opera went on with its fall season, which included an enchanting production of *I Capuleti et I Montecchi* as well as a widely panned world premiere, *Lilith*, by Deborah Drattell. The advance subscription sales for the fall season had been robust, but company leaders found it worrying when renewals for the spring season fell off substantially, even with the return of the former blockbuster *Porgy and Bess* on the program. "People were not making commitments for their time far in advance," Goldman says.

Subscription income is advance money in the bank for performing arts organizations. As Danny Newman put it in his influential 1977 book, *Subscribe Now!*:

> The subscriber is our ideal. In an act of faith, at the magic moment
> of writing the check, he commits himself in advance of the season's
> beginning (often many months in advance, and we then also enjoy
> the interest on his money which we have just put into banks or into
> short-term securities).

Subscriptions also cost less to sell than single tickets. For the purchaser, a subscription guarantees a seat at what might otherwise be a sold-out show and establishes a future attendance pattern—the subscriber knows where he or she will be, for example, on the third Thursday night of every month. The days were long gone when a City Opera subscription was highly sought after because it was the only way to be sure of getting a ticket to hear Beverly Sills. But still, at the beginning of the twenty-first century, the company's loyal subscription audience, albeit smaller, remained critically important.

But the shock of 9/11, and the subsequent unwillingness of operagoers to commit far in advance, was not simply a momentary phenomenon that would eventually dissipate. Rather, it amplified a trend that was already beginning to take hold all over the country. The generation that relied on subscriptions to organize their lives was giving way to another, made up of people who were often more inclined to make more spontaneous choices. Another factor was that entertainment options had expanded dramatically, both in live performance and, critically, in on-demand entertainment at home.

This disruption in selling patterns rocked arts organizations through-out New York, but it was particularly troublesome for City Opera, which operated with a razor-thin margin for error. Derek Davis, the company manager, who would later become director of business opera-tions, remembers that in January 2001, he was already concerned about a budget hole in the projections for the upcoming 2001–02 fiscal year. Indeed, the final audit for that year shows a $2 million increase in oper-ating expenses over the previous year—and the company's operations ended the year barely positive. To make matters worse, the Wallace endowment and City Opera's other investments had lost nearly $8 million that year, a consequence of the 2002 economic downturn brought on by the bursting of the dot-com bubble.

Still, there was nothing else for City Opera to do but to keep on with its artistic plans, including seven new productions for 2002–03. The fall season opened with a big new show: James Robinson and Allen Moyer created a cleverly updated *Il Trittico*. A production of Chabrier's buoy-ant *L'Étoile* came from Glimmerglass, as did Christopher Alden's appro-priately dark reading of Britten's *The Rape of Lucretia*, and the company performed *Salome* for the first time since 1976. The season's Handel offer-ing was a trivial, candy-colored *Flavio*, featuring the countertenor Bejun Mehta. With the success of *Porgy*, the company was now mounting Broadway musicals on a regular basis, and the big box office hope of the season was a revival of Sondheim's *A Little Night Music*, a produc-tion from 1990, which starred Broadway and film notables Jeremy Irons and Claire Bloom and was choreographed by Susan Stroman, who had recently won Tony Awards for *The Producers*.

The season also brought a major contemporary work to New York: Jake Heggie and Terrence McNally's *Dead Man Walking*, based on Sister Helen Prejean's searing memoir about the death penalty, which had premiered in San Francisco in 2000. Joyce DiDonato, a rising star, made her City Opera debut as Sister Helen, and Sheryl Woods gave a star turn as the death row prisoner's mother.

Dead Man Walking represented a new phenomenon—an American opera with legs. Several factors had made it a sell-out success in San Francisco: it treated a timely, controversial subject, ably distilled in McNally's trenchant libretto; it told a story audiences already knew, thanks to an acclaimed 1995 film version with Susan Sarandon and Sean Penn; and it was an ideal showcase for Heggie's lyric talents, which had already made him a popular collaborator for many well-known singers. New American operas tended to be premiered and forgotten, but a number of opera companies were quick to recognize that this one, which was both serious and accessible, had the potential to attract large audiences. City Opera immediately banded together with six other American opera companies to commission a new, more portable production of the opera, and over the next six years, each of them would perform the piece; additional productions were mounted at opera companies in Europe and Australia. Once launched, *Dead Man Walking* would never be out of circulation: by the end of 2017, it had been produced nearly sixty times and recorded twice.

The other contemporary work of the season, *Little Women*, by City Opera's composer in residence, Mark Adamo, was a coproduction with Glimmerglass. It, too, had enjoyed a meteoric rise. First mounted in 1998 for Houston Grand Opera's Opera Studio, excerpted at City Opera's 1999 Showcasing American Composers festival, given a main-stage production by Houston Grand Opera in 2000, and nationally telecast on PBS in 2001, *Little Women* was already extremely popular. A beloved novel combined with a tuneful score made it an audience attractor; even more critically, its female-centric cast and manageable vocal and instrumental requirements made it a natural for vocal training programs in universities. As a result, *Little Women* would have an even greater number of productions than *Dead Man Walking* in the years to come.

Heggie and Adamo, along with Tobias Picker, whose *Emmeline* had launched City Opera's new, accessible approach to contemporary opera in 1998, quickly became the go-to composers for opera companies hoping for hits. All three wrote more operas, but none of them managed to catch on as those initial scores had. Nevertheless, the success of *Dead Man Walking* and *Little Women* helped put new work on the agenda for opera companies that would not have considered it before, and even laid the foundation for a much broader interest in writing operas among young composers, who could now see the possibility of actually getting their works commissioned and performed.

But even with such a solid lineup, City Opera's overall attendance fell again. Ticket price increases kept the company's total box office income stable for the year, but the more significant problem was that fund-raising dipped an alarming $1.3 million. The investment income from the endowment again declined as a result of the economic downturn, and the company ended its seven-year streak of positive results with an operating deficit of $2.6 million.

The 2003–04 season saw some artistic retrenchment, with a slight reduction in operating expenses and only five new productions instead of the usual six or seven; none were from Glimmerglass. The September opening night was a new *Alcina*, directed by Francesca Zambello, intended as a showcase for Christine Goerke in the title role. But that plan backfired, as Goerke was not in good vocal shape. Although she did not realize it at the time, Goerke was in the throes of a transition into a heavier vocal category. Some years later, she would reemerge triumphantly as a spectacular singer of Strauss and Wagner, in demand at major houses such as the Metropolitan and Lyric Opera of Chicago, which would tap her for its brand-new *Ring* cycle. But in 2003, she was having trouble navigating the high, florid singing that the role of Alcina demanded. Critics were dismayed.

Other productions went more smoothly: the theater director Bartlett Sher, who would later become Peter Gelb's go-to director at the Met, made his City Opera debut with Marvin David Levy's *Mourning Becomes Electra*, starring Lauren Flanigan. (Based on Eugene O'Neill's reimagining of *The Oresteia* in Civil War–era New England, the opera was written for the Metropolitan's opening season at Lincoln Center and then disappeared from view for thirty years, until Levy revised it and gave it new life.) In the musical theater slot, the company brought back Hal

Prince's production of *Sweeney Todd* from 1984, with Mark Delavan in the title role, the West End actress Elaine Paige as Mrs. Lovett, and the young soprano Sarah Coburn as Johanna; for the first time, the Kellogg team doubled up on the musical/operetta titles with a revival of Jonathan Miller's *Mikado*. Stephen Wadsworth's famous *Xerxes* also returned, but without Lorraine Hunt Lieberson and David Daniels. Though still strongly cast and directed with the same meticulous care, it did not create the same audience furor. And at the end of the year, the numbers were the same: there was an operating deficit of over $2 million. Something had to change.

The company's leaders were grappling with the same problems that all of their predecessors had confronted. Its structure was inflexible, and there was little that could be done to bring down operating expenses unless the company cut back even more dramatically on new productions, which would likely have a negative impact on both the box office sales and City Opera's "innovator" image. The union contracts with the orchestra and the chorus were set up to cover a fixed number of weeks of work—so the falling attendance meant that ticket income was covering a smaller percentage of those contract expenses. Without a transformative renegotiation of the company's relationship with the unions—which would likely lead to a strike—the cost of the contracts would continue to climb. Sherwin Goldman recalled conversations with the head of the chorus union about the problem. "His answer in the end was: 'the membership is not going to accept any reduction in pay.'" But rather than grappling with these daunting problems head-on, Kellogg and his board were focused on the idea of a new theater as the cure for what ailed the company. After 9/11, Kellogg's dream of a new home received an unexpected boost. When plans for rebuilding the World Trade Center site were first discussed, some proposals were floated for the possible inclusion of an arts center. Kellogg saw an opening for City Opera, and by early 2002, he had begun discussions with the Lower Manhattan Development Corporation about the possibility. He found a champion in John C. Whitehead, an opera fan and the chairman of the LMDC. When questions arose as to whether a twenty-two-hundred-seat opera house would fit into architect Daniel Libeskind's design for the site, the company asked both Libeskind and the architect Rafael Viñoly to design opera houses that would work. Both came up with plans, including a design with part of the house cantilevered over the street.

But City Opera's bid was also met with significant opposition. Kellogg recalls that none of the politicians or community groups involved in the decisions about Ground Zero was in City Opera's corner. The company met with the governor, George Pataki, and the Speaker of the New York State Assembly, Sheldon Silver; neither was remotely interested. Indeed, when the final decision about which arts tenants to include was announced in June 2004, City Opera was out of luck. The *New York Times* reported that Mayor Bloomberg, influenced by his commissioner of cultural affairs, Kate Levin, and Beverly Sills, had opposed City Opera's move, citing concerns that the company's departure would hurt Lincoln Center financially. Instead, two other companies, the Signature Theatre and the Joyce Theater, were chosen as the performing arts organizations for the site, along with the Freedom Center and the Drawing Center. (As it turned out, City Opera was lucky to be overlooked. The wrangling over the cultural elements of the Ground Zero site would continue for years, and by 2018 only the National September 11 Memorial Museum had been built and opened.)

But Kellogg would not give up so easily on the new theater idea. After all, the new theater he had built for Glimmerglass (albeit on a smaller scale) had changed that company's profile profoundly. He was convinced the same would happen for City Opera. "This company is not going to survive until we get a new house," he said, "so we can schedule at our will, so we're not at the mercy of CCMD or the ballet."

> We have to have our own house and it has to be principally acoustically appropriate for opera, and it has to be smaller. That would make all the difference to the company's well-being. And it has to be away from the Met. We can't sit there and be constantly compared with our next door neighbor.

That fall he switched his focus to the American Red Cross building site, which is adjacent to Lincoln Center. A & R Kalimian Realty, a developer, had purchased the site and was planning a building to be designed by Christian de Portzamparc; City Opera met with the developers and the Department of City Planning to discuss putting an opera house beneath the residential tower.

As for how a $400 million new building would be funded, Kellogg had a few ideas: several board members were interested, the city was said to be open to the possibility (even though Mayor Bloomberg had ostensibly shot down the World Trade Center move because of concerns about a vacuum in the New York State Theater), and there was hope that some foundation or corporation might like to put their name on a new theater. Robert Wilson, the company's former chairman and its biggest benefactor, thought that the Red Cross site had potential since it was close to Lincoln Center and had ample transit and parking. He had promised $50 million when City Opera had first discussed the possibility of a new theater back in 2000 but had withdrawn it during the Ground Zero process because he thought the location was too remote. Now Wilson said that he might reinstate the pledge if the Red Cross site worked out. In the end, he didn't, ultimately deeming the site too small. But the company remained hopeful that Wilson—or someone else—would come through, and it spent a great deal on architect's fees and the like. It eventually wrote off nearly $3.8 million in pre-construction planning costs.

The pursuit of the new theater was not only expensive—it was enormously time-consuming. Some in the company felt that it distracted Kellogg from more urgent concerns, not to mention that it kept him from grappling with the larger question of how to ensure a more sustainable future for the company. As Mark Moorman, who worked in the development department, put it:

> I think he knew he wasn't going to be there forever, and he thought
> he had a working plan that honored the historical mission of the
> company—highlighting American artists, innovative repertory,
> theatrical production style—that was good enough, so that he could

devote himself to getting a new theater. I think he wanted to give us a home, like a father. [His thought was] "I will get you a home, and the next person will come in and put the company on a new path."

Fixing the company's income problems was proving no easier than solving its issues with expenses. Ticket prices had been rising steadily since before Kellogg took over, which helped to offset the decreasing attendance and keep the total ticket income flat. But as always, the company worried that if prices got too high, it would lose its appeal as a lower-cost alternative to the Met. Furthermore, the company was not producing any runaway hits, and it had reached its peak capacity for lighter fare with long runs of musicals and Gilbert and Sullivan operettas in both the spring and the fall. From the start of their tenure, Kellogg and Goldman had hoped that by revitalizing the company's repertoire and pushing for higher artistic standards, they might reap the rewards of an expanded audience. But the opposite seemed to be happening, and no one knew exactly why or what to do about it. Some observers suggested that Kellogg's single-mindedness about finding a new space was actually damaging the company's sales. If the theater was so bad that the company had to move, the thinking went, why should people buy tickets to see operas there?

In any case, though it was of little consolation, the company's financial conundrum—flat ticket income and rising expenses—was soon to become a national trend. It used to be that performing arts organizations could expect to cover their expenses with 50 percent box office sales and 50 percent contributed income. But now, across the country, that balance had shifted, as expenses increased and box office sales failed to keep pace. The income gap, forecast by the economists Baumol and Bowen in their 1966 study, was growing. Baumol and Bowen had pointed out that the expense of producing nonprofit performing arts would rise much faster than the ability of individuals to pay for them. By the early 2000s, the trend was exacerbated by changes in audience habits and the loss of reliable, returning attendees. This was more than just a post-9/11 hiccup, and performing arts organizations would have to address it with structural changes.

Contributed income would have to bear a larger share of the costs, and here Kellogg and Goldman ran into the difficulty that had plagued the company for its entire existence. "We needed to raise another $10 million a year," Kellogg says. The company's patron base, devoted as it was, was not made up of extremely wealthy people, and it was either unable or unwilling to give more money than it already had been. Corporate funding for operations had dried up long ago, and City Opera's access to foundation money seemed to have reached its limit. The company desperately needed to expand its patron base, bringing in more of the wealthy and the connected, who could contribute significant sums— but City Opera had never excelled in attracting that type of person. As the "second company" in New York, it had built its identity on being the alternative to the Met, and Kellogg's artistic program had continued to position it in that niche. But finding the people to pay for that vision was proving to be a problem.

Kellogg had been successful in fund-raising for Glimmerglass, and his first, innovative years at City Opera had attracted some new contributions, but fund-raising was essentially flat after 2002. For the development department, the months that Kellogg spent at Glimmerglass each year (he was, after all, still artistic director there) were essentially wasted. Some City Opera insiders felt that his elegant, country-gentleman-like demeanor, while appealing, ultimately impeded his ability to fund-raise. As Jane Gullong notes, "Paul Kellogg was too WASPy a fund-raiser, without teeth, a strong arm or a relentless strategy. In Cooperstown, his personal relationships with people like Eugene Thaw had a great impact on fund-raising. He brought no such seven-figure friendships to City Opera."

In its history, City Opera had had two major patrons. Lloyd Rigler and Robert Wilson, who had both contributed significant sums to the company in the past, were wealthy, eccentric entrepreneurs and loners, people who tended to drive away other contributors rather than encourage their participation. Both had been strong supporters of Sills, believing that her celebrity and her management could revitalize the company,

and they backed that belief with funds. But when the company's fortunes took a downward turn under Christopher Keene, Wilson cut back
his support, and Rigler turned his focus and his funds to his new satellite programming service for the arts. Rigler died in December 2003,
and within the past several years, Wilson had offered and withdrawn his
$50 million for the new theater. No individuals with similar means
had replaced them.

Irwin Schneiderman, the current board chair, was a different sort of
person. A Brooklyn-born, Harvard-trained lawyer at the white-shoe firm
of Cahill, Gordon & Reindel, Schneiderman was a self-described "kid
from the Jewish ghetto" who believed strongly in the company's mission as the People's Opera. It was Schneiderman who had recruited Kellogg in the first place, and he was enthusiastic about Kellogg's vision.
He was a generous contributor—his philosophy, Gullong recalls, was
"give until it hurts"—and in the early Kellogg years, he had stepped
up with additional money for Kellogg's initiative to raise artistic standards, the Fund for Artistic Excellence. However, he was not a multimillionaire; his annual giving was at the $250,000 level rather than the
$1 million level. "He kind of represented what NYCO was—self-made,
outer-borough. Successful and well-to-do, but not who you'd invite if
you wanted to get into social columns," Sherwin Goldman said. Schneiderman, says Gullong, "was not part of a social or business network in
which charitable favors were exchanged and institutions built."

None of the rest of the board gave or brought in $1 million gifts,
either. "We overestimated the viability of the NYCO board," Goldman
says flatly. "It was quite mature, and they didn't want to give the amount
of money that they were giving, or to give more money." When Gullong arrived in 1994, the expected contribution from a board member
was $25,000, and only half of them were actually paying up. Gullong
made the payments mandatory, and the amount was later increased to
$50,000. Building the board was a challenge, Goldman says. "The only
reason someone would go on the City Opera board rather than the Met
board was because it cost less."

In short, the City Opera board was not attractive to the wealthy New
Yorkers who join nonprofit boards for social reasons, and the people who

were on it did not tend to be socialites with lots of rich friends. Gold-man felt that the City Opera board was viewed as second class and that New Yorkers who wanted to be on an opera board would choose the Met, which, in recent decades, had become less restrictive about who it embraced. The new artistic profile under Kellogg had garnered enthu-siastic press, but it had not been significantly helpful in attracting major patrons. "It's because [patronage] isn't really about the art," Goldman says. "It is for some people, and maybe sometimes there's a coincidence of people with money. Occasionally you have a Bob Wilson—if he likes it, he'll pay for it. But that's very, very rare."

Jane Gullong thought that she had found another such person when James Marcus, a Metropolitan Opera and Juilliard School board mem-ber, brought Susan Baker to her attention. A former analyst at Gold-man Sachs, she was married to Michael Lynch, a partner at the firm who had acquired a significant fortune when it went public in 1999. Baker had been on the boards of the Brooklyn Academy of Music and the School of American Ballet, and she was looking for a new cause. Gul-long, in search of someone who would provide entrée to more multi-millionaires in financial enclaves like Goldman Sachs, thought she was a hot prospect for City Opera. Baker joined the City Opera board in 1999 and was soon elected vice chairman. She made some six-figure gifts to the company, and Gullong, who felt that it was time for Schneider-man to step aside after ten years, soon proposed Baker for the post of chairman, to which she was elected in May 2004.

Baker and Goldman clashed from the beginning over turf and man-agement style. "She never asked a question, which is the first thing you do when you come in," he says.

> She took notes all the time—it was like Madame Defarge. And when
> I asked her about the issues that interested me, such as, how are we
> going to expand the board and raise more money, her answer was,
> that's a board issue, not a staff issue [in other words, not Goldman's
> business]. City Opera always had a wonderful way, with board and
> staff working together, sharing these responsibilities, but she said
> only, this is not a staff issue.

Goldman was also troubled by some questions Baker had asked about the endowment, particularly regarding the legal restrictions on the company's ability to spend the funds. He suspected that Baker wanted to find ways to invade the principal of the endowment to use for current expenses.

When Baker interviewed the company's staff members individually, her discussion with Goldman did not go well.

> She asked me how I saw my job, and when I told her, she said, "A lot of those are responsibilities that we should really consider reassigning to the chairperson." She also said, "I think one of the problems here is that you and Paul are not working in an organizational manner. You're friends, and you work like friends, and that's not good in an organization structure." Clearly, she felt that she should be doing some of the things that Paul and I were doing. I said, "If you're going to discuss reassigning responsibilities, let's discuss it." She said, "We will in due course." I said, "No, let's discuss it now. I don't insist on my job being done the way I do it, but I do want to have a part in deciding what that is." She said, "No, that's my job." So I said, "Then it's all your job."

Goldman stepped down as executive producer later that year. He agreed to continue working on getting a new theater, which he saw as a "face-saving" arrangement, and Baker promoted Jane Gullong to the job of executive director, in which she took over many of Goldman's responsibilities.

The company's increasing financial troubles were reflected in the 2004–05 season opener, a new production of Richard Strauss's *Daphne*. The orchestra sounded underrehearsed, Stephen Lawless's staging looked cheap, and the principal singers, Elizabeth Futral and Robert Chafin, were vocally underpowered for those roles. The world premiere of Charles Wuorinen's *Haroun and the Sea of Stories*, based on a book by Salman Rushdie, was better produced and cast—a bright-voiced soprano, Heather Buck, sang the title role—but Wuorinen's complex, hard-edged music was not an audience-pleaser. That job went to the two musical revivals:

Rodgers and Hammerstein's *Cinderella* in the fall and the Hal Prince opera house version of *Candide* in the spring. As before, several of the season's productions came from Glimmerglass, including Tazewell Thompson's moving staging of *Dialogues of the Carmelites*, Lillian Groag's *La Fanciulla del West*, and Handel's *Orlando*, with Bejun Mehta, Amy Burton, and Jennifer Aylmer.

By the end of the season, the picture was again bleak. The total number of tickets sold had declined again—for the third year in a row—and expenses had increased, due in part to a $2 million hike in artistic costs (which takes into account anything that goes into opera productions, including artists' salaries) and $1.6 million in pre-construction costs for the new theater. Taken together, this added up to another huge operating loss—the third one in a row—of $4.7 million. However, the existence of the Wallace endowment gave the board some wiggle room. In the previous year, the company had begun borrowing, using the endowment as collateral, in order to fund its operations; by the end of 2004–05, the outstanding loan was over $6 million.

One bright spot in the year was the company's visit to Japan in May 2005 as a participant in the United States Cultural Program at the Aichi World Expo 2005. The New York City Opera gave four fully staged performances in Tokyo and Nagoya, two each of Mark Adamo's *Little Women* and the Mark Lamos production of *Madama Butterfly*. Fees paid to the company for the tour, as well as some additional corporate fund-raising related to it, boosted income. The experience also gave the company hope for future visits to Asia, which was expanding as a market for Western cultural exports as the options for domestic touring contracted.

Goldman's departure had inevitably brought about changes. He and Kellogg had operated as a good cop/bad cop team, with the conflict-averse Kellogg playing the popular father figure and Goldman the businessman in charge of keeping the budgets in line without worrying about whether anyone liked him. Goldman had often been difficult to deal with—"volatile and emotional," in the words of Gail Kruvand, who negotiated with him for the orchestra committee—and many in the company were afraid of him. His secretive, rule-by-fear operating strategy inhibited any kind of team building that might have helped the company weather hard times.

Mark Moorman felt that the leadership duo of Kellogg and Goldman (plus Thompson) was ultimately a problem for the workings of the company, since Goldman's seemingly arbitrary cost-control activities often trumped artistic ones, and the artistic people felt cheated. "It was a terrible combination," Moorman says.

> The wrong group of temperaments. And because Paul hated conflict, he provided no leadership, and everyone felt like a stepchild. If Paul had backed up Sherwin in those decisions, saying, "I agree that we have to decrease this budget, but I still think we can do a wonderful show," it would have helped. Instead, he soothed people, saying, "Let's have a drink, let's forget about it, it'll be fine."

With "bad cop" Goldman out of the picture, Kellogg receded even more. Gullong was more team-oriented and a more open manager than Goldman, but she lacked his tough-minded business sense. And she was plunged into a budget situation that required drastic measures, even a radical rethinking of the company's operations.

On Gullong's watch, a small, informal group of staff and board members formed an unofficial "new model task force" to explore some possible scenarios for total change. If City Opera's long-standing business and artistic model was no longer viable, what more sustainable one might take its place? And what existing structures would have to change in order for that to happen? One aspect of the discussion centered on repertory. The company seemed to have at least two distinct audiences: one that liked the moderately priced standard repertory and another that liked the rarities and contemporary works. The latter audience was more donor-heavy—and the task force considered the consequences of a scenario in which City Opera performed only new or unusual operas. They concluded that such a transformation would shrink the company and the audience too much to be feasible under the current system of labor contracts and could not be implemented without a major strike.

Wholesale reinvention seemed impossible in the short term, but for the 2005–06 season, Gullong tried a small-scale audience development initiative: a two-day festival called "Opera for All," which explicitly targeted the standard repertory audience. The idea was to play up the People's Opera identity by lowering ticket prices significantly and leaning on crowd-pleasers. The festival opened the season on September 8 with an eighty-minute concert of opera excerpts, featuring a special performance by opera lover and pop divo Rufus Wainwright. At a party on the State Theater mezzanine afterward, open to all ticket holders, the East Village Opera Company performed rock versions of opera arias. All tickets cost $25, as did all the seats at the following night's performance of *Madama Butterfly*, which was hosted by the actress Cynthia Nixon and featured behind-the-scenes videos between acts. Tickets were sold not only at the State Theater box office but also in Bryant Park during three public midday concerts with City Opera artists. Ticket buyers were offered the opportunity to purchase discounted tickets to any of the season's other performances. With the top ticket price for the rest of the season now at $110, this was a bargain. Tickets for the festival sold out quickly, and 71 percent of the purchasers were new to City Opera. Eleven percent of these first-time attendees returned for regular performances later in the season, a seemingly small number but a hopeful sign for future audience-building.

The experiment was expanded for the 2006–07 season, this time with eight $25 performances—another concert of excerpts with an after-party in the fall and seven performances of *La Bohème, Carmen, Butterfly,* and *Traviata* spread out over the season. These, too, sold out. A survey by AEA Consulting reported that the primary driver of the first-time ticket buyers was price, and 95 percent of Opera for All attendees were not subscribers. The audiences were ten years younger, on average, than the usual City Opera audience, and more diverse. It was a tantalizing hint about a new way to carry out audience development: opera was still something that people wanted to see—if the price was right.

If an entirely new model for the company was not a feasible option, another possibility was to examine how the existing model could be tweaked and improved. In 2005, a team from Boston Consulting Group (BCG), headed by Marc Powell, who was married to a company stage manager, undertook a three-month, pro bono assessment of City Opera, looking at the company's financial picture, its organizational structure, and the outside perception of it. Their findings, which were presented to the board at the September 14, 2005, meeting, painted a bleak picture: in four years, expenses had increased at nearly six times the rate at which revenue had grown; the company's investment in fund-raising was lower than that of any of its peers, and its inefficient decision-making and budgeting processes were hampering its ability to control costs and plan for the future. In addition, the company itself appeared conflicted as to its mission going forward, and a significant segment of donors and audience seemed unaware of what made NYCO special.

The BCG numbers were disturbing. The ticket sales analysis showed that sales as a percentage of capacity had been dropping steadily for a decade: in 1995, they were 84 percent; in 2005, 68 percent. In 2000, the year of the first *Porgy*, they had spiked to 82 percent but then resumed their downward trend. The percentage of subscription sales had also fallen, and City Opera, compared with fourteen peer companies, had by far the lowest percentage of capacity sold on subscription—27 percent—a challenging situation for a company giving 115 performances a year. It also had one of the highest percentages of unsold capacity: 33 percent. Cost increases were driven by performance payroll—some of which could be attributed to particular operas requiring extra singers—and theater costs, while the repertory planning process made it difficult to forecast expenses or to raise money for particular productions far enough in advance.

The lack of consensus within the company about its mission and future was also startling. Some BCG interviewees felt that City Opera should reclaim its People's Opera status, keeping ticket prices low, while focusing on outreach, accessibility, promoting young singers, and producing more shows with a broader audience appeal like musical theater and light opera. Others believed that the time for the People's Opera mission had come and gone—and the company should recognize that opera is a luxury product that necessarily commands high prices. Raising prices, some said, would give them the freedom to focus on exceptional singers and appeal to traditional audiences with money, while maintaining a position as a leader and innovator, with high artistic integrity.

The objectives that BCG spelled out for the company made the difficulty of its plight clear: achieve financial solvency, build new audiences, provide consistently innovative or accessible productions, become a destination for the artistic community. Every one of those goals was essential to its survival, and tackling any or all of them was an enormous task, particularly for a staff that was already stretched beyond its capacity trying to keep the lights on and put on 115 performances. The day-to-day struggle for survival certainly precluded any meaningful conversation about vision. Furthermore, at the same meeting that the report was presented to the board, Paul Kellogg announced that he would retire at the end of the 2006–07 season. At sixty-eight, he was exhausted and out of ideas about how to reverse a company in free fall.

CHAPTER 7

The Savior

DESPITE THE COMPANY'S financial woes and Kellogg's announcement, the 2005–06 season began on a positive note, with sellout crowds
at the Opera for All events and the artistic success of Stephen Lawless
and Ashley Martin-Davis's elegant production of Strauss's *Capriccio*,
updated to the 1940s, with Pamela Armstrong, Ryan MacPherson, and
Eric Halfvarson. Lovingly conducted by George Manahan, it made a
persuasive case for this talky piece, which can feel more like an endless
debate than an opera.

The *Capriccio* was Robin Thompson's pride and joy, even though it
was his third choice for the opening spot. His first choice would have
been a major coup: the US premiere of Thomas Adès's *The Tempest*, which
had played to rapturous acclaim in London the previous year. Thompson had gone to London on a whim to see it in February 2004, and he
said, "The crowd knocked my socks off. There were lots of young people
there. Alex Ross had just thrown two typewriters in the air writing about
it." Thompson swiftly secured the rights for the first American production and set about convincing his colleagues to stage it, giving CDs of

the London performance to Kellogg and Bartlett Sher, both of whom were enthusiastic. But the chair of the opening-night gala objected, and the idea was discarded. "That person hated it. So that was the end," Thompson recalls. "I was crushed. It would have been such a feather in the cap of City Opera." The loss of that premiere was just one sign that the company was no longer in the vanguard of the American opera world. The Santa Fe Opera ultimately gave the US premiere of *The Tempest* in the summer of 2006 and the Metropolitan produced it in 2012. (The Met's leaders were so enthusiastic that they decided to co-commission Adès's next opera, *The Exterminating Angel*.)

When *The Tempest* fell through, Thompson's initial plan was to replace it with a production of Jonathan Miller's *The Elixir of Love* set in a diner in the western United States, but this also fell through when Miller turned out to be unavailable for the period in question. "It was a lonely Saturday afternoon," Thompson recalls. "Paul Kellogg was in his office doing some paperwork, and we said, 'Now what are we going to do?' He had made a list of operas that he liked and wanted to do someday, and *Capriccio* was on the list." Thompson pulled together an artistic team and cast practically on the spot and built the show into an artistic success, although he acknowledges that selling tickets for it was an uphill battle. "But at that point," he says, "everything was an uphill battle."

The other new productions included Dukas's *Ariane et Barbe-Bleue*, an amusing novelty that was added to the season primarily because it was funded by patrons of Leon Botstein, the music director of the American Symphony Orchestra and the president of Bard College, who conducted it. That season included only two Glimmerglass imports: Richard Rodney Bennett's 1963 thriller, *The Mines of Sulphur*, and the Gilbert and Sullivan *Patience*. Two contemporary American works, Rachel Portman's child-friendly *The Little Prince* (2003) and Adamo's bawdy *Lysistrata* (2005) came from the Houston Grand Opera. Yet despite high hopes, ticket sales continued to decline, and the season ended with a $3 million deficit. The company's cumulative deficit was now $13 million for the last four years.

In the wake of the BCG report, planning for the 2006–07 season took a new turn. The report's list of recommendations was daunting and wide-ranging, but the most manageable suggestions had to do with expense control. After looking at the company's balance of fixed and variable costs, BCG's foremost suggestion was to give more performances of existing productions rather than investing money in new ones, and to present fewer titles overall.

Accordingly, the company scheduled just twelve operas that season, instead of fifteen or sixteen, but still spread over 115 performances. Also following BCG's recommendations, it presented 12 performances of Jonathan Miller's updated *Elixir of Love*, the same production that had fallen through for the previous season's opening night, instead of the 7 that it would normally expect this bel canto comedy title to sell. *Elixir* was an amusing show, set in "Adina's Diner" in the American Southwest circa 1960 (instead of on the farm of wealthy Adina in eighteenth-century Italy) with Nemorino, Adina's peasant suitor, as a grease monkey, and the charlatan Dulcamara, who sells Nemorino a "magic potion" that is supposed to make Adina love him, arriving in a two-tone convertible.

However, *Elixir* is neither a top-ten opera title nor a popular musical, and the ticket sales reflected that, falling well short of the overly ambitious goals set for the twelve performances. The same size audience that would have come to seven performances of the opera was now spread among twelve, with the correspondingly demoralizing effect of half-empty houses. The rest of the season had some artistic high spots: a clever Marilyn Monroe–and–JFK take on Handel's *Semele* for the opening night, starring a sparkling Elizabeth Futral; and a *Così fan tutte* led by Julius Rudel, who made his first appearance with the company in a quarter of a century. However, a new production of *La Donna del Lago*, planned as a showcase for the bel canto soprano Alexandrina Pendatchanska, looked cheap and ugly. Hampered by a gray, bare-bones set that was intermittently peppered with snow that sounded like pebbles as it hit the stage, a women's chorus that resembled a severe Presbyterian sewing circle, and mechanical directing, the cast sounded as dispirited as they looked.

The season may have cost less to produce, but the cuts had severe repercussions, which were felt at the box office. Subscription numbers had been declining steadily for the past decade (with the exception of the spike for *Porgy* in 1999–2000). But for this season, the decline became precipitous: the company lost over five thousand subscribers, dropping to just fourteen thousand, and sold twenty thousand fewer tickets on subscription than it had in the previous year. The one piece of good news was that there were more tickets sold altogether than in the previous season. However, the increase came entirely thanks to the eight sold-out Opera for All performances, for which ticket prices were significantly lower, which did not help the bottom line. By the end of the season, ticket income was $1 million short of the budgeted amount.

The idea that the BCG report had inspired—doing twelve rather than seven performances of *Elixir*—was a disaster, and one that experienced opera company managers should have predicted. As a result, in subsequent years, City Opera staffers would recall the whole BCG report as a debacle, a business-oriented process that fundamentally misunderstood the workings of an opera company. The *Elixir* idea had been based on an assumption that turned out to be incorrect: that more performances would produce more income at a smaller marginal cost. This failure called all of the assumptions and suggestions of the BCG report into question—and BCG's larger, essentially accurate diagnosis of the company's problems was tarred with that brush of failure.

And a new challenge had arisen. Across the Lincoln Center plaza, Peter Gelb had assumed the leadership of the Metropolitan Opera, beginning with the 2006–07 season. Gelb, the son of the legendary *New York Times* editor Arthur Gelb, had been the head of Sony Classical, and his artistic ideas, honed in the recording industry, were tuned in to the contemporary market. Now, it seemed, the Met was capturing all of the opera bandwidth in New York: the company had a splashy media campaign; a big, audience-friendly, all-day open house to launch the new season; a gorgeous—and highly photogenic—opening-night production of *Madama Butterfly*, directed by Anthony Minghella; and the promise of many new productions and exciting innovations to come. To lure new audiences who lacked the money for an expensive ticket, the Met instituted a Rush Tickets program, funded by Agnes Varis, which offered several hundred $20 seats for nearly every performance, available to those willing to stand in line. Questioned about their decision not to renew, some City Opera subscribers responded that they were "going to try the Met instead."

Perhaps the greatest irony of the situation was that Gelb had been handpicked for the job by Beverly Sills, who was named chairwoman of the Met board in 2002, six months after stepping down from her chairwoman post at Lincoln Center and "retiring" from arts administration. Sills's relationship with her old company had ranged from chilly to adversarial under Kellogg's regime. She had been deeply offended by the way the Met had treated her during her singing career—Rudolf Bing had refused to hire her during her heyday, and she only made her debut there in 1975, after he had retired—but the hatchet was buried when she joined its board in 1991, just months after she left City Opera's board. Now that she was the leading opera company's chairwoman, second-string City Opera seemed to be like dust under her shoes.

If the Met was going to steal City Opera's "brand," as some staffers complained, with lively productions and unusual repertoire, to say nothing of inexpensive seats and a newly welcoming attitude, it was all the more critical that the smaller company define its vision and its desired audience more precisely. What was City Opera now, and who was it for? What was the point of having two repertory companies with simultaneous seasons, next door to each other?

City Opera had evolved throughout its history, trying different strategies that enabled it to survive and positioning itself as an important alternative to the Met. While the Met was founded for the wealthy, the People's Opera was a creation inspired by 1940s populism: affordable entertainment for middle-class immigrants—like Fiorello La Guardia and Julius Rudel—whose association with opera was visceral, and went back to their countries of origin. Practical concerns shaped the company into a showcase for young American singers who weren't hired at the Met—and were happy to work for the small sums that City Opera could

afford to pay them. It was able to further carve out its niche by focusing on contemporary and American repertoire, both areas that the Ford
Foundation was interested in funding. With the rise of Beverly Sills, the
company became a destination for fans of New York's homegrown opera
star. And in the 1980s, when Sills was facing declining audiences as the
company's director, she attacked that problem by programming more
popular fare.

But in the past few decades, City Opera's core audience had continued to shrink. By the 1990s, the remaining grandchildren of the original 1940s audiences no longer felt any "old country" attachment to opera
as an art form. Those who *were* interested in opera would be more likely
to choose the Met, with its famous singers and lavish productions.
(Unlike the immigrants of the early and mid-twentieth century, who
came from war-torn European countries, New York's current immigrant
population primarily came from places like Latin America, Asia, and
Africa, where opera was not as culturally dominant—so even the People's
Opera was not likely to be their entertainment of choice.) As the "new
model" task force had discovered, there was still interest in affordable
standard repertory opera and novelties but no critical mass of attendees
that enthusiastically embraced the company as a whole. The numbers
were no longer adding up; there just weren't enough people to fill the
house for 115 performances a season. "It was a misalignment of supply and
demand," says Timothy O'Leary, who was a member of the company's management team under Gullong. But supply was fixed: the company was
locked into its union agreements.

Even with its tenuous bottom line and history of near-death experiences, the company had somehow managed to survive—and its scrappy,
underdog ethos was a key factor in that survival. "City Opera was always
the little engine that could," says Cori Ellison, a dramaturg with the
company in the late '90s and 2000s. The company owed its success and
continued existence, she said, to

a core of people who were incredibly workaholic, visionary, and quixotic. Any successful opera company has something of that, but at
City Opera, we always had this can-do kind of attitude. There was

always not enough of anything. Not enough time, not enough money. You couldn't have the right chairs in rehearsal, or the right props. Everyone was always thinking on their feet, able to improvise.

Marc Scorca, the president of Opera America, who worked at City Opera as director of special events in the early '80s, says the company had a "human deficit": too few people for the work that needed doing, so everyone worked "day and night—and weekends. They just lived there, and out of that crucible came eighteen productions, 115 performances a year. No company other than the Met has that level of productivity. It was a real bonding experience." Ellison concurs. "I lived there, in the basement, *in questa tomba oscura.* None of our offices had a window, and we spent so many hours down there, you felt as though you were growing mole eyes. You never knew what the weather was. You went down at 9 a.m. and came out at midnight. There could have been a nuclear holocaust, and you wouldn't have known." That intense bonding experience meant that the camaraderie of the City Opera staff and artists endured long past individual tenures.

However, Ellison points out, that very attitude may have kept the company in its scrappy, let's-put-on-a-show incarnation long past the time when it was a feasible model. "In a certain way, we enabled the board and the administration," she says. "We just kept rising to the occasion. They would say, 'You don't really *need* more money, you put on a perfectly wonderful *Capriccio* or *Vanessa* or *Xerxes* with that much money.'"

Kellogg and Thompson had worked hard to raise the standards at the company and change its image from a second-class, cheaper-option company into a modern institution with a distinct artistic profile. But the shoestring budgets persisted, and the audience of the 2000s, accustomed to the elaborate production values of film and television, was less tolerant of on-the-cheap staging than the audience of the 1970s had been. And now that the company was once again in serious financial trouble, austerity measures made it harder than ever for City Opera to maintain the fresh, innovative image it had presented during the early years of Kellogg's tenure. The Kellogg formula was looking tired.

———————

Even with all of Kellogg's efforts to reposition it, City Opera was still perceived as the second company in New York. Part of the problem, as Sherwin Goldman observed, was that the company "had no real institutional support. No one had a vested interest in City Opera. The City didn't say, 'this company can't fail'—neither did the state, nor the federal government, nor the Ford Foundation. It was, 'Oh, what a nice organization, but I'm not interested in opera.'"

Kellogg and Goldman had tried to solve the "second company" stigma by getting City Opera away from Lincoln Center where, they felt, that problem could never be overcome. As Goldman recalls, "I came to the conclusion that City Opera was not viable within the Lincoln Center operation, because Lincoln Center had its opera company, which was going to survive." Reynold Levy, who became Lincoln Center's president in 2002, was decidedly ambivalent about City Opera, Goldman says.

> He said, "We have an opera company, a symphony, a ballet, and you. You can stay, or you can go." On some days I thought he was being personally dismissive of the organization, and on some days, I realized he was right. From his point of view, what difference did it make? It would be better if [we] got out of there and [Lincoln Center made the State Theater into] a dance house.

The focus on finding a new building dominated the board as well. In 2004, Kara Unterberg, a young City Opera fan and Harvard Business School graduate who had trained as a singer, joined the board. She was at the time married to Roy Niederhoffer, a hedge fund millionaire and fellow opera enthusiast—their first date had been a City Opera performance. From the outset, Unterberg was aware of the company's difficulties and felt that little was being done, at least on the board level, to address them. "So much of the board's time was wasted," she said, on the new building project: "where to build, how to raise money to build—and all this stuff was fanciful." In her view, the board found the tangible building project easier to talk about than intractable problems like ticket sales, deficits, and the company's artistic future. As the youngest member by far, Unterberg recalls being intimidated by the City Opera board, which, she says, was very formal and not conducive to discussion. "People on non-profit boards often don't disagree because they are afraid to insult people," she says. Under Susan Baker's leadership, Unterberg felt that dissent was unwelcome. "Things were just presented, and if there was any kind of dissent or question, Susan had this amazing way of just getting off that topic." Unterberg began to feel that she had no power, that no one wanted her opinion, just her money, and that momentous decisions about the company's future were made in committee, where there was little that she could do to influence them.

Unterberg was particularly dismayed by the board's practice of approving budgets that included operating deficits. The budgets were also wildly optimistic, substantially overestimating both ticket and fund-raising income, so that the actual year-end results showed even greater deficits than those that were projected. Nomi Ghez, the board treasurer, would disapprovingly refer to this practice as "aspirational," but still it persisted.

The board went on approving the budgets because there were no immediate repercussions: the $55 million endowment—encompassing the $51.5 million from the Wallace Funds as well as some smaller, previously granted funds—had become NYCO's unofficial piggy bank. Starting in 2004, the company had been using it as collateral to borrow money to fund operations, paying significant interest fees. Then, late in 2005, two new sources of cash were identified. One was a serendipitous windfall: Ruth Klotz, a longtime, relatively low-level donor, who died in 2002, had left the company half her estate. This generous bequest became even more substantial when a painting she owned sold for $14 million at auction. The Klotz gift would eventually total $10.4 million and would be disbursed over three years, helping to bridge the ever-widening gulf between expenses and revenue.

In addition, the board had identified a provision in the Wallace endowment agreement that enabled them to take money directly out of the $51.5 million Wallace principal and use it for operations, without being required to pay it back—circumventing the rules that usually govern endowments. For three years, these so-called Special Projects withdrawals were used to pay off the company's loans (for which the endowment funds had previously been used as collateral). In all, the company withdrew a total of $9.6 million from the endowment. Susan Baker was particularly concerned about the loans since the company would have to demonstrate fiscal responsibility if it was to have any chance of receiving support from New York City for the proposed new building. So, for the 2005–06 season, the company used some creative accounting, offsetting the actual operating deficit of $5.9 million with the Klotz bequest and a Special Projects withdrawal from the Wallace endowment. On paper, the company had a surplus for the year. The following year, with the second multimillion-dollar installment from the Klotz bequest and another $4.24 million from Wallace, they did the same and again showed a surplus. The finance committee also decided to raise the percentage of the endowment draw from 5.5 percent to 6.6 percent, which is higher than customary, allowing the company to apply more investment income to its operations.

In the 2006–07 season, the company's investment committee had responded to the go-go Wall Street spirit and diversified the endowment portfolio, including moving 25 percent of it into risky hedge funds. Financial manipulation was the board's latest quixotic attempt to find a new strategy for survival. For a while it seemed to be working—the first year's returns were strong, with investment results up nearly 18 percent, and despite the Special Projects withdrawals, the endowment's value actually grew that year. Nomi Ghez, the board's treasurer, warned the other board members that the Wallace withdrawals were not "new money" and thus did not represent an increase in fund-raising, but the success of the new investment strategy did not help her case. If the company could replace the money by playing the stock market, what was the problem?

The board's approach to the search for a new general director was no more coherent, and a new leader was urgently needed. Kellogg was staying on through the end of the 2006–07 season, but from the time he announced his retirement in 2005, he had become increasingly remote from the company's operations. The search process for his successor had begun, without his participation, and it dragged on for months. A year after Kellogg's announcement, the search committee, comprised of nine board members and chaired by VP Mark Newhouse, reported that they had interviewed eleven candidates and had five more in the pipeline. The list would only continue to grow.

The interview process proceeded in fits and starts—and was, by many accounts, haphazard. When James Robinson, the artistic director of Opera Colorado, was invited to meet with some board members, he was not sure whether it was actually a job interview.

> They weren't really talking about the company itself, they were going around the table, saying things like, "I like Baroque music, would you do Baroque music?" or "I like the standards, would you do that?" I thought, they are not asking the right questions about moving City Opera forward.

Mark Weinstein, the former City Opera executive who had gone to the Pittsburgh Opera after Kellogg's appointment and was now its general director, also interviewed with the board and recalls the experience as "bizarre." "They were not listening to anything I said. I didn't think they were really interviewing me." Marc Scorca, the president of Opera America, had a first-round interview. The soprano Catherine Malfitano and Leon Botstein were interviewed. Board and search committee member Emilie Corey remembers a meeting in her apartment with George Steel, the head of Miller Theatre at Columbia; she was put off by his brash demeanor and his salary demands but says fellow board member Mary Sharp Cronson was eager for Steel to get the job.

Corey felt that the board's criteria for a new general director were vague. "They wanted a star," she says. "And there was the issue of the unions—who could work with the unions, hold back the unions, maybe even get rid of the unions, because the unions were what was costing so much money." Even that seemingly essential search criterion did not seem to be any more important than others. Corey recalls, "There was one guy who seemed strong enough to do that. But he didn't interview well. The board didn't think he was polished enough. He perspired during the interview." Another problem was that the idea of the new theater as the cure-all for City Opera's problems cast a shadow over the search. Weinstein recalls that, during his interview, the board seemed very focused on moving out of the New York State Theater, to the exclusion of any other ideas about how the company's problems could be addressed. "Susan Baker was leading the charge [for the new theater], and she was very excited by that," Emilie Corey says. The board hoped that the new theater would spark interest in the company and spur giving, since buildings are often more attractive to major donors than day-to-day operations are. The building seemed more important than who would actually lead City Opera. Then, in May 2006, the building project came to an abrupt halt when the Red Cross deal fell through. The developer wanted to get started and was unwilling to wait through the extensive New York City approvals process that would have been required if an eighteen-hundred-seat opera house was to be included. But no sooner had one magic bullet disappeared than another one took its place. In the spring of 2006, Susan Baker attended a dinner at the French consulate in New York. She was seated next to Gerard Mortier.

Mortier, who was then the general director of the Paris Opera, was a legendary figure in Europe. Belgian-born, he had begun his career by putting the backwater Brussels Théâtre Royal de la Monnaie on the map with his modernist approach to opera and dance, which included providing a nurturing environment for the fledgling Mark Morris Dance Group (he also left large deficits behind). In his next post, as the director of the Salzburg Festival, where he succeeded the legendary Herbert von Karajan, he spent the 1990s deliberately and happily ruffling the feathers of its traditionalist audiences, taking aim at its elite stuffiness with provocative stagings of classics, like a *Die Fledermaus* that featured Nazis, incest, and cocaine, and a *Così fan tutte* in which Karita Mattila, as Fiordiligi, had to sing "Come scoglio" while holding the leashes of two men, scantily clad in leather and chains, crawling on all fours and nipping at her heels. At Salzburg, Mortier also championed such composers as Kaija Saariaho, whom he persuaded to write a first opera, *L'Amour de loin*, and directors like Peter Sellars, whom he engaged to mount major projects like the resurrection of Messiaen's huge and challenging opera *Saint François d'Assise*. After leaving Salzburg, Mortier launched the Ruhrtriennale, a home for avant-garde, genre-breaking productions. True to form, his tenure at the Paris Opera was controversial and attention-getting. He was also approaching his sixty-fifth birthday, when he would be obligated, by French law, to retire from his post.

"Susan met Mortier and fell in love," says Emilie Corey. A worldrenowned impresario, brilliant producer, and charming person—what could be more game-changing for City Opera than Gerard Mortier as general director? As Jane Gullong points out, Baker did not subscribe to the second-best, underdog view of the company and didn't see how some could take pride in it. "She thought NYCO could be the best; she had high standards for it. She also had a business school mentality, and one of her philosophies was that you make the best decision if you postpone it." True to that philosophy, she had dragged the search for a new director on for eighteen months, and now, having met Mortier, Baker was ready to move. "From the minute she met him at the French consulate, this was in process," Gullong recalls. "She asked me what I knew about him, and said she was going to Paris to talk to him. I don't think she consulted any other board members."

Alexander Neef, a longtime protégé of Mortier, who was then the casting director of the Paris Opera, recalls that Mortier was "flattered and intrigued" by Baker's wooing but not yet persuaded that moving to New York was feasible. "He said no a number of times. I think he was pretty aware of what it would mean to become a [lesser] neighbor of the Met, when in Paris he was more like an equal—these two are the biggest opera companies in the world, in terms of volume of activity and budget size. [In 2006–07 the budget of the Paris Opera was about $240 million; it gave over 350 performances, both opera and ballet, in two theaters, each year.] New York fascinated him, but I think he struggled with the idea." Once Mortier decided that the offer was worth considering, Neef says, he thought long and hard about

> what it would mean for him, having had this history with some of the most prestigious arts organizations in Europe. That's the reason he was asked—to somehow transfer or translate that prestige to City Opera. I think he was very mindful of what he thought was needed in terms of resources, to do something that would satisfy his level of quality, and that would replicate in New York what he stood for in Europe.

Baker was ready to promise her big fish whatever he wanted, and he wanted a lot: Mortier insisted that if he were to accept the post, he would need a budget of $60 million per season. Such a figure was way out of line with NYCO's finances. Its most recent operating budgets were in the neighborhood of $40 million, and income was not keeping pace with even that number. The development department was raising $14 million annually, and the company was taking in about the same amount in ticket sales and other earned income. With the addition of $3–$4 million in its regular endowment draw, the company's actual income added up to just over $30 million. The resulting deficits were being masked by the Klotz money and the Special Projects withdrawals from the endowment—and neither solution was sustainable in the long term. Reaching a $60 million budget would require at least another $20 million in annual fund-raising, but despite all indications to the contrary, Baker assured Mortier that this could be done.

Having spent his entire career in the state-subsidized theaters of Europe, fund-raising was a new concept for Mortier. On one of his early visits to NYCO, he asked the staff how much of the annual fund-raising was guaranteed. The answer—"None of it"—was a surprise to him. So was the need for earned income. "I think he had never been asked before to consider revenue, and you need to do that in America," Neef says.

> In Paris, he might have a 150 million euro budget with a 100 million euro subsidy and 800,000 tickets to sell. It's not hard to make

50 million euros with 800,000 tickets. That's what public subsidy allows you to do—to create an enormous amount of activity. Activity means tickets. You don't have to be very expensive; the sheer number of tickets allows you to make a lot of money off them.

Baker persuaded the board to go along with her choice, $60 million guarantee and all. "Susan could convince you that a white wall is actually black," Corey says. "She is a very compelling person. She's smart. And she talks a lot. She can talk people into things almost by hypnotizing them." Mortier impressed the search committee, Corey says, and at a subsequent cocktail party, he charmed all the guests, which persuaded the board that he could raise money. He was officially hired.

The hire, which was announced in February 2007, sent shock waves around the opera world. Reactions ranged from excitement at the prospect of having Europe's biggest enfant terrible loose in New York to bewilderment at how such a marriage could be possible. Some City Opera staffers were cautioned by colleagues across the Atlantic who knew Mortier or had worked with him that he would not be a good fit for the organization, that he would never come, and that he would "blow your budget in no time."

Once Mortier was chosen, however, the day-to-day leadership of the company became an issue. Paul Kellogg would depart after the spring of 2007, but Mortier would not be starting full-time in New York until the beginning of the 2009–10 season, when his contract in Paris was up. During this interim period, Mortier would visit New York every other month and work on planning his inaugural season. Several assistants, including Alexander Neef, who was slated to move to New York with Mortier, would also make regular trips. For these intervening two years, Susan Baker decided that she would run the company herself (aided by Jane Gullong) rather than bringing in an interim executive to take over the general director's functions. A memo from Baker dated May 7, 2007, featured an organizational chart placing her as the "liaison" between the absent general manager (Mortier) and the staff. As a management strategy, this left much to be desired, particularly since Baker had no significant administrative experience. She was also entirely

focused on Mortier and his future plans, to the exclusion of the immediate challenges of keeping the company functioning.

Whatever changes Mortier would put in place for the future, there were
two years of opera seasons to put on before his arrival, and the financial
picture remained bleak. The 2007–08 season, largely planned by Robin
Thompson, was a repudiation of the previous year's BCG-style cheaper
season. This time, there were thirteen operas—six were new, including
two that were built by the company; the other four rented or purchased.
One of the new productions was an important New York premiere: Richard Danielpour's *Margaret Garner*, the tale of a fugitive slave who kills
her children rather than have them returned to captivity. The libretto
was by the renowned novelist Toni Morrison, who had used the same
tale for her novel *Beloved*, which won the 1988 Pulitzer Prize. Morrison
won the Nobel Prize for Literature in 1993, and the opera had attracted
considerable attention at its 2005 world premiere in Detroit. The City
Opera production would be an important event and had the potential
to attract some new African American audience members and supporters to the company, but it would be hard for it to compete with the
splashy opening night the Met was planning: director Mary Zimmer-
man's house debut with *Lucia di Lammermoor*, featuring the electrifying
French soprano Natalie Dessay in the title role. After the debacle of too
many *Elixir*s, City Opera returned to its practice of devoting ten or
more performances only to the tried and true, such as a double bill of
Cavalleria Rusticana and *Pagliacci* in a production by Stephen Lawless
that referenced the shabby realism of mid-twentieth-century Italian
films, and the company's old, truly shabby *Carmen*.
     But returning to a more exciting slate of productions—and, it was
hoped, increased ticket sales—would mean higher costs. As always, new
productions required more rehearsal time. Productions with special
requirements—like an associate chorus of African American singers for
Margaret Garner or associate dancers for the new production of Purcell's
King Arthur, directed by Mark Morris—also increased expenses. The
projected budget for 2007–08 thus included a hike of nearly $5 million

in expenses and was correspondingly optimistic about both fund-raising and ticket income. It assumed 75 percent capacity, even with the number of inexpensively priced Opera for All performances cut from eight to three. And even taking these generous assumptions into account, it still anticipated an operating deficit of $8 million, which would, presumably, be filled by the last installment of the Klotz bequest and another Special Projects withdrawal from the Wallace endowment money.

The original plan for the season also included a teaser for what the company hoped would be a new source of revenue: multi-week runs of American musicals. City Opera had been presenting musicals as part of the regular season since the Sills era, but this new initiative, the "American Musical Theater Project," represented a more substantial commitment. It was planned to eventually become a separate season of musicals that would run during the summer, after the regular opera season. City Opera had begun working with Marty Bell, a Broadway producer, on the project, and the first full summer season was slated to take place in 2009. City Opera had, of course, been down this road before, under Beverly Sills, with the Lawrence Wien grant that subsidized a long spring run of a musical in each of the five years from 1986 to 1990—it had been an effective way to fill the orchestra guarantees but had mixed artistic results.

City Opera planned to launch the project with a new production of Lynn Ahrens and Stephen Flaherty's Tony Award–winning *Ragtime* during the regular spring season in 2008: it would be the tenth anniversary of the show's 1998 Broadway premiere and the company's first new production of a musical since Kellogg took over. But in March 2007, a month after it was announced and included in the subscription brochure, the *Ragtime* project fell through. It was replaced with a revival of the Hal Prince *Candide*, last seen in 2005, which could not compare to the *Ragtime* project as a buzz-worthy event. The idea of the summer musical series was dropped as well.

By the time the season began in September 2007, the company was already projecting an even higher ($9 million) operating deficit, which increased as the year went on and ticket sales and fund-raising again fell perilously short of projections. The minutes of the September 20, 2007, board meeting contain the dispassionate statement: "Ms. Baker stated that she hopes that a new business model would allow City Opera to operate without these deficits in the coming years."

This "new business model," as yet undetermined, was to be the result of the radical changes that Mortier planned to institute with the 2009–10 season. First, he wanted to run operas in stagione rather than repertory. Chuck Giles was one of the City Opera staffers who worked closely with Mortier. In their first conversations, Giles says, Mortier asked his opinion about the idea. "I said, we spend two-thirds of our money on work, one-third on the shows," Giles recalls. "With stagione, we'll do bigger shows that cost more, but we will not be spending as much on labor [because we won't have the constant changeovers] so I think you can probably reverse that equation and be able to pay for it."

Mortier had also decided that the New York State Theater was not the liability that Kellogg considered it to be. In his view, another renovation could solve its remaining structural and acoustical problems, and as for needing distance to distinguish City Opera from the Met, his artistic plan and persona would be differentiation enough. Being across the plaza from Peter Gelb's Met was not a disadvantage—rather, it stoked his competitive fire.

However, a stagione system, with dark nights between performances, required more theater time than would be available in the State Theater, and, in any case, Mortier had another, even more radical idea: he would use multiple theaters of different sizes and configurations. In Mortier's vision, the season's ten operas would be performed in slightly staggered pairs, in different theaters: while one opera was being performed in one space, a second opera would be teched and rehearsed in another. The technical teams would then move on to the next pair of shows.

"Mortier pushed envelopes for a living," says Giles, who found working with the Belgian impresario to be an exhilarating experience. Mortier, Giles, and Jürgen Höfer, Mortier's technical director from Paris,

began a hunt for theater spaces in New York. The places they investi-
gated had plenty of operational challenges. The Park Avenue Armory,
for example, was raw space, not yet the trendy, unconventional performance mecca it would later become: "We spent a lot of time making
architectural drawings to create a workable theater at the Armory, meeting with architects and conceiving where we would we have dressing
rooms and put projectors." The Guggenheim Museum theater had no
real orchestra pit, the Rose Theater at Jazz at Lincoln Center, which is
on an upper floor in the Time Warner Center at Columbus Circle, had
a challenging load-in and backstage setup. Other spaces under consideration included the Apollo Theater in Harlem, the Palace Theater on
175th Street, the Hammerstein Ballroom in Midtown, and several other
armories, including the Armory Track athletic facility in Fort Washington and one in Kingsbridge in the Bronx. Theaters more accustomed
to accommodating opera included the Beacon Theatre, the Brooklyn
Academy of Music, and the company's old home, City Center on Fifty-
Fifth Street, which was now used primarily for dance.

"Those two years were the most fun I ever had," Giles says. "I wasn't
producing a thing, but I worked harder than I've ever worked in my
life." He was negotiating stagehand union contracts (some of the spaces
had none), establishing schedules, doing drawings, figuring out how to
staff all the shows—the production staff would be nearly doubled—and
how to work in theaters that were not theaters. Everything was different and had to be planned anew.

The 2009–10 season of operas to be presented in those spaces would
also be completely new in every respect. Every title would be from the
twentieth century or later. The season, which the company dubbed
"The Good Old Twentieth Century," was to be Mortier's calling card,
featuring titles and artists associated with him, and his declaration of
opera as a contemporary art. His signature offering was the gigantic
production of Messiaen's lengthy *Saint François d'Assise* from the
Ruhrtriennale, featuring a massive, dome-shaped, lit sculpture by Ilya
Kabakov, which would be staged in the Armory. Philip Glass's *Einstein
on the Beach* would be remounted, in its famous Robert Wilson production, and Wilson's *Pelléas et Mélisande* would come from Paris, as would

Krzysztof Warlikowski's staging of *The Makropulos Affair*. Deborah Warner's production of Britten's *Death in Venice* would be brought from the English National Opera. Warlikowski would also direct *The Rake's Progress*—Mortier's plan was to reopen the renovated State Theater with it, as an homage to Balanchine and Stravinsky. (The State Theater had been built originally for Balanchine, who had choreographed many important ballets to the music of Stravinsky; by underlining the relationship, Mortier was making an association between City Opera's work and that of City Ballet's legendary choreographer.)

Even more exotic pieces included *Reigen*, an opera—based on Schnitzler's play *La Ronde*—that had premiered at the Monnaie in Brussels in 1993, directed by Christopher Alden, which would be at the Guggenheim, and the world premiere of Bernice Johnson Reagon's *The Parable of the Sower* (later completed by her daughter, Toshi Reagon), to be directed by Peter Sellars, at the Armory. An avant-garde choreographic piece, created by director Alain Platel with children in Harlem, using music by Verdi, was slated first for the Apollo Theater, and then for BAM. (This addition was Mortier's response to concerns about an all-twentieth-century season.) Some preliminary projects that did not appear in the final season plan included Weill's *Mahagonny*, Prokofiev's *The Love for Three Oranges*, and Emir Kusturica's *Time of the Gypsies*. Mortier had also hoped to mount John Adams's *Nixon in China*, but Peter Gelb got there first, securing the piece for the Met. The productions would be staggered, beginning in September and running through April, giving the company a presence in New York throughout the regular season, rather than the stop-and-start fall and spring footprint of the past. The plan was to mount some eighty performances in six different theaters, most of them with less capacity than the twenty-seven-hundred-seat New York State Theater. There would be many fewer tickets to sell, potentially giving City Opera a rarity factor for the first time in many years.

Mortier was also determined to get the company's executive offices and rehearsal spaces out of the State Theater basement. Giles had located a space: two high-ceilinged floors in a utility building in the Inwood neighborhood of upper Manhattan. He mapped out a design that would include a rehearsal studio the size of the stage and an orchestra rehearsal room big enough to accommodate the orchestra (124) and chorus (140) for *Saint François*. There was also a chorus lounge, coaching rooms, and storage, as well as artistic and executive offices. "With rehearsal space so tight in New York, I figured we could rent it out," Giles adds. The neighborhood was closer to where many of the musicians lived anyway, making it a popular prospect.

Starting in 2009, City Opera was to have an entirely new identity—cool and fabulous. The scrappy People's Opera image was to be expunged, replaced by the brave new world of Gerard Mortier. In Baker's view, the company's financial and audience challenges could be solved only by a total remake, and for her, the tatty old *Carmen* was no great loss. Mortier would challenge the Met on its own ground and win. In the meantime, the company was in a holding pattern but, Baker calculated, all they had to do was get through the next two years, and with the stock market booming and the Wallace endowment to draw on, all would be well.

Mortier unveiled his initial plans for "The Good Old Twentieth Century" to the board at the September 2007 meeting, along with some aspects of the "new business model." While the budget would be considerably increased—more new productions, higher fees for conductors, greater rehearsal costs—he also suggested that there would be savings in stagehand costs, due to the stagione system in the multiple theaters, as well as savings from doing fewer performances overall (80 instead of 115), and that he hoped to gain some income by selling productions and costumes. A meeting with the Andrew W. Mellon Foundation, resulting in a promise of $2.5 million for the inaugural season, had also encouraged Baker and Mortier to believe that more foundation support of that magnitude would be forthcoming.

But it would be up to the development department, headed by Jennifer Zaslow, to manage the heavy lifting for that $60 million season. The fund-raising consultant Dory Vanderhoof had been engaged to help refashion the department's efforts into a comprehensive campaign that would include future production underwriting, capital projects, and endowment as well as annual support. Vanderhoof's analysis of forty-nine

thousand households in City Opera's donor database promised a staggering capacity of $19.7 billion in charitable contributions. Even after
limiting the screening to the four thousand households that were already
donors or subscribers, the number was still a hefty $4.6 billion, and Van-
derhoof told the board that in his experience, a campaign could be
expected to yield 5–10 percent of that capacity, that is, $230–$460 million. The next step, he said, was identifying one thousand households
with $1 million in capacity, and winnowing the list to the best three
hundred prospects.

   This was heady stuff for the hand-to-mouth City Opera, a company
that had raised, at most, about $14 million in annual giving and had
never seriously contemplated an endowment campaign. Vanderhoof laid
out some of the strategies for accomplishing these goals, including the
expansion of the department, advance planning, and new ways to counter
problems like the company's unfocused business plan, inconsistent artistic quality, low-price reputation, and weak ticket sales, all of which
would be red flags for big donors. He also emphasized the importance
of the board in the success of the campaign, stressing that each board
member would have to help financially and help in identifying and cultivating more donor prospects.

By December 2007, yet another facet of the new vision for City Opera
had come into focus. Ongoing negotiations with the New York City Ballet about renovations to the New York State Theater had reached an
agreement. The renovations would include Mortier's priority—a new,
larger, moveable orchestra pit—as well as a new stage lighting and media
system. The Ballet was, as before, not particularly keen on changing the
acoustics, which worked perfectly for its purposes—that is, dampening
the sound of footfalls on the stage—and in order to get to an agreement on any renovations at all, the Opera agreed to leave aside the acoustics question for the moment. It's worth noting that neither of Kellogg's
core issues about the theater—acoustics or autonomy—was addressed.
Mortier, in any case, did not seem terribly concerned about the acoustical issues in the hall. He just wanted an orchestra pit that was big enough

for Strauss's *Elektra*, an opera that the "old" City Opera would never have dreamed of undertaking.

Neef claims that Mortier actually liked the State Theater and that the renovation had a lot to do with public relations. "We were fighting the bad reputation that [the company] had created for itself," he says. "If you tell your audience for years that the theater they are coming to is really terrible, and you are going to give them a new theater and that never happens, it's pushing people's noses into the problem." The renovation was, thus, "a way of giving the theater back some credibility by saying, we are doing this big renovation, making the pit flexible, adjusting the acoustics."

The renovations would require the theater to be closed for much of the 2008–09 season, and the Ballet was not going to give up any of its performance weeks to accommodate construction. The BCG team and the staff had worked up several alternative scenarios for City Opera's activities during that time. Marc Powell explained to the board that financially, it made the most sense for City Opera not to perform in the State Theater at all during the construction year. Instead, the company "could use alternate venues and joint ventures to compensate for a loss in ticket sales." Mortier added his endorsement to that plan, saying that he felt it was "important for the State Theater to be closed during all of the City Opera's performance months so there could be a complete transformation in advance of his opening season in the fall of 2009." He also stated that it was important to honor the union guarantees—the payments due to the artists under their current contracts—and that the staff would investigate the costs and possibilities of performing in other venues around the city. Ideas for programming during the theater's dark year included operas in concert, or a series of educational concerts on various themes.

During her time at Goldman Sachs, Susan Baker had specialized in collateralized debt obligations, and she was adopting a similar high-risk, high-reward strategy with City Opera. Taking the company out of its theater for a year was yet another giant step in the transformation that she believed Mortier could effect. As always, Baker was prepared to give Mortier whatever he wanted in order to accomplish this feat, and what he wanted was an enlarged, moveable orchestra pit. He was also under-whelmed by ordinary City Opera productions like the cheesy *La Donna del Lago*, which he saw in the spring of 2007, and did not particularly wish to be associated with another season of them. A dark year with no activity at the New York State Theater would, in theory, draw a line under the "old" City Opera. In 2009, it would be born anew, a phoenix from the ashes.

In investment banking, the money can always be found, and Baker believed that Mortier's vision and celebrity would open the purses of the wealthy to pay for this new, cutting-edge, high-quality City Opera. With Wall Street healthy and climbing, why shouldn't it be a success? Hadn't City Opera's newly diversified investments increased their returns by 18 percent in the last fiscal year? There were rumblings of change to come: at that same December 2007 meeting, Nomi Ghez, the board treasurer, reported that current earnings on the endowment were flat. But in late 2007, the total economic collapse of 2008 was still in the future, and optimism ruled. Susan Baker, believing City Opera to be unsalvageable in its current artistic and financial incarnation, had bet the ranch.

CHAPTER 8

Salvation Denied

MICHAEL GARY JOINED the City Opera fund-raising team in the summer of 2007, coming from the New York Botanical Garden's development department. When he was offered the job, his colleague at the Botanical Garden, Claudia Keenan, who had previously worked for City Opera, warned him not to take it. "She said, 'They have a $9.5 million deficit, it's systemic, they're going to crumble,'" Gary says.

> I didn't care. I was so excited and jazzed by the idea of Mortier. I thought hiring him was a brilliant idea. I thought he was going to set up a dialogue between the Met and City Opera in a way that had never really happened, because Mortier's forward-looking vision was in stark contrast to the more traditional values of the Met. It could create a city-wide conversation about art and what it meant. And opera would be at the center of it.

A heady thought, but how could this radical vision fit into the realities of the New York City Opera? It was up to Susan Baker to single-handedly reconcile the two. Having landed this starry fiancé, she had to keep persuading both parties—the company and Mortier—that the marriage was possible. And as the long engagement unfolded over 2007 and 2008, she kept careful control over all interactions between the general director–designate and the company.

Mortier, who was still running the Paris Opera, came to New York every other month for several days, and during this time Baker was his constant shadow. When he met with the senior staff, she was always present. George Manahan, who had been offered an ongoing contract to conduct one opera with the company each season, says, "I remember going into meetings with him and [orchestra manager] Dave Titcomb, and he would say, 'George, won't it be wonderful when you conduct *Elektra* with 110 musicians in our new pit?' And Susan Baker would always be sitting next to him, taking notes. We didn't get private face time." Michael Gary recalls, "She was in constant communication with him. I can't tell you how many meetings I was in where she would get a call from him, and she'd get up and walk out and take the call. My gut tells me she was probably parceling out access to him." Staffers found Baker's demeanor around Mortier to be odd—"Girlish," one called it, "like the little girl talking about the big boyfriend."

Even the board was kept at arm's length. "The board was terrified of Mortier," Kara Unterberg recalls.

> He was European, the *artiste*. Susan was propping him up, saying we are so lucky that he is coming and we don't want to do anything to jeopardize his coming. [There was] the fear of his leaving, the fear of disappointing him, because "He is so special, and he will save the day. We are so lucky that he would even think of us. We don't want to upset him."

The board's agreement to a dark season, with no activity in the State Theater, despite the inevitable financial difficulties it would cause, was one example of their compliance. "People were afraid to speak up, because it was Gerard Mortier insisting on this."

Shielding Mortier from any bad news, or potential objections, was in keeping with Baker's secretive leadership style. One staffer compared her performance at board meetings to a "geisha dance," complete with a Japanese fan that she would sometimes use to cover her face.

> She would put the agenda face-down on the table; then she would turn it up, just glance at it and say, and say, very quietly, so people could barely hear her, "We're now going to have a resolution of the next item on the agenda. Can we have a vote on that?" followed with a flutter of the fan. The normally very talkative, smart people on that board, who were very invested in the company, said nothing in these meetings. There was no discussion. It was like she sucked the energy out of the room. People did not feel empowered to speak—or to challenge her.

Monumental decisions, such as moving the company completely out of the State Theater for a year, or red-flag items like budgets showing huge deficits, were passed without debate.

The key challenge for the Mortier regime was, as always, the money. Robert Meya, who joined the company's development department in June 2008, points out that the challenge was probably even greater than the board realized. "Nonprofits define budget by expenses, not revenues," he says.

> City Opera's expense budget was in the $40–$45 million range. But revenues were more like $30 million. Mortier was promised an operating budget of $60 million. [The change was presented as an increase] from an operating budget of $45 million to one of $60 million. But they were actually doubling their projected revenue. That is impossible, even for extraordinarily well-run organizations.

No one was going to say this to Mortier, however. "They tiptoed around the issue," as Mortier's deputy, Alexander Neef, later recalled.

Mortier could not have been entirely unaware of just how heavy the financial lift would be. At a breakfast meeting, he had asked Marc Scorca, president of Opera America, to research how much money other performing arts institutions in New York were raising. Scorca found that with the exception of the Metropolitan Opera and Carnegie Hall, no arts group was raising more than $20 million—including American Ballet Theatre, New York City Ballet, and the New York Philharmonic. Scorca sent his findings to Mortier, which Neef confirms, though Scorca received no response. In 2008, making projections for the inaugural season, Mortier estimated that ticket sales would bring in $15 million. Thus, even assuming that the endowment draw of $3–$4 million could continue, annual fund-raising would still have to bring in over $40 million, more than double the highest level achieved by the majority of New York institutions. And, in addition to the season operations, both Baker and Mortier spoke grandly about another $100 million fund for artistic experimentation.

The development team was hopeful that foundations, which tend to like cutting-edge projects, would be a healthy source of funds. The quick response from the Andrew W. Mellon Foundation encouraged those hopes: its president, Don Randel, had met with Mortier and committed $2.5 million on the spot for his initial season. Several arts-oriented foundations were in the process of closing down, with the prospect of substantial terminal gifts. Ultimately, the Alice Tully Foundation came up with $1 million to support Mortier's planned production of *Saint François*, and the Mary Flagler Cary Charitable Trust, a longtime supporter of the company, promised $500,000.

Other foundations were not as forthcoming. Neither Mortier nor Baker was comfortable asking for money, and an experience with the Starr Foundation was a case in point. Mortier and Baker met with Florence Davis and Paula Lawrence, the president and vice president of the foundation. Michael Gary, who went along, says,

> When you sit down with a foundation you are there to ask for money—to pitch something, to explain why it's a great project and why you hope they will support it. It's pretty cut and dried. This meeting felt like we were at tea—very slow to get moving. Then Susan introduced Gerard who proceeded to speak for 35 or 40 minutes just on his biography. Florence Davis looked at her watch repeatedly during the meeting. Then she got up and excused herself. I was

mortified. We were there to ask for half a million dollars, and this could not be going worse. Paula was able to pull out of Mortier something about the program. Then, the meeting was almost over, and I was thinking, are they going to make the ask or not? So I said, "What we're here for is to ask you for half a million dollars to support"— whatever it was. Mortier turned beet red. When we got into the elevator, he turned to me immediately and excoriated me for broaching the topic of money. To her credit, Susan defended me, and said, "That's how it works here, Gerard." But it should have been decided before we went who was going to do the ask.

The Starr Foundation did not give a grant.

Individual donors were not lining up to contribute large sums, either. In the summer of 2008, when the campaign had already been under way for months, Robert Meya was surprised to see how little had come through. "I was thinking, where is all this money going to come from?" he says. The fund-raising effort seemed backward to him. "When you launch a campaign, first you need a group of board members to come together, and plant the seed for fund-raising, with each one committing $5 million, or $10 million, whatever it takes." But the board had not done that. Baker had made no pledge, nor had any of the other board members. Without those leadership commitments, the development department was having difficulty lining up other major donors, which would normally be the second phase of a campaign. "We were trying to tap the people [outside the company] who might have affection for Mortier's artistic style," Meya says. "We set that into motion, but you don't just start giving millions of dollars to Mortier's artistic vision before he has even shown up if you are not one of the insiders on the board." Since the board insiders weren't committing, no one else was, either. Baker's reluctance to ask for money meant that she did not foster a culture of giving and outside fund-raising on the board, a fatal omission.

Mark Moorman, who worked in the company's development department at the time, found that some of their prospective donors were not as impressed by Mortier as Baker had expected. In the course of his work, Moorman would hear a variety of dismissive sentiments directed at Mortier: "He *was* a big name, but he's not relevant anymore. He's not really doing such interesting work. We've seen his work in Paris, and we hated it. He hires mediocre singers in productions that are not beautiful. Am I going to be able to bring my niece? I don't want to bring my niece to go and see some political statement on tradition vs. modernity in contemporary culture." Moorman also heard a lot of concern about Mortier's professed disdain for the operas of Puccini and thought that was a bad sign as well. He couldn't see a way forward. "New Yorkers are so tough," he said, "and Mortier couldn't crack that code."

Art as an intellectual endeavor, in the European mode, proved not to be an easy sell in New York. Moorman had put together a presentation on "The Good Old Twentieth Century," which was aimed at convincing the City Opera audience and donor base that the program was not frighteningly modern, but rather—with pieces like *The Makropulos Affair*, *The Rake's Progress*, and *Pelléas et Mélisande*—fully in line with the City Opera tradition. Mortier was simply curating the repertoire, like an art exhibition. But, as Moorman recalls, people were resistant.

> They said, "It's too much, I don't want to be lectured to. It's not a school." Mortier wanted to compete with Gelb—"They're doing the *Ring* cycle, we'll do the anti-*Ring* cycle!" He would say this to people and their response would be, "Why would you do that? Who wants to go and see that? How much is it going to cost?" He talked about introducing every opera with a press conference that has a panel discussion with New York intellectuals, like you see in Europe. Susan Woelzl, the press director, would say, "There are no intellectual press conferences in New York. They are as short as possible." I think he could see the writing on the wall, that New York was not going to be what he thought it would be for him.

Moorman believes that Mortier was hurt by the fact that his vision was not immediately and unconditionally embraced in New York.

There were other ominous signs as well. In October 2007, the Dow Jones Industrial average had reached a high of 14,000. As the subprime mortgage crisis emerged, the Dow began to decline, then imploded. By

March 2008, Nomi Ghez reported that City Opera's investments were down 4 percent. In May, board VP Mark Newhouse reported that personal fund-raising meetings with board members to try to shore up the faltering annual fund had brought in an additional $1.2 million—a positive sign for the current year, considering the economic downturn, but only a drop in the bucket in the face of the $40 million in contributions that would be needed for Mortier's inaugural season in 2009–10. Newhouse also noted the development department's belief that, given hard financial times, donors might be adopting a "wait and see" attitude. And with no subscription renewal campaign for the dark season of 2008–09, there was a falloff in low-level donors, who typically include a contribution with their renewal.

The original budget for the 2007–08 season had anticipated an operating deficit of $8 million, but the final results were even worse. Ticket sales and donations fell millions of dollars short, and even with the addition of a last $2 million from the Klotz estate, and another Special Projects withdrawal of $1.72 million from the Wallace endowment, the company ran a deficit of nearly $9 million for the fiscal year. As the market continued to fall, City Opera's investments lost value, going from a gain of over $5 million in 2006–07 to a loss of over $6 million in 2007–08. At the end of the fiscal year, the company's total net assets had dropped by $17 million, to $40.9 million. By contrast, at the end of 2000–01, the year that the company added the Wallace endowment funds to its balance sheet, its net assets totaled $69.8 million.

The plan for the $32 million dark season of 2008–09 was to break even, but this goal relied on some tenuous assumptions, including an unconfirmed tour to Japan and $4 million in reimbursement for some of City Opera's expenses from the capital campaign that was under way to fund the State Theater's renovation. (City Opera felt this was only fair, since the company had given up its performance income in order for the renovation to take place, but no deal for reimbursement had yet been made with the Ballet.)

There would be very little income from performances. Preliminary ideas about presenting multiple operas in concert had given way to an even more modest plan that would not require renting so many expensive venues. Instead, there would be only one opera in concert—Barber's *Antony and Cleopatra*—at Carnegie Hall, plus a five-concert series for the orchestra, along with a few singers and chorus members, dubbed "Looking Forward" (that is, to the inaugural Mortier season), which would feature works by twentieth-century composers. The orchestra concerts would be performed in halls in Queens, Brooklyn, the Bronx, and Staten Island, with a final one at Alice Tully Hall at Lincoln Center. Thus, ticket income for the company's local New York activity that season was projected to be just under half a million dollars, down from the $12 million it had earned in 2007–08. And for that very limited activity, the cost would still be a whopping $29 million—primarily because of City Opera's high fixed costs and Mortier's insistence on honoring the union contracts by paying for work the company couldn't use. The guaranteed payments that the company owed the unions came to nearly $9 million. (According to bass player Gail Kruvand, the head of the orchestra committee, no one even raised the possibility of reducing these payments for the dark season, even though the orchestra and chorus would have only a few weeks of actual work.) There would be an additional $4.5 million in income if the proposed Japan tour went ahead, but that still wouldn't bring the company anywhere near breaking even.

As spring wore on, more of Mortier's plans were revealed. In June, the company announced the commission of a new opera based on Annie Proulx's story "Brokeback Mountain" for a future Mortier season. The tale about a secret, twenty-year love affair between two gay cowboys had been made into an enormously successful, award-winning film by Ang Lee in 2005. However, the choice of composer, the seventy-year-old Charles Wuorinen, known as a thorny serialist and a throwback to another era, did not seem like a fresh start. During a presentation at the June 2008 board meeting, Mortier appeared confident and resolute about the inaugural season. He said, for example, that *Saint François*, though it required thirty-four orchestra rehearsals (an enormous number, and very expensive), would be a great artistic triumph for the company and the city. One positive augury came in July, when the company announced that the oil-and-gas billionaire David Koch had pledged $100 million to the $200 million campaign to renovate the New York State Theater; it would be renamed for him. James Marlas, a longtime board member, had made the connection with Koch, who was beginning to put out feelers in the New York cultural world.

But there were less positive developments as well. In May 2008, Alexander Neef, who had been working closely with Mortier on the plans for his first season, and had been expected to move to New York as Mortier's second in command, accepted a job as general director of the Canadian Opera Company in Toronto. Having gotten the measure of City Opera and its fund-raising capabilities, he had started talking to the Canadian company, which was known as a more stable operation, earlier that year. "It already seemed to me that for me and my family, it would be very hazardous to leave a completely safe job in Paris, relocate everybody to New York and hope for the best," he explained. Given City Opera's precarious finances, "It would have been very risky to embark on that project with the very limited security that was there." Another defection was Frederick J. Iseman, the private equity mogul, and one of the few City Opera board members with significant philanthropic capacity, who resigned from the board after six years to join the board of the Metropolitan Opera.

Some staffers who had been initially dazzled by Mortier found that the doubts they had suppressed were now beginning to resurface. While the plans seemed exciting and transformative, and Mortier's skill as an experienced impresario and man of the theater resonated with those on the artistic side, the disconnect between the reality of the past and his vision for the future was easy to see, particularly as the company struggled with its finances during the 2007–08 season. "It was like Joe Torre coming to manage Little League," says Manahan.

And by the end of the summer, Mortier finally got wind of the fact that the board had not secured the funds to cover his first season—the only commitments had come from foundations, and they were far from enough. His response was a feint. The famous Bayreuth Festival, founded in Germany by Richard Wagner for the presentation of his operas, was in the process of deciding on its future leadership. Wolfgang Wagner, the composer's great-grandson, had announced his intention to retire as the festival's director after the 2008 summer festival and wanted his thirty-year-old daughter, the stage director Katharina Wagner, to succeed him. The succession was up to the festival's governing board, however, and in late August, Mortier offered himself as a candidate, teamed with another descendant of the Wagner family, Nike Wagner, to strengthen his bid. The Bayreuth board quickly named Katharina and her half sister Eva as codirectors, but Mortier had made his point. It was, he confirmed later, in e-mail messages to members of the press, a deliberate warning message to the lukewarm members of the New York City Opera board.

Baker did her best to shore up the relationship between Mortier and the company after this public display of pique. Michael Gary remembers the tense September board meeting, at which Mortier forcefully issued an ultimatum: the company would come up with the $60 million, or he would not come. Unterberg remembers that Mortier was angry; she says, however, "The board had never voted on that $60 million. It was just a number Susan told him." In early October, the public narrative was still positive, with Baker insisting that Mortier *could* have run both City Opera and Bayreuth, which is a summer festival, simultaneously. Mortier also assured Anthony Tommasini at the *New York Times* that the board was now solidly behind his plans and he would be staying to carry them out.

Meanwhile, the company continued to hemorrhage money and, with no real ticket income in sight, found itself short on cash for the 2008–09 season. The terms of the Wallace gift had allowed the company to make withdrawals from the endowment for "Special Projects"—but the same terms prohibited reducing the endowment below 80 percent of its original value. And that limit had already been reached. The company seemed to have no further way to exploit those funds. But at the end of the summer, Susan Baker and Nomi Ghez took a radical step and retained counsel to draft a cy pres application to the New York State attorney general, who is responsible for the assets and governance of nonprofits incorporated in the state of New York. This "application for cy pres relief" asked that City Opera be released from the restrictions on the Wallace endowment that were a condition of the gift from the donor, thus enabling it to borrow a large sum from the endowment. With these funds, the company could pay off the substantial debt it had accumulated and cover the losses that were already being anticipated for the upcoming year—among other issues, the Asia tour was still unconfirmed. Anticipating that the request would be granted, and the company would ultimately be able to access the endowment funds, the board also began to move its investments from stocks to cash in order to prevent further losses in a plummeting market.

Kara Unterberg was aghast at the idea that the company would invade its nest egg. "I didn't go to the endowment vote. I said, I'm not voting on that." Unterberg says that she had tried to raise objections to the cy pres application in small meetings but got nowhere. "The answer I always got was, 'what's the alternative?' And I didn't have an alternative." The cy pres petition said that the funds would be "borrowed," and thus required a plan for eventually paying the money back into the endowment, which the staffers recognized was probably impossible. However, the assurance of repayment was included, and the petition was submitted.

In early October, eleven staff members were laid off, and it was announced that Jane Gullong, the company's executive director, would depart at the end of the year, her position having been eliminated by Mortier. A few weeks later, the dire cash flow situation led to a two-day furlough for all company employees except some finance and development staff, who were frantically soliciting donations in order to cover the payroll and enable the rest of the staff to return to work. To make matters worse, the economic downturn was now a crisis, with bank failures, including the Lehman Brothers bankruptcy filing in September, and steep stock market declines. The board, already jittery about Mortier's expensive plans, became more so. Even Mortier recognized that circumstances had changed, and he agreed to work with Giles to cut the budget for 2009–10. They got it down to $54 million.

The staff was left in the dark. On October 22, the senior staff sent a memo to the executive board begging for a meeting to clarify the plans for the future. The inaugural 2009–10 season was still under construction, with everything from the negotiation of venue contracts for the multiple theaters to the securing of performance rights for the works still pending, making it impossible to design subscription brochures and donor materials, or proceed with labor negotiations. "We need guidance as to who is leading the staff of City Opera until Gerard's full-time arrival in New York," the memo pleaded. "Most importantly, we want to discuss the scope of our future plans to understand our way forward in the short term and long term, and how we convey this information to the larger staff."

On November 4, 2008, the second shoe finally dropped: Mortier was out. The board, finally facing facts, had offered him a budget of $36 million—less than the smallest opera company in France, as Mortier put it, and a long way from the $250 million budget he was accustomed to at the Paris Opera—and he would not take the job under those circumstances. Mortier told Dan Wakin of the *New York Times* that he suggested the company run a deficit on purpose and borrow money to put on a first season that would show potential new donors what the company could do. The board refused.

Some company staffers, including George Manahan and David Titcomb, had always assumed that Baker would come up with the money for the first season herself, with a personal donation, and believed that Mortier thought the same. This would have been a logical assumption, given that she was not only the board chair but also Mortier's champion. But Baker never offered any financial pledge. Instead, she apparently expected the major donations to come from others—such as unspecified billionaires in Dubai and Abu Dhabi, or New York philanthropists with no previous connection to City Opera—who would be so impressed by the prospect of Mortier, or the triumph of his initial season, that they would sign on, though no actual overtures had been made. The reality, of course, turned out to be more complicated. The endowment investments in hedge funds had produced exciting returns for a year, but the economic crash put to rest any hopes that they might provide the magic solution. The board had effectively taken those endowment funds to Las Vegas, spun the wheel, and lost.

The economic crisis, conveniently, took much of the blame for the failure of the Mortier plan, but City Opera's weak board, low fund-raising capacity, and lack of leadership were the real culprits. "The board was very much on the fence, they wanted to wait and see," Emilie Corey says.

> Instead of embracing the thing, increasing their investment, everybody was very tentative. I thought that was too bad. If I had promised someone $60 million, I would have done anything. I would have sold my apartment. I would have sold my jewelry. I would have done everything I could. And I would have made a major gift myself so that I could say, I'm doing this, I want you all to do it too. But [Susan] didn't do that.

And even if the first $60 million had been found, and Mortier had come, the chances of success were slim. Marc Scorca says,

> I've seen many companies make an Arts Management 101 error, which is, "If we do the work, and it's good enough, people will flock to us and support us." That's what City Opera was saying: "Somehow, if we can just pay for Gerard Mortier's first season, it will be so great that we will be supported through box office sales and philanthropy." That doesn't work. You have to have the base. You have to have the investment capital. You have to be prepared for sustained investment in a new concept, a new direction, and it doesn't happen overnight. Betting on the good reviews, betting on the word of mouth as an institutional strategy is not a good idea.

In the process of reimagining the New York City Opera according to Mortier's vision, too much appears to have been done backward. The appointment of Mortier himself was essentially an impulse choice made by one person, Susan Baker, and never received the full buy-in of the company's other leaders and stakeholders. The board, accustomed to a culture that rubber-stamped decisions and took no responsibility for the company's plight, went along with Baker's selection. The staff, hopeful that a professional opera house impresario might be able to rescue the company, suppressed their doubts. Patrons were presented with a fait accompli and given a choice—to either support it or not. The audience was not consulted.

Indeed, Baker's fascination with Mortier blinded her to the complexities of the opera audience in New York and City Opera's audience in particular. Mortier appeared to be fixated on a book he had read about the culture wars in America during the 1980s, when provocative artwork like Serrano's *Piss Christ* provoked ructions in Congress over government funding for the arts. He was looking forward to shaking things up in a similar fashion, as though America were a giant, conservative backwater in dire need of his sophisticated, avant-garde, European sensibility. The plans for his first season, heavy with projects imported from Europe, sent that message clearly. Mark Moorman recalls,

> Among my opera friends, the feeling was, New York City Opera doesn't need some hifalutin European. New York City Opera is a source of pride for America—Rosenstock and Rudel were immigrants, but they were proud Americans. Mortier was playing a different kind of game, trying to change New York rather than building on it to create something different.

The fact that Mortier wasn't even a resident in New York yet, wouldn't be for the foreseeable future, and was, if anything, dismissive of the company's current activities, made him seem even more disconnected. His visits, controlled by Baker, and featuring first-class airfares and hotel rooms, compounded the image of the privileged outsider, swooping in to instruct the hoi polloi.

The folie à deux of Baker and Mortier would have enormous consequences. It fed the confusion about New York City Opera's identity. Operational decisions that were made in deference to Mortier's ego cost the company a substantial percentage of its audience. And the "silver bullet" fantasy of a billionaire savior meant that the already overwhelming financial problems were never addressed and would only get worse.

From the time that she took over the chairmanship of the City Opera board in 2004, Susan Baker appeared to be out of her depth, harboring ambitions that did not correspond to reality. Sherwin Goldman believed that she wanted to run the company herself; indeed, she quickly pushed him out, thus marginalizing Paul Kellogg, who had depended on his "bad cop" counterpart. The ensuing leadership vacuum left the company without a strong artistic or managerial hand on the tiller, particularly when the search for a successor to Kellogg was allowed to drag on. At the same time, in areas such as fund-raising, or in coming up with a sustainable plan to deal with the company's growing deficit, where a board chair's leadership was urgently needed, she relied too much on questionable exploitation of the company's endowment, including withdrawals and risky hedge fund investments.

The choice of Mortier represented the pinnacle of Baker's magical thinking. His price tag was impossibly high for the company, and Baker did not raise the money, even as she promised him that it was all under control. She ensured that doubts about the City Opera's financial capacity were kept from him, even to the extent of paying for some of his first-class airfares and hotel rooms herself. She made bad deals to give him what he wanted, like the renovation of the New York State Theater with no guarantee of compensation for the loss of performance income during the dark season. Baker's confidence in her own acumen seemed to be her undoing. As one staffer put it, "She believed that she could be the puppet master and that no one was as smart as she was. She thought she could keep pieces of information from people, and that she was somehow going to make it all work out. It was a terrible strategy."

The collapse of Baker's elaborate Mortier fantasy was the beginning of the end. A few years later, when things had gotten even worse, Alan Gordon, the notably pugnacious head of AGMA, representing the company's singers, choristers, dancers and stage directors, would tell *Opera News*, "They ought to hang Susan Baker in front of the State Theater."

CHAPTER 9

The Man of Steel

CHUCK GILES REMEMBERS November 4, 2008, as a day of extreme emotions. There was joy—Barack Obama was elected president of the United States. And there was grief—Gerard Mortier would not be coming to City Opera. Eighteen months of planning and excitement about a glorious future had come to an abrupt end. "My dreams were crushed," he recalls.

The shocked staff tried to manage the day-to-day operations of the company. "We were rudderless," Cori Ellison says. George Manahan was named interim artistic director; he and his colleagues worked to ensure that the Carnegie Hall presentation of *Antony and Cleopatra* and the other "dark theater" season concert performances would continue as planned. They also began to assemble some programming ideas to fill the massive hole left after the collapse of Mortier's plans for the 2009–10 season.

Financially, the company was on perilous ground. The board was still negotiating with the Ballet to access funds from the theater renovation capital campaign. City Opera wanted the money to make up for some

of the $12 million in ticket income that it was forgoing by not perform-
ing in the State Theater during the dark season—but so far, no deal
had been reached. Even though it wasn't able to use the theater, the company still had to pay its share of the upkeep expenses. The guaranteed
payments for the unionized artists were proving higher than previously
budgeted. Adding to this already challenging budget picture was a sev-
erance payment of $335,000 to Mortier, who was entitled to compensa-
tion since the board's failure to guarantee the $60 million budget was
a deal-breaker. As feared, the Japan tour had not materialized, and in
early December, the anticipated deficit on the dark season—once characterized as "break-even"—was at $13 million.

    With no current opera performances and no future program to inspire
giving, the fund-raising staff had a near-impossible task. "We were in
shock when we got the news that Mortier wasn't coming," Michael Gary
recalls. "There was no Plan B." He says that Jennifer Zaslow, the director of development, who was normally calm and centered, gathered her
team and told them, "Your job is to find a new job." Zaslow herself left
shortly thereafter for the New York Public Library, and Robert Meya,
who had headed Major Gifts, took her place. Somehow, the team was
able to keep institutional giving at 70 percent of what it had been, and
the company's most loyal individual supporters did not desert it. Under
Meya, the fund-raising staff launched a new campaign—"I Am City
Opera"—with videos from current and former singers, directors, staff,
and patrons all talking about what the company meant to them personally. It was an attempt to recapture the old People's Opera spirit—
something, Gary says, that had been "lost along the way" with Mortier.

    More than that had been lost: the impression left by the dark the-
ater season was hard to combat. Mark Moorman saw the decision to save
money by not performing operas during the dark season as a negation
of what an opera company stood for. It could have been done differently:
a decade earlier, when the San Francisco Opera was exiled from its home
so that the War Memorial Opera House could undergo a seismic retro-
fit and renovation, the company performed its full 1996–97 season of
staged operas in other theaters. The fact that City Opera had chosen to
go dark, he felt, was a betrayal.

We are a mission-driven organization. We have a mission to produce opera. Our donors are not ATMs meant to support administrative costs. They are there to support the art we make and that's our pledge to them. Everyone at every level understood that, and was proud and eager to participate, but our leaders were very dismissive. Their view was "No, we'll just shut down, we'll pay the singers, they don't have to sing, and come out on the other side." We didn't feel that was right. The chorus was upset that they couldn't sing for a year. The orchestra was upset that they couldn't play. We were upset that we didn't have operas to go to, and that we didn't have a respectable story to tell donors. There are many reasons for the downfall of NYCO, but I think one of the most compelling stories of NYCO is, "who oversees the overseers?"

The dark season was just one of the questionable decisions that the company's overseers had made. The cavalier attitude toward the endowment was another, and the board was about to take the most critical step down the road of abrogating its responsibility for the fund's preservation. It had been clear for years that the company's business model was in serious trouble, but rather than making hard choices about how to solve the financial problems, the board, under Susan Baker, allowed the deficit pattern to continue, masking it with a windfall bequest and, even more disturbingly, withdrawals from the endowment.

Between these "Special Projects" withdrawals and millions in losses from the recession, the value of the Wallace endowment was already down from its original $51.57 million to just over $27 million when the company's cy pres petition was approved by the office of New York Attorney General Andrew Cuomo in October. This gave City Opera permission to make a massive $17.5 million withdrawal, which would be used to fund current operations and pay off the $9.5 million of debt incurred the previous season. A second cy pres request, of $6.6 million, would be approved the following spring, all but depleting the endowment. The funds were supposedly "borrowed," but the likelihood of the company being able to pay the money back into the endowment was small to none.

All along, City Opera's board had viewed the endowment as expendable rather than as an asset to be preserved, which is the fiduciary responsibility expected of a nonprofit board. The pattern of borrowing today to pay for tomorrow had begun even before Baker's Hail Mary hiring of Gerard Mortier. And it was the prospect of using the endowment as a piggy bank that had set the whole debacle in motion, first emboldening Baker to promise Mortier a vastly expanded budget, and then encouraging the complacency that led to her failure to raise sufficient funds for the fantasy. It was with this same attitude of nonchalance that she agreed to wait two years for Mortier to arrive, and to squeak by with a dark, no-income season in the meantime. The invasion of the endowment through the cy pres petition was originally intended to provide the cash to keep the company running until Mortier came; supposedly, his enormous success would then open the floodgates of donations and enable the company to pay it back. Worst of all, the invasion was done at the most inopportune moment, when the financial markets were in free fall.

If the only alternative to the final pillaging of the endowment was bankruptcy and reorganization, that might have been a better solution. For example, two and a half years later, the Philadelphia Orchestra would file for Chapter 11 and reemerge a year later having renegotiated its labor contracts and its rental agreements and altered its pension arrangements. In any case, days after the cy pres request was granted, on October 28, the Mortier fantasy was reduced to rubble, and the company's prospects for repaying the money were, if possible, even bleaker than before. With the granting of the cy pres petition, the company was required to engage an outside adviser to consult on its efforts to stage a comeback. Michael Kaiser, then president of the John F. Kennedy Center for the Performing Arts and author of the newly published book, *The Art of the Turnaround*, which chronicled his history of remaking troubled arts institutions, was tapped to fill that role. His recommendations included immediately hiring a general director, shrinking the season from its former 110-performance length, renegotiating the union contracts, building the board with people who would be better able to make large donations, and developing a new long-term artistic plan.

Hiring a new leader was the first order of business, and for the second time in three years, the board assembled a search committee to interview candidates for the general director position. Emilie Corey says that she was asked to be part of it but refused—"since Susan did exactly what she wanted the last time, what was the point?" Kara Unterberg, despite the fact that she was going through a divorce, did agree to participate. "I was giving it one last shot," she said.

Candidates like Neal Goren, founder of Gotham Chamber Opera, Michael Capasso, founder of Dicapo Opera, and Leon Botstein, president of Bard College and the music director of the American Symphony Orchestra, were interviewed. The City Opera staff was consulted, and their overwhelming choice was Francesca Zambello, an experienced opera stage director who had worked at major international houses including the Metropolitan, Paris, Covent Garden, La Scala, and Munich. At the time, she was working as a consultant for the San Francisco Opera. Having directed theater on Broadway and at Disneyland, she had a keen sense of how popular culture and high art could intersect—and she boasted an A-list Rolodex of artists. She was also known to be outgoing and a straight shooter. After Kellogg's gentlemanly reticence and Mortier's European abstraction and provocation, she seemed like the kind of person who could rally support for the company inside and out. Unterberg more than liked her. "I thought she was the only person who could do it," she said.

Zambello was among those who had also been interviewed for the job during the previous search, but she had decided then that she was not interested. This time, she was. As she recalls it, "Susan Baker and Mark Newhouse met me in my office on Fifty-Second Street and said, we would like to offer you the job of artistic director." Zambello wanted to work as a team with an executive director, and it was agreed that she would start looking for possible candidates. Zambello came up with several possibilities for the executive director slot—but then, suddenly, things changed. Mary Sharp Cronson, a longtime board member, had another candidate in mind for the general director position—George Steel—and she threatened to withdraw her funding if Zambello was hired.

Cronson had some leverage. She was the company's connection to the Peter Jay Sharp Foundation, a charitable entity set up by her brother, a prominent real estate developer, when he died in 1992. The foundation, which had been a generous, longtime contributor to the company, was in the process of liquidating its real estate holdings and distributing its considerable assets. Arts institutions like the Brooklyn Academy of Music had already received eight-figure gifts. Although Cronson did not control the Sharp Foundation's giving, her continued participation on the board fueled the expectation that City Opera might receive a significant closing gift.

Cronson had gotten to know Steel, who was forty-two, during his eleven-year tenure as executive director of Columbia University's Miller Theatre. A supporter of new music herself, she liked his unconventional programming. Steel was also the part-time conductor of Vox, an early music vocal ensemble which he had founded, and was credited with making Miller a destination for new and different presentations, ranging from Renaissance choral music to contemporary chamber concerts. Steel had been interviewed for the City Opera job during the previous search, and had recently become general director of the Dallas Opera. After Cronson made her wishes known, the conversation in the search committee shifted abruptly. "Mary Cronson pushed hard for George Steel," recalled Unterberg.

> People started saying that Francesca was too busy and doing too many other things, that she wouldn't be focused, and the only reason that Mortier didn't work out was because he wasn't here full time. George Steel would be here full time. So instead of someone with a lot of opera experience, you take someone who doesn't have any, and isn't all that well thought of in Dallas.

In fact, it appeared that Steel's new job leading the Dallas Opera was not going smoothly. He had not endeared himself to the staff, and his lack of practical knowledge about opera was often glaringly apparent. However, with Cronson's adamant support for Steel, the search committee's selection had become a foregone conclusion. Unterberg remembers that there was no advance warning that a committee vote on the choice of general director would be taken. "It was just supposed to be a meeting. There wasn't any real discussion, and people who hadn't even met all the candidates were voting." According to Zambello, Baker withdrew the offer to her on January 7. The full board met for final approval of Steel on January 14. He would be starting work right away. Soon thereafter, Unterberg resigned.

On January 15, City Opera gave the first of two concert performances of Barber's *Antony and Cleopatra* at Carnegie Hall, featuring Lauren Flanigan and Teddy Tahu Rhodes. The company made a brave showing, declaring its continued existence with an important but rarely heard contemporary score. The performance also marked the end of the ancien régime: it was the last day for Robin Thompson, who had arrived with Kellogg. He was due to be supplanted during the Mortier regime and had not been asked to stay on even after Mortier opted not to come. The incoming general manager and artistic director also attended the performance. In the *New York Times* story that announced the company's selection of its new leader, Baker called Steel "scrappy, flexible, adaptable, charming and innovative."

Steel started at the company on February 2. He recruited some staff: Edward Yim, who had worked at the Los Angeles Philharmonic and was currently a manager at IMG Artists, representing performers, came on board as director of artistic planning. Yim loved opera and opera companies, though he had never worked in one. What is more, he says, "I thought, this is a great opportunity, because if we can fix City Opera and save it, we'll be heroes; and if we can't, no one will blame us." Steven Blier, a well-known pianist and vocal accompanist, was hired as a consultant to provide expertise in casting singers. He joined Kevin Murphy, who had worked previously at the Met and had been brought to City Opera from the Paris Opera by Mortier the previous year. The team would have to quickly organize a new season from scratch, as the expensive Mortier projects all had to be jettisoned. In April, Steel announced a program of five operas for the 2009–10 season, two in the fall and three in the spring, all of which would be performed in the New York State Theater: Mortier's ambitious multi-venue plans had been abandoned along with his productions. Four of them would be NYCO revivals, and a new, bare-bones *Don Giovanni* would be directed by Christopher Alden.

The drop in activity—from City Opera's previous schedule of twelve to eighteen productions and at least 110 performances per season to 32 performances of five operas plus one concert—was dramatic. The company's fixed costs were still high, however: the board approved an operating budget for the year of $30.4 million, about two-thirds of previous budgets. With only a quarter of the performances of previous years, projected ticket revenues were slashed to just $3 million—down from the $12–$14 million of the pre-Mortier years. The difference was to be made up by extra fund-raising: On top of the regular annual donations, the company leaders were counting on a newly established "Turnaround Campaign" to bring in another $7 million for the year. The budget also included the $9 million in reimbursement that Baker was still hoping to extract from the Koch Theater renovation capital campaign. Once again, hope triumphed over experience.

Steel, whose blond, cherubic good looks recalled the choirboy he had once been, had never run a large organization. Nor had he ever been obliged to raise significant funds, given that Miller Theatre is mostly subsidized by Columbia University. His artistic tastes were also offbeat. "He'd rather hear Chabrier than Bizet," Yim points out. "And if it were Bizet, it would be *Djamileh* rather than *Carmen*."

Many of the remaining City Opera staff members were bemused and confused by Steel, whose casual, even flippant, manner and lack of opera house experience did not inspire their confidence. "He was like the weird stepdad who starts driving the car," says one. Another recalls that at the first senior staff meeting, Steel told the group that he did not like opera and that he did not want to hear about how things had been done in the past or what City Opera had done because this was a new era. Steel viewed himself a new broom, and while there was clearly a need for radical change in City Opera's way of operating, Steel, like Mortier before him, seemed to be operating without regard for the company's traditions or the people who had maintained them for many years. Gail Kruvand, the head of the orchestra committee, felt that Steel didn't understand or respect the company's history. "We wanted so much for this to work and to survive. The organism was fragile, but he didn't have an appreciation or recognition of that."

On top of all this, the orchestra and chorus contracts were expiring. Kruvand, who handled the orchestra negotiations, recalls, "George didn't know what he was doing. We said, 'Are you going to make us a proposal?' He never did. So we said, 'We'll give you a proposal. We understand the financial constraints; we're going to propose that you pay us for twenty-two weeks.' So he looked like a genius." (Steel got the credit for the orchestra's proposal, a new two-year contract that reduced the guarantee from twenty-nine weeks and cut the number of regular orchestra players covered under the guarantee from fifty-nine to fifty-two.) In the AGMA negotiation, the chorus contract guarantee was also reduced from twenty-six weeks to twenty-two. Overall, the reduction in pay and benefits for the artists' unions amounted to 16 percent. But with the drastic reduction in the number of performances, the company was still paying for more work than it could use.

Thanks to the pillaging of the endowment, however, City Opera had survived. In other parts of the country, the economic crisis had shuttered half a dozen opera companies, with Opera Pacific, Connecticut Opera, Baltimore Opera, and Orlando Opera falling like dominoes over the six months from November 2008 to April 2009. All were much smaller than City Opera, with budgets under $10 million, but like City Opera, they had all had been in various stages of financial trouble for some time. The downturn merely exposed weaknesses that had been present all along—exacerbating their problems with bad ticket sales, reduced contributions, and defaults on pledges. There were some interesting parallels between the largest of these regional companies, the

Orange County–based Opera Pacific, and City Opera. Opera Pacific also focused on young singers, presented some contemporary American titles, and had a bigger and fancier company (the LA Opera) as its neighbor, if not exactly across the street. However, Opera Pacific's downfall was that it had depended on just a few donors (three) for the lion's share of its contributed income.

Larger opera companies with more resources were better able to weather the economic collapse since they could trim their budgets without jeopardizing their operations. LA Opera had layoffs; the Metropolitan Opera imposed a 10 percent pay cut for staff, used the iconic Chagall paintings in the opera house lobby as collateral for a loan, and replaced four expensive revivals, including Corigliano's *The Ghosts of Versailles* and Berlioz's *Benvenuto Cellini*, with more economical (and popular) titles.

On November 5, 2009, City Opera reopened the renovated New York State Theater, renamed the David H. Koch Theater, with *American Voices*, a concert of American arias and musical theater numbers. The most dramatic visible change in the auditorium was the addition of two new side aisles on the orchestra level. The original Philip Johnson design had continental seating, with rows that stretched uninterrupted from one side of the auditorium to the other. City Ballet had long resisted changing this configuration, not wanting to lose any prime central viewing space, but had finally agreed to the aisles, which made audience circulation easier. The other major change was the expanded, movable orchestra pit that Mortier had demanded. These alterations resulted in the loss of about two hundred seats, reducing the theater's total seating to twenty-five hundred.

The concert showed off the orchestra, which sounded bright and present in the renovated pit, which could now accommodate up to one hundred musicians. But the proceedings didn't feel entirely festive, given the simple presentation—most of the selections were performed downstage in front of a black curtain. And while bigger voices, like those of Lauren Flanigan and Measha Brueggergosman, carried well, the acoustical improvements, including the removal of carpeting from the walls and floors and new seat materials, did not noticeably aid those with slimmer instruments. The enhancement system that Kellogg had installed was gone.

For the singers, the hall felt different. Amy Burton, who had last sung with the company in 2005, gave a poignant performance of "Les feux d'artifice t'appellent" from Rufus Wainwright's *Prima Donna*. "It was way better. I heard the orchestra like I had never heard it before," she says. "It was like making chamber music. Taking the carpet off the back wall and expanding the pit made such a difference. I'm so glad I got to sing on that stage again, and experience something that was acoustically pleasant."

Performances by some City Opera veterans—Joyce Castle hamming up her signature number, "I Am Easily Assimilated," from *Candide*, and Samuel Ramey exhorting the congregation in the revival scene from *Susannah*, conducted by Julius Rudel—evoked the past. In the lobby, an exhibit by the artist E. V. Day, in which opera costumes from the company's warehouse were reimagined, using miles of fishing line, as flying sculptures hovering over the promenade, suggested how tradition might be tweaked for the future.

One of the company's most anticipated productions that fall was Hugo Weisgall's grand, twelve-tone *Esther*, which had its world premiere in 1993 as one of the three works presented to mark City Opera's fortieth anniversary, and hadn't been staged since. Lauren Flanigan, the original Esther, once again headed the cast, and the original Christopher Mattaliano/Jerome Sirlin production, featuring projections that evoked ancient Persia and permitted quick segues between scenes, was resurrected. The novelty value of this obscure opera generated enough interest that a fifth performance was added to the originally planned four.

For *Don Giovanni*, the only new production of the season, Steel engaged Christopher Alden, whose transgressive aesthetic matched his own. The bare-bones scenery made a virtue of necessity: Chuck Giles says that the show was budgeted at $25,000, far less than the cheapest production ($90,000) that he had ever supervised for the company, and he had been there since 1986. Yet the production's two walls, angled to create a triangular playing space, helped project the voices into the theater, and Alden's dark concept of unrepentant wickedness, featuring explicit sexual activity and violence, played out in 1930s costumes, and the implication that the characters were members of a kind of evangelical church, was a hit with critics and audiences. The cast was strong as well: six of the eight principals were making their company debuts, and singers such as the suave baritone Daniel Okulitch in the title part and the rich-toned Keri Alkema as Donna Elvira demonstrated City Opera's continuing, critical role as a showcase for young talent.

By the end of 2009, things seemed to be looking up. All of the fall programming had done well, and with the addition of a fifth performance of *Esther*, ticket revenue was about one-third higher than the $1 million projected for the two fall operas. Additionally, the *American Voices* gala event had taken in over $2 million, an impressively high number for a City Opera fund-raiser. And the company finally reached an agreement with City Ballet and City Center for $9 million in funds from the capital campaign for the theater renovation. As part of the agreement, City Opera would relinquish its early fall weeks in the theater to the Ballet. Since the opera company had cut back so drastically on its performing weeks, it did not, for the foreseeable future, need the theater time.

All three spring operas were revivals of City Opera productions that had originated at Glimmerglass and each represented a different strand of the company's tradition. The iconic Mark Lamos *Madama Butterfly* reflected the company's commitment to standard repertory operas, but it was weakly cast, and ten performances proved too many. The company's historical role in revitalizing Handel's operas was represented with *Partenope*, which brought the City Opera debut of Christian Curnyn, a major early music conductor, and featured two rising young countertenors, the British Iestyn Davies, who had appeared with the company in *King Arthur*, and Anthony Roth Costanzo, a Met Auditions winner in 2009. Finally, the company affirmed its role as a champion of unusual repertoire with Chabrier's frothy *L'Étoile*, sung in French with English dialogue, and featuring the irrepressible Jean-Paul Fouchécourt, the radiant Jennifer Zetlan, and Emmanuel Plasson in the pit. Although the twenty-two spring performances did not meet their sales goals, the total ticket income for the year was over $3 million, slightly higher than projected, thanks to the robust sales in the fall.

But the hot ticket of the spring was across the plaza at the Met, where the South African artist William Kentridge's spectacular production of Shostakovich's *The Nose* had galvanized the art world as well as opera lovers. And while not all of Peter Gelb's new productions had been equally successful, his biggest innovation—HD transmissions of live operas into movie theaters—had been a runaway success. Gelb, coming from the recording business, had recognized the potential of media as a way to enlarge the company's audience, and one of his first priorities upon joining the Met had been to renegotiate the company's media agreement with its unions, persuading them that a new, revenue-sharing arrangement, instead of the old, prohibitively expensive model in which artists were paid up front for any media work, would be in everyone's interests. To the surprise of many, the HD program had proved hugely popular and had expanded exponentially into theaters across the United States and around the world. In the 2009–10 season, the series had sold 2.4 million tickets, dramatically expanding the company's audience, to say nothing of the reach of its brand. By transmitting the Met's high production values and top singers, the HD program raised the bar for opera companies everywhere. And with an HD cinema ticket costing about $20, the Met could, at least in terms of price, claim the People's Opera title.

At City Opera, the fund-raising team had been able to meet its annual fund goals. Much of the foundation money that had originally been pledged to support Mortier's first season had been saved: the $2.5 million Andrew W. Mellon Foundation grant, instead of arriving as a one-year gift, would be given over several years, and the Mary Flagler Cary Charitable Trust closing grant was also preserved, albeit somewhat reduced. The healthy showing for the fall gala also buttressed the bottom line.

However, the company needed much more for both the present and the future. The five-year Turnaround Plan that Michael Kaiser had drawn up for City Opera was intended to position it as a midsize company whose activity was more in line with its budget size than had been the case in the past. Its previous level of activity—106 performances of thirteen operas in 2007–08, and even more before that—had been second only to the Metropolitan in the United States. However, its $45 million budget was considerably smaller than those of the next busiest opera companies—San Francisco, Chicago, and Los Angeles—all of which gave many fewer performances than City Opera had.

The Turnaround Plan had City Opera gradually rebuilding from its current, reduced level of $30 million and thirty-two performances of five operas to reach a budget of $36 million and seventy-two performances of eight productions in 2014–15. (It would still be a lean operation: by comparison, Lyric Opera of Chicago had a budget of $58 million for approximately the same level of activity.) But with fewer performances than it had given in the pre-Steel days, ticket income would be lower. By the fifth year, it was expected that contributed income would cover nearly three-quarters of the budget. The notion of a fifty-fifty split between ticket sales and contributed income was an artifact of the distant past—and not just at City Opera.

Before Steel arrived, City Opera's annual fund-raising had been stalled at approximately $14.5 million for nearly a decade. The Turnaround Plan aimed to gradually increase this number over five years, finally arriving at $26 million a year in annual fund contributions. However, since achieving this level would be an incremental process, an additional $30 million in major gifts would be required in the meantime to fill the gap in the company's operating budget. It was hoped that the ongoing "Turnaround Campaign" (a component of the Turnaround Plan) would secure such gifts. Survival required a colossal increase in contributions.

Once again, City Opera faced the same situation that had helped doom the Mortier directorship. It had no deep-pocketed board members who were able or willing to come up with multimillion-dollar gifts. It had no rich friends who would use their networks to secure more funds. This time, it didn't even have the rock-star prospect of Mortier to sell; it had George Steel, whose profile was considerably lower. A big expansion of fund-raising had worked once—with Beverly Sills, who was able to leverage her star power and deep association with the company to save it—but Sills and her era were long gone, and there was no one who represented City Opera as she had. What is more, the dark season had called into question the need for the company's existence: when it was gone for a year, did anyone miss it? Did anyone care enough about the People's Opera to pay big money for its resurrection? In the 2009–10 season, it seemed the answer was no. The company raised only $2.2 million of the year's $7 million Turnaround Campaign goal.

That was not the only shortfall. That season, City Opera got only $4 million of the $9 million that it had expected to receive from the David H. Koch Theater (DHKT) capital campaign. In the end, even with a reduction in administrative expenses, Steel's first season ended with an operating loss of $4.6 million.

George Steel's vision for the "new" City Opera became clearer during his second season in 2010–11. The first had been planned collaboratively, with input from company veterans, and quickly—out of necessity. For the second, Steel made the decisions himself. With no standard repertory titles, it reflected his taste for the offbeat.

The subscription brochure, designed with an eye toward trendy modernity, featured contemporary art pieces, including a cover image of Kehinde Wiley's *Portrait of Andries Stilte*, in which a young, black rapper is posed like the wealthy burgher of a Golden Age Dutch painting; the idea was to demonstrate City Opera's role of "infusing traditional grand opera with New York swagger." (The previous season's brochure had been similarly offbeat, using contemporary art photographs, like Rachel Papo's image of a young female soldier in battle gear against a desert background for *Esther*. However, since much of the programming had been conventional, there was some confusion between the identity the company was attempting to project and what it actually put onstage. With the new season, the imagery was more aligned to the product.) The company's logo, which dominated its website and marketing, was a large black dot, an economizing carryover from the expensive rebranding campaign that had been done for Mortier. It was supposed to seem edgy and modern, but unfortunately it looked like a black hole, and the connotations were not lost on some observers. It was, as Kara Unterberg put it, "where all the money goes."

Three of the 2010–11 season's five shows would be new productions of twentieth-century operas. In the fall, Christopher Alden would direct the New York premiere of Leonard Bernstein's opera *A Quiet Place*, first performed in 1983, but since neglected. In the spring, there was *Mono-dramas*, an evening of three solo works for soprano by Arnold Schoenberg, John Zorn, and Morton Feldman, staged by the visual artist and director Michael Counts. It would be followed by Stephen Schwartz's *Séance on a Wet Afternoon*.

A Quiet Place, Leonard Bernstein's only full-length opera, which incorporated his earlier one-act hit, *Trouble in Tahiti*, as a flashback, should have been an important New York event, given Bernstein's association with the city and the reverence in which he was held. But the production, though beautifully produced and sung, was a box office disaster, with its eight performances—too many for a modern opera—averaging only 43 percent capacity, barely half what had been projected. The other fall opera, a revival of Strauss's *Intermezzo*, did even worse.

But Steel was still thinking big. At the November board meeting, he elaborated on his ideas for future seasons, which included such massive undertakings as the Robert Wilson production of Debussy's *Pelléas et Mélisande* (one of the Mortier projects from Paris) and Francesca Zambello's production of *Showboat*, to say nothing of new productions of *Tristan und Isolde* and Britten's *Gloriana*. In 2011–12, Steel planned to increase the season to seven operas, and, like the current season, there would be no warhorse repertoire (the closest being Puccini's *La Rondine*). The selections included *Damon* by Telemann (Steel found Telemann's operas "richer than Handel's"); *The Golden Ticket*, by Peter Ash, based on the Roald Dahl children's book *Charlie and the Chocolate Factory*, which had successfully premiered at Opera Theatre of Saint Louis the previous spring; and Rufus Wainwright's *Prima Donna*, which had been originally commissioned and then dropped by the Metropolitan Opera. *Prima Donna* had premiered—and been panned—in Manchester the previous year, but Steel thought that bringing in Wainwright and his following would offer some new blood.

It wasn't long, however, before more bad financial news undercut this optimism. The Turnaround Campaign goal for the year had already been reduced from $7 million to $5 million, requiring several layoffs and a 10 percent salary reduction for all senior staff. With no immediately accessible reserves to draw on, cash flow depended on fund-raising. The process had begun to liquidate several small non-Wallace endowment funds—the Rigler fund and the air rights fund—for use as operating money, and a third cy pres application to use the rest of the Wallace money was under consideration.

One potential bright spot was that the board had a new chair. With Susan Baker tied to the Mortier debacle, the company needed a new leader, and Robert Meya had recruited Charles Wall, a retired lawyer and executive who had been vice chairman of Philip Morris International in Switzerland and had served on the City Opera board from 2001 until 2008. Wall rejoined the board in September and took over the chairmanship in January 2011, with Baker remaining on the board.

But things looked even darker in the spring. By March 2011, Peter Gee, the CFO, was already forecasting a $1.4 million deficit for the year due to a shortfall in ticket sales. The future was no rosier—Gee told the finance committee that if the company continued in its present business model, the structural deficit could grow to as much as $10 million in future seasons. In the meantime, the pension benefit plan was frozen, and Wall offered a $2.5 million matching grant to help plug the deficit and raise additional funds. Gee and Steel were tasked with preparing business model alternatives.

On March 30, Steel reported to the board that he had discussed the company's financial troubles with Reynold Levy, the president of Lincoln Center. Their conversation had covered ideas about restructuring, changing the performance calendar, and reducing fixed costs. The possibility of City Opera performing outside Lincoln Center, Steel said, would be explored. The time for the company to announce its 2011–12 season came and went, and reporters began asking questions. In early April, the *New York Times* and the *Wall Street Journal* reported that City Opera, facing a potential $5 million deficit, had embarked on an exhaustive review of its finances and would not schedule future programming until it reached a balanced budget.

Meanwhile, the results of the ongoing spring season were helping neither the bottom line nor the narrative. A revival of Jonathan Miller's *Elixir of Love* was lively and well cast but sold less than half the house over its seven performances. *Monodramas*, the evening of three solo works for soprano, was Steel's baby, but it turned out to be an even bigger, and very expensive, bust. Intended to attract the visual arts community and the downtown music crowd, it alienated nearly everyone else, particularly with Feldman's *Neither*, a forty-five-minute ordeal of single, unconnected notes and simple phrases, most of them very high, valiantly performed by Cyndia Sieden. Visual artist Michael Counts's abstract accompanying presentations provided little illumination over the (very) long haul. Though the production received some critical praise for its audacity, it sold poorly at 36 percent.

Perhaps the biggest disappointment of the 2010–11 season was Stephen Schwartz's *Séance on a Wet Afternoon*, starring Lauren Flanigan. Hoping for interest from Schwartz's Broadway fans, the company scheduled ten performances of the production, which had originated at Opera Santa Barbara. But the preteen and family crowds that made *Wicked* so successful did not turn out for an opera about a demented, unsuccessful psychic who kidnaps a child, and it, too, underperformed. This was not surprising: the story was B-horror-movie creepy, the characters unsavory, and Schwartz's melodic gifts translated to the opera stage as a string of interchangeable power ballads.

Despite the season's forty-three performances, nine more than in 2009–10, ticket earnings were down: $2.9 million, disastrously lower than the $5 million projected for the season. The audience clearly was not flocking back to the company in its edgy George Steel incarnation. In 2007–08, its last year under the "old" model, with over one hundred performances of a dozen or more titles, City Opera had roughly thirteen thousand subscribers. In 2010–11, it was down to about three thousand. Nor were donors increasing their support to the degree that the company had counted on. Although Wall's $2.5 million matching grant had succeeded in putting the special Turnaround Campaign (the extra push for major gifts beyond the usual annual fund) over its goal of $5 million, there were shortfalls in other fund-raising areas. A particular disappointment was the season's spring gala, built around a concert of music by Stephen Schwartz and featuring some Broadway luminaries; it did not attract the expected support from the composer's theater network. Once again, the company ran a significant operating deficit.

By April, with the prospect of an even more reduced season in 2011–12, Ed Yim was looking for an exit strategy. "I told George, 'I love the work we have done, but I don't think you need me—or can afford my salary—to put on a three-opera season. Also, my sense is that the stuff I can bring to the table, you want to provide yourself.'" In June, Yim went to the New York Philharmonic as director of artistic planning.

In retrospect, Yim believes that Steel needed someone to put the brakes on. "I think George might have been better served by a more experienced opera administrator than me," he says. "Someone who might have had a more tempering influence on George's visionary, progressive view, who would have been able to say, 'George, you can do one of these [ambitious contemporary operas], but not three.'" No one in the company had the standing to say that, and Steel remained persuaded that his impulse toward unusual repertory was the right way forward. Gail Kruvand recalls being horrified at a board meeting in May, when Steel presented a specious chart tracking City Opera's performances of what he called "The Twelve"—the most familiar standard repertory titles—over the six years before the dark season. The chart, he claimed, supported his conclusion that producing traditional operas was overly expensive and led to greater budget deficits.

In the most basic terms, the budget model of the "new" New York City Opera made as little sense as that of the old one. Because of its fixed costs in labor contracts (it was still paying for work that it wasn't using) and Koch Theater expenses, the company was spending a disproportionate amount for the number of performances it was giving. It had a budget of $31 million for five operas and forty-three performances. By contrast, the Seattle Opera's budget was about $21 million for the same activity—and it was earning much more in ticket sales. City Opera's enormous fund-raising requirements, now nearly double what they had been before the dark season, were just as unrealistic as they had been when the company tried to raise huge sums for Mortier. The company needed to reduce its fixed costs, but that was a process that required sophisticated and transparent negotiation.

One draconian option for that reduction was already on the table: leaving the Koch Theater. "We knew they were talking about it, because of the cost of the theater," Kruvand says.

> But we weren't really asked, "What are your thoughts about this?" We were marginalized. George couldn't deal with people, and I think he didn't really want input. I don't think Chuck Wall did either. Silly me, I thought, "They can't just leave, they have almost another two years on their lease." Then I heard Wall say exactly that at a board meeting: "We're going to leave, and the ballet can sue us if they don't like it, but we don't have any money."

Preliminary conversations about the upcoming expiration of the orchestra contract had also begun. "I think Steel stonewalled Local 802 [the orchestra union] and AGMA," Kruvand says. "He never made proposals. Maybe George thought that if the contract expired, the company would have no more obligation to us. He was not a guy that lived in the real world. If he wanted it, that's what it was going to be."

The board meeting of May 19 lasted all day and resumed on the morning of May 20. That afternoon, the company dropped the bombshell: it told the *New York Times* that it would leave Lincoln Center and perform in different venues around the city. The budget for the upcoming 2011–12 season would be considerably less than the current $31 million; two of the five operas planned would be smaller-scaled works, suitable for three-hundred-to-nine-hundred-seat houses; and the company would move its offices from the Koch Theater's basement. Steel said, "We love Lincoln Center, but the reality is that the fixed costs of living here are simply too high." He estimated those costs at $4.5 million per year.

"That board meeting went on for hours and hours, and it was horrible," Emilie Corey recalls.

The tension in the room, the stress, and then, to finally vote, and say we were going to go, was awful. The truth was, we had no choice. We couldn't afford to be there. And nobody at Lincoln Center gave a shit. The silence was deafening. There was no, "Oh, we're one big happy family here, one of our constituents is hurting, let's see if we can help them." No way, José. Couldn't care less. Bye-bye.

As Goldman had realized years earlier, Lincoln Center had its opera company, the Met, and didn't really see the need for two. Meya concurs. "We were like the battered stepchild. We didn't feel the love."

Purely in real estate terms, the idea that Lincoln Center needed only one opera company turned out to be sound. With City Opera gone, the New York City Ballet returned to the primary position envisioned for it back when the theater was built. The Koch Theater became a dance house, welcoming many visiting and local companies, including the Paul Taylor Dance Company, Alvin Ailey American Dance Theater, and American Ballet Theatre. David Titcomb recalls the former house manager of the theater telling him, "If we had known how many people were interested in renting the Koch Theater, we would have kicked City Opera out a long time ago."

It soon became evident that the company would seek to lower its fixed costs in other areas as well. Now that it was leaving Lincoln Center, and would no longer be the same kind of repertory operation, City Opera was hoping to leave behind some of the most onerous elements of its union obligations as well. The changes would be draconian: The company's first proposals to union representatives ended guarantees for the number of weeks of employment and the number of members hired. Instead, the singers and players would be paid per service for rehearsals and performances, which would give the company the flexibility to program only what it could afford. The proposed new contract would also eliminate vacation pay, tenure, leaves, instrument insurance, and the current health insurance plans. Not surprisingly, the unions objected strenuously. The transition was not going to be easy.

City Opera veterans were enraged by both the proposed changes to the labor contracts and the move from Lincoln Center. Julius Rudel penned a scathing op-ed in the *New York Times*, recalling the company's sixty-eight-year history, including its brush with bankruptcy in 1956, and concluding, "If the board and management of City Opera cannot finance, produce and support full seasons of standard operas in interesting productions with first-rate casts as we once did, they should be replaced, so that [in another] 68 years . . . no one will wonder what ever became of City Opera." Soprano Catherine Malfitano circulated an open letter, signed by more than 120 artists including numerous prominent City Opera veterans such as Placido Domingo, Carlisle Floyd, Samuel Ramey, Hal Prince, and June Anderson, asking the company to reconsider the move and accusing the management of "the dismembering of the company, piece by piece and person by person." The letter characterized an opera company as "a team, a cohesive family . . . which brings with it a shared point of view, a richness of context, ensemble values and a nest for nurturing young artists" and said that City Opera would lose its identity and importance if it were transformed into "a small ad hoc presenting organization forced to deploy pickup orchestras, choruses and soloists."

On July 12, at the Guggenheim Museum, to the counterpoint of a vehement demonstration outside by chorus and orchestra members and their supporters, Steel officially unveiled his plan for the 2011–12 season, which would not begin until February 2012. There would be a total of sixteen performances of four operas, including a Jonathan Miller production of *La Traviata* from Glimmerglass (the board had insisted upon one A-list standard repertory piece) and Rufus Wainwright's *Prima Donna*, both of which would be performed at the two-thousand-seat Brooklyn Academy of Music. *Così fan tutte*, directed by Alden, would play in the six-hundred-seat Lynch Theater at John Jay College, and Telemann's *Orpheus* would be staged in the equally small El Museo del Barrio. (Steel also announced a future initiative: a series of Shakespeare-based operas, in partnership with the Public Theater, to be presented in the outdoor Delacorte Theater in Central Park with free tickets, to begin in fall 2012 as part of the 2012–13 season.) The $13 million budget would be less than half of the previous season's $31 million.

Fourteen of the company's forty-eight staff jobs had already been eliminated, and the exodus continued as the summer stretched into fall. Peter Gee, the CFO, resigned and was replaced by Andrea Nellis, who had been general manager at the Public Theater. Others followed, including the directors of marketing, education, and press, as well as the artistic administrator. Robert Meya told Steel that he, too, was planning to leave, though he stayed until February, when he moved on to the Santa Fe Opera. Several longtime board members also departed: Nomi Ghez did not stand for reelection and Roy Furman, whose principal association was with Lincoln Center, resigned. Artist board members also left: mezzo Joyce Castle quit in June in objection to the move, and conductor Jonathan Sheffer, who had been brought onto the board by Steel two years earlier, left, citing disagreements over the company's artistic direction and saying that he felt it had "broken faith with the audience."

Key artistic staff departed as well. Kevin Murphy, the respected director of music administration, seeing the writing on the wall, accepted an offer to head the opera program at Indiana University, though he would remain a casting adviser to the company. And the post of music director, held since 1996 by George Manahan, was eliminated. Manahan says that he had asked his agent to negotiate him out of the last year of his contract even before the company's efforts to end the orchestra guarantees were revealed. "I was nervous that any day, they were going to declare Chapter 11," he says. He took seriously the company's contention that City Opera could no longer afford to exist as it always had, even if others he spoke with did not. "The answer that you would always hear from players and other people was, 'We've been hearing that for 25 years.'" But Manahan could see that this time was different.

By the fall, the company still had no agreement with its artists' unions, and on November 30, talks with the unions broke down—a federal mediator was called in. Meanwhile, Steel's contract was extended for three years, and the company found office space to rent downtown, at 75 Broad Street, not far from Steel's home.

With chorus rehearsals for *La Traviata*, the first opera of the season, due to begin on January 9, negotiations resumed early in the new year but quickly reached yet another impasse. The company declared a lockout on January 8, saying that it could not afford to pay for rehearsals since the unions had pledged to strike the performances, which were scheduled to begin on February 12. But ten days later, the unions capitulated and took the per service deal, in which they would be paid by the rehearsal and performance, and would keep some health insurance. The long-standing guarantees were history. Kruvand says, "Our legal counsel wisely suggested that, should the company die, we didn't want the story to be 'the unions killed City Opera.'" The Local 802 spokesman said that the union had accepted "deep concessions" in the hope of raising City Opera "from the ashes." The concessions, Kruvand says, meant a reduction in the average pay for orchestra members from $40,000 annually to just $10,000.

The end of the guarantees seemed inevitable, given the company's greatly reduced schedule—eight weeks of rehearsals and four weeks of performances—its need for flexibility, and its precarious finances. But the acrimony of the process and the poisonous atmosphere between the musicians and management resembled a battle between factory owners and workers having their jobs moved to Mexico. The musicians were already upset by the artistic direction of the company and the move from Lincoln Center, and they were dubious about the sustainability of the projected financial plans, which would see ticket income comprising barely 10 percent of the organization's budget. And now they saw the institution to which they were committed losing its place in the cultural firmament. They did not trust Steel or Wall to be its stewards.

"Paul Kellogg really felt like this company was his family," Kruvand says.

> There was a huge amount of respect for the artists, and not just their artistry, but the fact that they were a part of this, just as his job was to be the general director. George Steel just dismissed any sense of responsibility to the performing artists. Chuck Wall didn't have that connection to the performing artists in the company either, which

I think allowed him to accept what was going on, the diminution of the work. Our position was: "It's our passion, but it's also our livelihood." George Steel had no empathy for that, and I think his fatal flaw was that he felt *he* was NYCO; that it was his show.

After the fiasco with Mortier, City Opera desperately needed a reset, but Steel's style of leadership, as it turned out, was remarkably similar to Baker's: rule by fiat rather than openness and inclusiveness. He was used to running a small operation, Miller Theatre, in a hands-on way, and City Opera was a different animal. One staffer commented that Steel's often micro-managerial focus on small artistic details was a way for him to stay in his comfort zone, escaping from the increasingly out-of-control big-picture problems of fund-raising and managing the board. Furthermore, Steel was not attracting major donations for City Opera. In an ironic twist, the company never received the transformative, eight-figure gift from the Peter Jay Sharp Foundation that seemed to be the quid pro quo when Mary Sharp Cronson pushed for Steel to be hired. As Baker had done with Mortier, Cronson had imposed her choice on the company without supplying the money or the muscle to support that choice.

Allen Moyer, a designer who had worked with the company, said in retrospect, "If they had wanted someone to put them out business, they could not have found someone to do it faster than George Steel. I met him a few times, and I always felt he was totally overwhelmed. I think his decision to leave the State Theater was the beginning of the end. He seemed to never really grasp the enormity of the situation."

CHAPTER 10

Down the Drain

WITH THE UNION negotiations settled, City Opera's first itinerant season opened on schedule at the Brooklyn Academy of Music in February 2012, but the two productions did not bode well for its future artistic health. The Jonathan Miller *Traviata*, rented from Glimmerglass, looked cheap and threadbare, and its lackluster singing, unsubtle conducting, and deliberately low-key acting made for a dispiriting evening (the expiring Violetta, for example, taking realism a step too far, spent the entire last act motionless in bed). The US premiere of Rufus Wainwright's *Prima Donna* was no more encouraging. A compendium of operatic clichés about a depressed diva, sung in French, it reflected its pop celebrity creator's affection for the genre but failed to infuse it with any of his originality. The opening performance and party did attract a healthy contingent of celebrities, including Anjelica Huston, Yoko Ono, Marina Abramović, and Laurie Anderson, who told the *New York Times* Style reporter that she loved the opera.

Advance sales had lagged, so City Opera decided to sell every ticket to the performances at BAM, a two-thousand-seat house, for

$25—company leaders secured an extra $122,500 from donors to sub-sidize the inexpensive seats. At that price, all eight performances of the two operas sold out. Since ticket sales made up such a minimal percent-age of the operating budget anyway, the good PR of the full houses outweighed the income lost. Price was clearly a factor: casual purchas-ers were more likely to take a chance for $25 than for $100, as had been the case with the successful Opera for All experiment a few years earlier. However, like the Met's subsidized Rush Ticket program, those earlier Opera for All sales represented only a small percentage of the total num-ber of tickets available in the season. The sold-out BAM performances—half of the company's season—suggested that one way forward for City Opera might be to sustain itself entirely on similarly subsidized, afford-ably priced performances, effectively returning to its People's Opera roots.

The other two productions, however, staged in theaters that were less than half the size of BAM, sold out without the benefit of reduced ticket prices. Christopher Alden had another go at Mozart, this time a bleak and carnal *Così fan tutte* in the six-hundred-seat Lynch Theater at John Jay College. In May, the company mounted Telemann's *Orpheus*, a lively novelty piece, at El Museo del Barrio. It looked like an inexpensive col-lege production—modern dress, some metal tables on wheels, fluorescent lights, and a few bare branches—and only a few of its singers had any feeling for its period style.

The different theaters presented a number of problems. "The Museo del Bàrrio was a rat trap," Chuck Giles says. "Gerard Mortier and I had looked at that theater and rejected it." Giles says that David Zinn's com-plicated original set design for *Orpheus* was not just unaffordable but unworkable in the space; it had to be rethought, especially since the stage crew was inexperienced. Even BAM, though it had a good stage crew, had problems: "no wings, a horrible loading dock, and you can hear the trains going under it." With *Traviata* in performance while *Prima Donna* was being rehearsed, the crew did a "shuffling act to get one set in and the other out."

Conditions were also challenging for the artists. "You never knew what you were going to find," says Gail Kruvand.

You never knew if there were going to be chairs that were comfortable to sit on, or stools, or how much space there would be. At John Jay, it was so crowded, with no room to pack and unpack, that I dropped the bow case on my bass and broke a hole in it. There was no consideration for what the artists needed. I don't mind schlepping around town, but you've got to have space to play, a stool to sit on, and you have to be able to get easily in and out of the pit.

In April, the company announced that for the 2012–13 season, it would establish a pair of "home bases," splitting its activity between BAM and its original home, the City Center theater on Fifty-Fifth Street, which Giles found entirely inadequate, particularly given its lack of wing space. For him, City Opera had taken a giant step backward. "The reason City Opera left City Center is that it wasn't a good theater."

And even though the company had left the fixed costs of the Koch Theater behind, it still had to pay for space and labor, and most New York theaters capable of presenting large, complex opera productions were unionized. Giles notes, "BAM and City Center, the places we used most, were both union. John Jay paid union rates. We had to rent office and rehearsal space. There was no storage for supplies, as we had in Lincoln Center, so we had to find and rent that." The company also had to work within the scheduling structures of multiple theaters instead of just one.

The greatly diminished performance schedule affected not just ticket sales but donations and the potential for cultivating more donors. "Leaving Lincoln Center was the death knell for the company," says Michael Gary.

In the fund-raising pyramid, the base has to be broad—that includes any ticket buyer who has any affiliation with your company. At the top are your board, your biggest donors, the people who are closest to the company. But you need that broad base in order to identify people who have an interest in your company, so you can funnel them up to higher levels of support. When that base was removed, we became like a pillar—our audience was so small. At the Museo del

Barrio, with six hundred seats, four performances totaled twenty-four hundred people, less than we had for one performance at the Koch Theater.

Cash flow problems persisted, and a few board members, including Wall, stepped in to cover expenses, which included substantial legal fees from the protracted and difficult union negotiations. The numbers were less extreme than in previous years: the fiscal year finished with a smaller operating deficit of less than $1 million. But this new model put enormous pressure on fund-raising. The company had taken in $10.7 million in donations for the year, a robust number but lower than the original goal, and it had only done so with the aid of several large, onetime gifts. One plan that Steel presented for the 2012–13 season had five operas, the other had four; the board chose the more conservative option.

Cuts were still needed, and the next target was the storage cost of the company's warehoused productions. Steel described the warehouse at the October 2012 board meeting as "67,000 square feet jammed to the rafters with stuff. Most of the productions are incomplete." It cost about $500,000 a year to maintain what he called "an inventory of junk." The decision was made to dispose of it all with an online auction in January 2013. City Opera's share of the proceeds came to $233,000.

Many City Opera stalwarts believe that this decision was the final nail in the company's coffin. In practical terms, it meant discarding millions of dollars' worth of stage material. Even if many of the pieces were part of incomplete production sets, Giles pointed out that they were still valuable: stock like props, costumes, and decks could have been kept for reuse and stored less expensively. "That toy box—one hundred trailers full of scenery, props, and costumes—is what allowed City Opera to do what it did as efficiently as it did."

But on a more philosophical level, the Steel administration was jettisoning the company's history, effectively announcing that the old City Opera was no more. Gail Kruvand went out to the warehouse before the sale. "It was like a walk through the history of NYCO," she says. "The fabulous Hal Prince production of *Don Giovanni*. *Haroun and the*

Sea of Stories. The Lamos *Butterfly.* The loss is so deep—there's nothing left."

Indeed, Steel seemed to have no interest in the company's rich past. Leaving the Koch Theater was a big step in the deliberate process of leaving that past behind; so was the warehouse auction. The designer Allen Moyer, who had created several shows for City Opera, believes celebrating the company's past could have been a plausible route forward.

> So many of us constantly talked about the organization—if I were George Steel, and didn't have money to do new productions, I would have said, "Why don't we turn this into a virtue, do a whole season of some of our biggest successes. We own the productions, so let's take what we already have, do a little renovation, freshen the costumes, make sure there's enough rehearsal time, and cast them well."

Moyer thought that Steel missed opportunities by ignoring assets that City Opera already had. "I kept saying, it's an election year, everything is about the rights of gay men and women to marry, and *The Mother of Us All* is about rights. Why not do it, when everyone is talking about that? Maybe Mr. Steel hated those productions, but the common consensus was that he didn't even know about them."

The decision to liquidate the warehouse was of a piece with Steel's view that the remade company would focus on presenting new productions rather than reviving old ones. It would also be disposable and ad hoc. "He had a presenter's, or small-scale producer's, mentality," one staffer says. "The meetings were always like, 'Why do we need to save those costumes? We'll never do that production again. Why do we need sets? Why do we need the orchestra? I can get people. I know people. I can just pull people together.'"

A further blow to the company's past fell on October 29, 2012, when Hurricane Sandy roared up the East Coast, whipping up storm surges that flooded lower Manhattan and shut down its power grid. The new City Opera offices at 75 Broad Street were in the flood zone, and the remains of the company's archives were stored in the building's basement

level. As the storm approached, Steel and other staff members trans-
ported some of the boxes to the upper-floor offices, but much of the
material, including the company's music library, with its years of accumulated performance notations, was inundated.

The 2012–13 season opened at BAM in February with a predictably
attention-getting choice: Thomas Adès's 1995 opera *Powder Her Face*,
about the sexually insatiable Margaret, Duchess of Argyll. Jay Scheib's
production left little to the imagination: it included twenty-four naked
men who wandered about onstage during the opera's infamous oral sex
aria. Britten's *The Turn of the Screw* followed: the bland production,
updated to the 1980s, missed the opera's creepy menace. For the second
pair of operas, the company moved to City Center. First up was a rarity,
Rossini's *Moses in Egypt*, directed by Michael Counts in a production that
used video, with images like a scrolling desert panorama and a cave that
the singers appeared to step inside, as its only stage design. (One board
member, in justifying the warehouse sale, pointed to this show, noting
that it could be stored on a hard drive.) There were some lively singers
in the cast of mostly debut artists, but Counts's slo-mo directing and
Jayce Ogren's pedestrian conducting let the piece sag. Next, Christopher
Alden turned Offenbach's effervescent *La Périchole* into slapstick, with
distracting gags and over-the-top physical comedy that upstaged the
splendid leading lady, Marie Lenormand, and the idiomatic conductor,
Emmanuel Plasson.

That season looked especially sad compared to the much livelier opera
events going on elsewhere in the New York area. In the realm of the
new and unusual, Peak Performances in Montclair, New Jersey, presented
the world premiere of David T. Little's searingly original *Dog Days*.
A ferocious, heavy-metal-infused tale of a family struggling to survive
after an unspecified apocalypse, it ended with an eleven-minute epilogue
of wordless, increasingly loud noise. *Dog Days* was fiercely directed by
Robert Woodruff and sung by an outstanding cast including the cross-
over opera/Broadway soprano Lauren Worsham as a teenager and John

Kelly in the silent role of a man in a makeshift dog suit, whose mere existence brutally exposes the fractures in the family. A remarkable departure from the musically conservative new works typically presented by mainstream opera companies, it electrified the opera world.

The world premiere of *Dog Days* had grown out of work done by Beth Morrison, an offbeat young impresario. Over the last several years, Morrison had become a new force on the opera scene and a symbol of its increasing openness to new ideas about repertory. She had studied voice and then switched to business, and had run City Opera's Vox program for a few seasons before founding her own company, Beth Morrison Projects (BMP), with a mission of supporting creative artists. Clad in tutus, fishnet stockings, and high-heeled boots, Morrison was an outlier in the (very male) opera world, and she had new ideas about how to get around the daunting challenges of helping young composers create new operas without needing to rely on rare commissions from big institutions. Morrison's method was to find seed money for projects by composers and librettists who interested her and then create partnerships with bigger organizations to launch full commissions and productions of their works. She had helped Little and his librettist, Royce Vavrek, develop *Dog Days*—and then brought it to a larger institutional presenter, Peak Performances, which commissioned the full work.

And she was thinking even bigger. January 2013 saw the debut of the Prototype Festival, created by Morrison and HERE, a producer of multidisciplinary art. Prototype showcased an eclectic range of chamber operas by a new generation of composers, and its tour-ready productions were designed to tempt opera companies and presenters to try something off the beaten track. The offerings in the first year of Prototype ranged from a world premiere about an honor killing in Egypt by Mohammed Fairouz to a multimedia exploration of the Bluebeard story, and another disturbing work by Little, *Soldier Songs*, an intimate exploration of what it feels like to be a soldier.

Other New York opera producers were also presenting imaginative work. Gotham Chamber Opera, a lively company founded in 2001 by the conductor Neal Goren, specializing in overlooked chamber operas, had been gradually expanding both its activity and its ambition. Gotham's experiments with nontraditional spaces had included a Haydn opera in the American Museum of Natural History's Planetarium in 2010; and in the spring of 2013, it put on Cavalli's *Eliogabalo*, an opera about a teenage Roman emperor with rapacious and omnivorous sexual appetites, at The Box, a Lower East Side nightclub known for all-night raunchy burlesque shows. The deliberately tawdry and over-the-top production featured topless dancers writhing on a central runway within arm's length of the audience. Meanwhile, on a grander scale, the Metropolitan Opera mounted Adès's 2004 opera *The Tempest*, which NYCO had let slip through its hands seven years earlier. It also presented the hit David McVicar/British Raj staging of Handel's *Giulio Cesare* from Glyndebourne, musically splendid and featuring soprano Natalie Dessay dancing a Bollywood number, as well as a stunning production of Wagner's *Parsifal*, directed by François Girard, with the star tenor Jonas Kaufmann and a startling set with a lake of blood in act 2. City Opera's niche as a place for the new, unusual, and theatrical was being squeezed from both sides.

And the company was still struggling to raise money. Board members continued to defect—by January 2013, there were only twenty, down from thirty-seven five years earlier—and the company was not finding new, reliable sources of donated funds. As it had the previous year, the company was able to secure some onetime major funding—an emergency infusion of cash at the end of 2012 from the Ford Foundation, Bloomberg Philanthropies, and the Andrew W. Mellon Foundation, who put in $500,000 each, enabled the season to go on. But this was not a long-term solution.

"People started leaving the board and holding back on the contributions," Emilie Corey says.

It was a negative, spiraling whirlwind. I think they didn't want to be associated with a doomed organization. City Opera lost any cachet it had left. Some years back, people could say they were proud to be on the NYCO board. Now, people were saying to us, "What are you doing?"

According to Corey, there were still people on the board who had the capacity to contribute more, but they were not inspired to do so.

In March, Steel announced the 2013–14 season: it would open BAM's Next Wave Festival with Mark-Anthony Turnage's *Anna Nicole*, based on the story of the *Playboy* model and tabloid celebrity, which had been a surprise success at the Royal Opera in London in 2011. Next was a return to El Museo del Barrio with J. C. Bach's *Endimione*, an English National Opera production of Bartók's *Bluebeard's Castle* at St. Anne's Warehouse in Brooklyn, and finally, Alden's production of *The Marriage of Figaro* at City Center.

Even with the uncertainty, the board thought that the company was safe for the moment. Emilie Corey remembers, "There was a sense in June [2013] that we had turned a corner, we had made it through the year and we were going to be okay. The staff was decimated, there were not so many expenses, and things had really been pared down. It felt like, if we exercised as much discipline as we could, maybe we'd be okay."

They were not. In August, board members began receiving frantic phone calls: some expected pledges, about $1.5 million, had fallen through, and the company did not have enough money to put on *Anna Nicole*. Corey did not want to "leave BAM in the lurch" and she, and some others, contributed once again, to enable the show to go on. But in early September, a week before the *Anna Nicole* premiere, City Opera announced that it would be unable to complete the rest of the season unless it raised $7 million by the end of the month. Furthermore, if it could not raise an additional $13 million by the end of the year, the 2014–15 season would be canceled as well. As part of the effort, the company launched a $1 million Kickstarter campaign, hoping to appeal to younger donors. But the Kickstarter effort had a whiff of desperation about it—this was a move more appropriate for a scrappy start-up than a long-standing institution.

Roy Niederhoffer, the hedge fund entrepreneur who had joined the board in 2010, described the August crisis as an "ultimatum" given to the board. "George [Steel] said, 'I can't do this anymore, I have a company to run. I don't want to be, for the third consecutive year, down to the wire begging people for money.' He said, 'You give me the money up front, or I'm shutting down the company.'"

Crowdfunding aside, the real hope was that a savior would come forward with the necessary millions. It had happened in the past: the Ford Foundation bankrolling of the American seasons under Rudel and the bailouts by Lloyd Rigler in the Sills years kept the company running when it might otherwise have folded. And throughout the company's history, serendipitous events seemed to occur with remarkable frequency: the air rights sale; the 1985 warehouse fire that produced insurance funds and extra donated income under Sills and then, with the settlement of the class action suit, another windfall in 1998; the release of Wallace funds in 2001, which created the endowment; and finally, the Klotz bequest, which kept the company afloat for several years in the mid-2000s. Looking for saviors had become part of the company's modus operandi. Even when the quest proved disappointing, as with Gerard Mortier, City Opera was not deterred. Board chairs were also expected to be saviors: many had hoped Susan Baker would help fill the fundraising pool with her Wall Street connections; and Chuck Wall, less connected but personally generous, had already poured millions of his own money into the abyss.

But now, the much-diminished company was struggling in an unprecedented way to make its case and demonstrate why it deserved to survive. It had lost subscribers and supporters during the dark season—and the eccentric presentations of Steel's first two years had not brought them back. The departure from Lincoln Center had created a negative narrative, alienating many company veterans who went public with their unhappiness in the open letter, making things even more difficult. In its current, itinerant incarnation, City Opera was producing a mere sixteen opera performances a year, whereas in the not-too-distant past, it had done more than one hundred. As a result, it was now barely visible on the New York scene. Steel's vision for the company, in many ways a repudiation of its history and a rejection of its old audience base, positioned City Opera as a niche operation, specializing in the offbeat. It was, perhaps, a worthy idea, but it was one that had more in common with the boutique-sized Gotham Chamber Opera with its budget of under $2 million. The dowager had put on Goth makeup and piercings, and very little was left of the old People's Opera identity. A more charismatic and outgoing general director might have been able to make the case to funders for the continued survival of the New York City Opera, but after four years, Steel had lost the company more friends than he had gained.

Anna Nicole opened as scheduled on September 17 for a seven-performance run. Colorful and entertaining, if rather unpleasantly stereotyping American lower-class culture, it was popular with audiences and critics. But the desperate fund-raising push had not produced the necessary cash; even the Kickstarter campaign had raised only a fraction of its $1 million goal, although Niederhoffer had primed the pump with a significant donation of his own. And David Koch, who had previously made substantial contributions, was unwilling to help after discovering the subject of *Anna Nicole*: the title character's octogenarian oil tycoon husband, J. Howard Marshall II, who was unflatteringly portrayed in the opera, had once owned 16 percent of Koch Industries.

Mayor Michael R. Bloomberg also refused to help. On September 26, the board voted to begin bankruptcy proceedings if the $7 million goal was not reached by Monday, September 30. Bloomberg declined to intervene, either as mayor or as billionaire philanthropist. Launched as a populist enterprise by another New York City mayor seven decades earlier, City Opera no longer had its People's Opera status to appeal to the politician, who might have supported it out of a sense of civic pride, and the businessman had doubts about the sustainability of its business model.

The September 28 performance of *Anna Nicole* was widely expected to be the company's last, and indeed it was. New York City Opera filed for Chapter 11 bankruptcy protection on October 3. "It didn't happen like anyone projected it was going to happen," says Emilie Corey. "It was very sudden. We were dying. Then, in June, we had a little sense of remission. And then, we died."

CHAPTER 11

The Aftermath

THE SUDDEN DEATH of the New York City Opera caught the opera world by surprise. How could it just be gone? In its seventy years of activity, it had become an iconic New York institution. Time and again it had come close to perishing, but somehow it always survived. During one of the worst of these crises, the orchestra strike of 1989, Donal Henahan traced the dizzying roller coaster of its fortunes in the *New York Times*: "Lacking a master plan," he concluded,

> City Opera may continue to muddle through . . . but fewer and fewer
> discerning opera lovers are likely to care. Coming back from the dead
> is a good trick, yes. But if Lazarus had done it again and again, the
> public would have yawned and moved on.

Amazingly, the company had hung on for almost twenty-five more years. But now, it was all over.

Blame could be, and was, liberally assigned. Should the honors go to George Steel, woefully underqualified for his leadership position in a major opera house, who transformed the company's programming but failed to build an audience or a donor base? Had his decision to leave Lincoln Center, with its convenience and cachet, been the kiss of death? Or had the death blow been struck earlier? Many pointed to the dark season of 2008–09, when the company abandoned its loyal subscribers, who, in turn, abandoned it. Was the culprit Susan Baker, whose choice of Gerard Mortier as general director and whose failure to raise the funds to support his vision set the final desperate years in motion? Was it the board, which did not come up with a plan to fix the company's struggling business model in the 2000s, when the deficits began to grow, and instead obediently followed Baker's lead in the steady pillaging of the endowment, and also allowed for the leadership vacuum after Paul Kellogg left? Could the finger be pointed at Kellogg, whose initial burst of artistic energy was quickly sidetracked into the quixotic search for a new theater, and whose leadership abilities were no match for the company's worsening circumstances? Or was it Sherwin Goldman, whose "bad cop" methods contributed to a lack of transparency and trust within the institution?

The company had been through several key turning points, but the decision to shut down for the year of the dark season was widely thought to be the most catastrophic. With one stroke, City Opera lost its audience, its endowment, and its place, however tenuous it may have been, in New York's cultural life. The decision, like so many others in the company's recent history, pointed to a weak board with a habit of acquiescing to the determinations made by its leadership. So did the board's ill-fated decision to go along with Mary Sharp Cronson's insistence on hiring George Steel—without a firm, eight-figure pledge from the Peter Jay Sharp Foundation to back it up. Like many nonprofit boards, City Opera's was made up of mostly well-intentioned people who were paralyzed by inertia and did not step forward when questionable decisions were made. Following the company's long history of "we'll get through this somehow," they rubber-stamped the chair's decisions at every turn.

It would have taken a Herculean leader to come back from the debacle that the company faced at the end of 2008: someone with strength and credibility, who could be straightforward about the company's plight, including the need to do something about the crippling union and the-ater agreements, and rally support for it. With its built-in financial fragility and weak leadership, City Opera was especially vulnerable to the pressures of falling attendance and diminishing fund-raising that were increasingly troubling nonprofit arts institutions in the wake of the economic collapse of 2008. One factor that was unique to City Opera was its position as a second company; as opposed to the Met, with its big donors who give in many cases for reasons of social status or civic pride, City Opera had to cultivate givers who were passionately and specifically invested in its mission. Clarity of mission, therefore, was paramount.

This made City Opera's perpetual identity crisis—that "lack of a master plan" that Henahan noted back in 1989—all the more trouble-some. What was City Opera in the 2000s? The BCG report of 2006 diagnosed a profound confusion about the company's mission, and that confusion was never addressed. Efforts to capitalize on nostalgia for the so-called golden era of Julius Rudel, when City Opera launched American stars like Beverly Sills, were just that—nostalgia. As general director, Sills had kept the organization going through her star-power fund-raising. But in the absence of any "master plan," the only fixed element guiding the company seemed to be the repertory model, which brought with it inflexible labor costs and an enormous number of performances that could be sold only through a healthy subscription system. Without Sills, the company started to look like a collection of labor contracts in search of a vision.

Keene, Kellogg, and Steel all made a special effort to continue the company's tradition of artistic risk-taking, but they were only intermit-tently successful with the public, and their programming did not, for various reasons, adequately fire the imagination of donors. Tickets that were truly cheap enough to make City Opera the People's Opera would have necessitated funding the company almost entirely with donations—an impossibility without either a very deep-pocketed backer or govern-ment support. And who were the "people" anyway? The opera-loving Italian and Jewish immigrants who had been the company's original audience were long gone, and their descendants were not as interested. Who wanted City Opera now? No one had been able to find an answer to that question, and soon enough the clock had run out.

For all the particularity of the circumstances behind City Opera's demise, the chill that fell across the opera world had elements of "there but for the grace of God, go I." Like the canary in the coal mine, City Opera had fallen victim to pressures that were besetting the opera world as a whole. The historical business model of the opera company—the repertory system, the enormous theaters, the labor requirements, the balance of earned and contributed revenue—was being challenged by profound shifts in audience habits and donor behavior. Audiences could no longer be relied upon to buy season-long subscriptions and, by comparison, selling single tickets was more expensive and unpredictable. The symphony orchestra and the opera company were simply no longer the default choice for a large swath of the population. Instead, the audience had to be wooed and persuaded, which was itself expensive. Special events, like the staged *St. Matthew Passion* performed by the Berlin Philharmonic at the Park Avenue Armory, prized for their one-of-a-kind cachet, were ascendant; a week-in, week-out repertory system could not compete with their pizzazz.

On the fund-raising side, many opera companies were finding that major donors who grew old and died were not being readily replaced by a new generation of opera supporters. The new rich—the hedge funders and the tech billionaires—had a different attitude toward philanthropy than the old-school industrialists and financiers. Having generally acquired their wealth swiftly, and at an earlier age, they were more inclined to take on sexy, world-changing causes than provide operating support for legacy civic cultural institutions. Prominent younger philanthropists, following in the steps of Bill and Melinda Gates, felt that the entrepreneurial skills they had employed to dramatically innovate in technology and generate unprecedented wealth in the finance sector could be used to disrupt in philanthropy as well. They wanted to be hands-on in their efforts to eradicate diseases or re-create the American public school system. Funding an orchestra or an opera company was not nearly as exciting.

As income streams faltered, and the product grew ever more expensive, the ratio of earned income to contributed income was shifting dramatically. The once standard fifty-fifty split was long gone, and the share of ticket sales was shrinking. Now 25–30 percent was viewed as a respectable percentage; some companies earned even less. This put new pressure on fund-raising and also forced companies to think more broadly about their community relevance. If tickets only supplied 20–30 percent of their operating capital, how could they persuade donors other than their devoted patrons that they deserved to survive?

Some of the biggest opera companies had already confronted these stresses and made changes. In 2011, when David Gockley signed on for a second five-year term as general director of the San Francisco Opera, he tackled head-on the multimillion-dollar hole in the company's budget and the unsustainable growth of its expenses. "I think there is a hope that what you see happening won't happen," he said, "and an unwillingness to extrapolate certain trends, like how union contracts are increasing every year, how your prices can't increase as much as that, how your subscription rate is 38 percent whereas in 1980 it was 80 percent." He rightly noted that these trends, projected fifteen to twenty years into the future, were "pretty scary." Under his leadership, the company worked together with the unions to find $8 million in cuts to its annual budget; for example, changes in orchestra retiree health care, an expensive provision that had not previously taken into account the existence of Medicare. Gockley also set in motion an endowment-building campaign, growing it from $45 million when he arrived to $174 million when he retired in 2016.

Lyric Opera of Chicago, with a budget similar in size to San Francisco's $79 million in 2016, had sold out entirely on subscription until 2002, a remarkable record. However, it, too, began to see its audience numbers decline, and it faced that challenge by cutting back on performances. In 2013, Chicago introduced a new revenue stream: it added an annual, multi-week run of a classic musical to its schedule, as City Opera had so many years before. Lyric's musicals were cast with Broadway performers rather than opera singers, and, after several years of Rodgers and Hammerstein favorites, it tried out a new genre with Andrew Lloyd Webber's "rock opera," *Jesus Christ Superstar*. The musicals helped boost the company's earned income and brought new audience members to Lyric. But on the fund-raising side, it still needed to raise much more money each year in order to meet its operating expenses.

Even the mighty Metropolitan Opera was not immune. In February 2014, a few months after City Opera threw in the towel, Peter Gelb, the Met's general manager, sounded the alarm, declaring that the company's fixed costs were too high, and if it continued on its present course, it would be looking at bankruptcy within several years. The Met, too, was spending more than it was taking in. It had run an operating deficit of nearly $3 million the previous year, the current year's loss was going to be considerably higher, and its audience numbers were falling, causing a drop in revenue that was compounded by an ill-advised hike in ticket prices. As was the case elsewhere, this meant increased reliance on contributed income. The Met's stable of donors remained robust but not inexhaustible.

Furthermore, the Met board was concerned that the company's endowment was shrinking rather than growing. Since 2007, the company had been taking over $20 million from the endowment each year to fund operations, amounting to a higher percentage than nonprofit organizations conventionally draw. The endowment's growth was not keeping pace with the drain, and it had already incurred significant losses during the financial crisis. As a result, the endowment's value had shrunk from $345 million in October 2007 to just $253 million in 2014—considerably less than the company's annual operating budget, which had ballooned to $327 million. To remedy the situation, the board was preparing to undertake a big fund-raising drive that would build the endowment back to a sustainable level, but first, costs would have to be cut in order to ensure that the funds weren't wasted.

As it turned out, Gelb's message of doom was at least partially tactical. The contracts for fifteen of the sixteen unions representing the company's workers would expire on July 31 that year. A full two-thirds of the Met's budget was devoted to the wages and benefits of unionized employees—logically, this would seem a place to make cuts. But since 1980, the company's strategy had been to essentially buy labor peace by giving the workers what they wanted, within reason. This meant that the unionized workers had never once taken a cut in pay for thirty-four years; orchestra and chorus members averaged annual salaries of over $200,000, plus generous benefits. Gelb's stated goal was to cut labor costs by 16–17 percent, largely through changes in benefits and the byzantine structure of work rules.

The battle was ugly and protracted, with the union representatives accusing Gelb of mismanagement, overspending, and flawed artistic choices that had driven down attendance. Some favorite targets were the $169,000 cost of a field of poppies in the new production of *Prince Igor* and the expensive and controversial 2010–12 Robert Lepage *Ring*, which had not been the box office bonanza that the Met had hoped for, and which Alex Ross of the *New Yorker* had savaged as "pound for pound, ton for ton, the most wasteful production in modern operatic history." But the City Opera bankruptcy was on everyone's mind, as was another brutal labor fight in the music world: the Minnesota Orchestra's fifteen-month lockout, just resolved that January. It seemed intolerable that the Met, with its thousands of employees and international significance, might be similarly wounded by a labor action. The *New York Times* weighed in with an editorial, urging the Met and its unions to talk and compromise. A federal mediator and an independent financial consultant were brought in. In mid-August, an agreement was reached: there would be a 7 percent—rather than 16 percent—cut in pay for the unions (with some of that restored at the end of the contract) and the work rules and benefits would remain in place. Though not anywhere near what Gelb hoped for, the agreement represented a new understanding on both sides that sacrifices would have to be made. It also included significant cuts in management expenses. Altogether, the cost reductions were expected to trim $90 million from the budget over the course of four years.

The Met had dodged the bullet for the moment, while across the country, the San Diego Opera had been resurrected from its own near-death experience. In March 2014, Ian Campbell, the company's general

director for thirty-one years, announced that the company was no longer sustainable and would close. Like the New York City Opera and the
Met, it had been filling the gap between its income and its $17 million
in annual expenses with large withdrawals from a $10 million bequest.
Those funds had now run out, and Campbell, whose approach to opera
was grand productions with big stars, persuaded the board to shut down
the company, since it could no longer afford to produce at the lavish
level to which it had been accustomed.

However, a local coalition of opera fans, labor unions, and community leaders mobilized a rescue operation, raising funds and joining forces
with board members like Carol Lazier who had second thoughts about
the vote to close down. National figures—like Marc Scorca of Opera
America; Kevin Smith, former head of the Minnesota Opera; and William
Mason, former general director of Lyric Opera of Chicago—came in to
advise. Campbell was ousted, and Lazier, who had helped bankroll the
effort to save the company with a $1 million challenge gift, took over as
board president. But many of those who had been in favor of closing
resigned, taking their money with them. The company cut its budget,
moved to more modest space, reduced its staff, and simplified its production schedule. The drama of San Diego's death and resurrection was
considered to be another example of opera board dysfunction: in this
case, a board in thrall to a general director with a generous salary who
knew only one way to produce and was not interested in investigating
alternatives.

Questions about San Diego did not end there. In June 2015, David
Bennett joined the company as its new general director. Bennett's previous berth had been the Gotham Chamber Opera, the nimble, forward-
looking New York City company that operated on a modest budget
and specialized in chamber opera. Bennett's experience with a smaller-
scale operation and flexible producing seemed to be a good fit with San
Diego's new ethos. But just a few months after Bennett arrived in California, Gotham suddenly announced that it was closing down. Edward
Barnes, its new general director, had uncovered a substantial number
of unpaid bills, as well as thousands of dollars from a dedicated grant
used to cover other opera needs—and apparently the board hadn't known

about any of it. Gotham's productions had become more ambitious in recent years, but it now appeared that its revenues had not kept pace with its expenses.

Gotham's board and funders proved unwilling to make up the arrears in addition to funding the upcoming season. Again, the specter of City Opera loomed, this time with fatal results. Barnes told the *San Diego Union-Tribune,* "I think people sensed an opera company in financial crisis, and to them it was New York City Opera all over again and they did not want to get involved. They didn't want to take the risk, which was understandable." After Gotham's abrupt shuttering, questions were raised in San Diego about Bennett's management of his former company, but Lazier and her board proclaimed themselves unworried about his skills and said that San Diego would operate under a system of complete financial transparency.

The closing of City Opera provoked considerable soul-searching in the opera world and raised questions about whether the institutions that produce it would be able to adapt substantially and quickly enough to survive. Opera companies had begun to tweak their operations, but the institutional model, particularly of the largest, most complex companies—the Met, Chicago, and San Francisco—was going to be hard to adjust. All three are burdened with enormous opera houses (between three thousand and four thousand seats), and their workers' union contracts make it difficult to be flexible in response to changing times. Smaller companies often have more leeway. The Dallas Opera, for example, cut its seasons from five productions to three, beginning in 2011, when it encountered financial difficulties after moving into a new theater. In 2014–15, on an even financial keel again, it returned to a five-opera schedule. Since Texas is a right-to-work state, its opera companies can more easily contract and expand their activity without running afoul of union obligations.

Seasoned observers did not believe that the pendulum would ever swing all the way back, however. In 2014, David Gockley, having announced that he would retire as general director of the San Francisco

Opera at the end of 2016, looked back on the changes he had seen in his forty-five-year career. During the 1970s and '80s, when opera was expanding in the United States, Gockley had put the Houston Grand Opera on the map with bold repertoire choices and a new theater. Later at San Francisco, he had managed to stem the cataclysmic increase in expenses—keeping the abyss, as he called it, at bay. But the last ten years, he said, were worse than anything he had ever seen before.

> The traditional audience, most of whom are subscribers, are being replaced by younger people who are more casual, less loyal attendees. Subscribers contribute, nonsubscribers do not contribute. There are more individual people seeing opera, but they are not seeing as much of it, because there are so many other things to do.

Asked what a sustainable opera company would look like if he were to create it today, Gockley envisioned a company with a budget of $10–$12 million, performing five productions over six to eight weeks, possibly in a festival configuration. "It would be a company that had access to a number of different venues, performing a broad diversity of repertoire, and it would be totally flexible in terms of the performing personnel it could use. You wouldn't be paying for people you don't need." Since this opera company would be hiring on a pickup basis, it would have to be located in a market with a lot of musicians. Gockley also saw hope in the robustness of festivals like Opera Theatre of Saint Louis and Aix-en-Provence.

That formulation marks a radical departure from the established urban opera company that employs artists year-round. It is more nimble economically, but in relegating the artists to freelancer status, it diminishes not only their income and economic stability but also their ensemble cohesion. How does one calculate the value of artistic entities like the Metropolitan Opera orchestra and chorus who work together on a regular basis? However, the growth of such entities, like the many fifty-two-week orchestras that took root across the United States in the 1960s and '70s, may well have been a historical anomaly, fueled by foundation grants and burgeoning civic pride. These institutions transformed the lives of many musicians, who had once lived from gig to gig, into upper-middle-class professionals with steady jobs, salaries, benefits, paid vacations, health insurance, and pensions. The establishment of the National Endowment for the Arts in 1965 offered some hope that government might take over the responsibility of subsidizing full-time artistic institutions, and thus, their artists, as many European countries did. When that did not happen, the transformation of this segment of American artists into a professional class was left without a reliable source of ongoing support. How does one justify to donors the continuing obligation to support upper-middle-class incomes for musicians? For decades, donors were asked to close the gap between income and expense. Now, however, with only a small percentage of income coming from box office receipts, patrons were being asked to take on the responsibility of supporting the livelihoods of large numbers of well-compensated artists indefinitely into the future. City Opera had given up the struggle. Would others do better?

CHAPTER 12

Reinvention

THE SEISMIC CHANGES in attendance patterns and expenses that helped bring down the New York City Opera and forced opera companies across the United States to tweak their operating models also pushed some innovators in the industry to think about more substantive change. If filling a giant theater for multiple productions of grand operas was no longer an achievable goal, what were the alternatives? Some opera companies approached this dilemma by rethinking what an opera company is, what it does, and who it serves. In so doing, they tried to reach beyond their traditional audience demographic—older, white, middle class—into new communities. For decades, opera companies have had education and outreach programs that supplemented their core activities, but these newer efforts represented a redefinition of what core activity actually was.

One of the first to embark on this kind of mission was Houston Grand Opera. Under Anthony Freud, who succeeded David Gockley in 2006, it reached into communities around the city with projects like "The Song of Houston," in which composers were commissioned to write operas based on stories from particular ethnic groups in the area.

The mariachi opera *Cruzar la Cara de la Luna* was an early hit; pieces about Houston's Vietnamese, Iranian, and other populations were presented in venues around the city, often in neighborhoods where these groups lived. The project later morphed into collaborations with such Houston powerhouses as NASA (an opera about the *Challenger* disaster) and the Menil Collection (an opera about the Rothko Chapel). The point was to demonstrate that the opera company belonged to the city, even if the people who attended these targeted productions never came to the Wortham Center. When Freud took over Lyric Opera of Chicago in 2011, he brought the idea along, pushing Chicago to undertake its own community-focused projects with a new arm, Lyric Unlimited.

Second stages became an important tool for companies like Houston and Chicago, which wanted to present repertoire other than grand opera. By using smaller venues, they could present more experimental fare and attract people (often younger ones) who would be unlikely to buy tickets to *Tosca* in a big opera house. In 2009–10, Boston Lyric Opera, best known for traditional fare on its main stage, launched Opera Annex. For these annual presentations, BLO created site-specific productions in non-theater locations as diverse as the John F. Kennedy Memorial Library (Peter Maxwell Davies's *The Lighthouse*), an ornate, domed, nineteenth-century synagogue (Frank Martin's *The Love Potion*), and the Boston Cyclorama, the former home of the giant Gettysburg painting (Philip Glass's *In the Penal Colony*).

In 2016–17, BLO became completely itinerant, leaving its longtime home, the Shubert Theatre, which had become too expensive, to perform in various venues around the city. One advantage of the departure was that BLO was able to take over its ticket-selling function, which had previously been controlled by the Shubert, and market directly to its audience: its gross receipts for its first vagabond year were the highest that they had been since 2008, and its single-ticket sales were up by 32 percent. The company has said that it would like to have a permanent home, but none of the existing Boston theaters fit its needs. Esther Nelson, BLO's general director, told a radio interviewer, "Those older theaters are really kind of a holdover of the nineteenth- and early twentieth-century theater culture. And let's face it, most of them were Europeans and it was a system of elitism. That's not the world we live in anymore. We live in an increasingly diversified society. The theater needs to reflect that."

To attract the unconventional audiences, opera companies looked to produce unconventional work in alternative spaces. LA Opera launched its Off Grand series in 2012 at REDCAT, a two-hundred-seat black box theater attached to Disney Hall. Here the company could present work like David T. Little's *Dog Days*, which came to LA in 2015 after its initial success several years earlier in Montclair, New Jersey. In LA, *Dog Days* again found great success, selling out every performance. Unlike LA Opera's principal venue, the Dorothy Chandler Pavilion, with its three thousand seats, REDCAT offers its audience an intimate performance experience. As such, it helps change the idea of what opera is: rather than something remote, it is as up close and personal as the media that younger audiences watch on their cell phones, with the added advantage of being live.

LA Opera's president and chief executive officer Christopher Koelsch believes that the REDCAT series and other Off Grand productions—like the annual Halloween screenings of films such as *Dracula*, *Nosferatu*, and *La Belle et la Bête*, all with new scores, performed live, in a renovated 1927 movie theater in downtown LA—have been an ideal means of rebranding the LA Opera as hip. They have also expanded the company's footprint by appealing to new audiences and, critically, new donors. While the intimacy of the small spaces means limited ticket income, LA and others have found new donors interested in nontraditional fare who are willing to support these projects and, thus, the opera company as a whole.

LA Opera continued to enjoy the best of both worlds: its general director, the former star tenor Placido Domingo, is one of the few remaining opera performers whose name on the program (either as conductor or as a baritone in a singing role) reliably sells tickets. Company leaders made sure that one opera out of the six main-stage titles it offered each year would be headlined by Domingo—and they could always count on strong box office sales for that production. But for the productions that did not include Domingo, Koelsch noted, sales were unpredictable, with hits hitting big and failures failing big. Like other companies, LA has worked to maximize its single-ticket sales with dynamic pricing (changing the cost of a seat based on demand); one staffer's job includes daily monitoring of the "heat map" of sales in the opera house.

Other companies altered their production schedules to create a more festival-style format. A pioneer in this effort was the Fort Worth Opera, which hired Darren K. Woods, a former operatic tenor, in 2001, with the expectation that he would shake things up. And indeed, he did. In 2007, Woods converted the company's year-round schedule to a concentrated spring festival that would not compete with the bigger, nearby Dallas Opera. He was also ahead of the curve in introducing a focus on contemporary opera, including commissions, main-stage productions, smaller projects, and an annual Frontiers program that presented readings of excerpts from unproduced operas. In 2016, the company presented a successful world premiere, *JFK*, which it had commissioned. To the shock of the opera world, Woods was abruptly fired the following February, ostensibly because of the budget deficit of the previous season, though the new board chair noted that there were some disagreements about artistic policy as well. The new general director, hired in 2017, had no experience with opera companies.

In 2017, the most watched company in the United States was Opera Philadelphia, which embarked on a radical change in format. Unlike City Opera's shots in the dark, however, this change had been carefully researched, planned, and paid for over several years. The company, based at the venerable Academy of Music, and performing five or six operas in stagione over the course of each season, had been losing its audience gradually for years; and Philadelphia's opera fans have long tended to get their fix in nearby New York. When David Devan took over as general director in 2011, he hoped to tackle the problem by raising the company's artistic standards, committing to new operas, establishing a composer-in-residence post, and putting on second stage shows like Ana Sokolović's intimate, folk-influenced *Svadba*, an a cappella opera in which five women prepare their friend for her marriage; it was staged in a repurposed power station and followed by a traditional Balkan wedding feast.

But after two years, subscriptions still didn't increase, and neither did annual giving, leaving the company to balance its budget with extraordinary gifts. An audience research study turned up a startling statistic: since 2009, the company had attracted three thousand new households each year, a seemingly large number, but only about three hundred of those returned within the next several years. If that state of affairs continued, Devan and his board concluded, the company could probably survive for only five to eight more years.

Funded by some large foundation grants, Opera Philadelphia undertook a fourteen-month contextual segmentation study of its consumer base, the first ever by an arts organization. This kind of marketing survey, typically used by major commercial brands, such as Coca-Cola, looks at the context that motivates a consumer to purchase a product. One of the study's core conclusions was that the subscription model, once the bedrock of the nonprofit performing arts, was truly obsolete. While many in the industry had suspected this for some time, Opera Philadelphia's data offered hard proof. Some subscribers—the most devoted opera lovers—remained, but the whole premise of subscription, in which consumers are made to buy things in advance that they don't want in order to get the one thing that they do want, or to reserve their seats, was actively repelling other consumers. The young, single-ticket buyers to events like *Svadba* did not buy far in advance. They liked the shows they saw but did not consider the company as a whole as something important to them on an ongoing basis. "Those three thousand people loved us, but they didn't come back, because they didn't perceive that there was something interesting for them," Devan says. Furthermore, the data segmented the company's attendees into a far more complex array of groups than the old subscriber/single-ticket buyer dichotomy, each with different motivations for buying a ticket.

Based on the research, Devan and his team decided that Opera Philadelphia had to find new ways to attract and keep all these kinds of potential and actual audience members. One idea was to create a new sales model—something more along the lines of Netflix or HBO, in which consumers could choose among varied "product lines." "The younger cohort are binge consumers," Devan says, who are more drawn to events and happenings than regular programming. With that in mind, Opera Philadelphia devised a new artistic model as well: a festival, with a broad range of innovative content, like Sundance, a "dense, urbanized festival, on different stages, all happening concurrently, in a cacophony of activity," says Devan. The research indicated that consumers, allowed to curate their own experience within that happening, would buy tickets to more events.

In September 2017, Opera Philadelphia launched the O17 Festival, a twelve-day whirlwind with six different operas, including three world premieres, plus a vocal recital and a free outdoor broadcast of *The Marriage of Figaro*, in six different venues. It was conceived as a giant, two-week opening night, animating the city with opera. For the repertory, the company stretched the borders of the genre and collaborated with other Philadelphia institutions. The world premieres were dramatically different from one another. *We Shall Not Be Moved*, inspired by the story of the 1985 armed standoff between the Philadelphia police and the activist commune MOVE, combined classical, jazz, spoken word, dance, and video; it was created by artists with little or no previous association with opera and was performed almost exclusively by artists of color. David Hertzberg's *The Wake World*, a hallucinatory seventy-minute opera with two female principals and chorus, was staged on a catwalk in the main gallery of the Barnes Foundation, whose impressionist collection inspired it. The third world premiere was *Elizabeth Cree* by Kevin Puts, who had won the Pulitzer Prize for his earlier opera, *Silent Night*; the tale of a Victorian music hall celebrity turned murderess, it was the most conventional of the three. *War Stories*, a double bill of pieces by Monteverdi and Lembit Beecher, originally staged by Gotham Chamber Opera, was presented at the Philadelphia Museum of Art. The audience heard the Monteverdi in a cloister and moved to the museum's grand interior staircase for the Beecher. The only standard repertory work, *The Magic Flute*, was presented in the production by Barrie Kosky, whose playful use of silent film and animation had made it a hit in LA and Minnesota.

As exciting and dynamic as this type of festival format may be, it is also more expensive than a standard season. Devan had raised an additional $15 million in "venture capital" to support the budget expansion of the three years leading up to and including O17. Included in the $15 million were funds for publicizing and selling the festival in adjacent markets, like Baltimore, Washington, DC, and New York City. By attracting out-of-towners, Opera Philadelphia could build its audience, donors, and board by reaching beyond its own metropolitan area.

O17 was an artistic triumph and, Devan says, "an unmitigated success." Not only did the company hit its attendance targets, but the three unusual shows in small and nonstandard venues sold out immediately and had waiting lists, even though they were new works with no title recognition to help drive sales. The research data showed that attendees were excited about "the ambitious and innovative programming and high quality" of the festival: its "net promoter score," another statistic drawn from the commercial market research world, which measures consumer enthusiasm on a scale from -100 to +100, jumped from 58, in the company's former model, to 87. Eighteen percent of the audience was under twenty-nine, up from 9 percent previously, and two thousand new households purchased tickets. Out-of-towners made the trip and attended multiple events, and the festival attracted an unusually high percentage of attendees who were young and/or nonwhite.

Devan was encouraged by the response and all the positive data indications. However, he knew that the real test would come the following year, with Festival O18. Would the attendees return? And if they did, would they become donors? Opera Philadelphia's $15.5 million budget, which includes both the fall festival and two productions later in the season (for 2017–18, they were George Benjamin's highly praised *Written on Skin* and *Carmen*), is nearly 80 percent funded by contributions. Devan acknowledged that the festival, however data-driven, still represented a risk in a famously risk-averse industry. But risk, he says, is essential. "Did Uber know what was going to actually happen with ridesharing?" he asks. "No. But I don't know how you can approach the classical arts in this century without becoming comfortable in managing ambiguity. You need to figure out some things to hang on to, but also be totally cool with not having some of the answers."

Opera Philadelphia may have reinvented the festival format, but it was far from the first opera company to make use of it. The Santa Fe Opera and Opera Theatre of Saint Louis (OTSL) had been successful summer festivals for decades. In addition to their compact schedules and potential for cultural tourism, both operated with a tradition of balanced budgets. This precedent was established by John Crosby, who founded Santa Fe in the 1950s; his protégé Richard Gaddes went on to start OTSL in 1976. The third major US summer opera festival, the Glimmerglass Opera, which Paul Kellogg had put on the map in the 1980s, had fallen on difficult times after he left for City Opera. But in 2010, Glimmer-glass was taken over by the indomitable director Francesca Zambello, who had been turned down to run City Opera just eighteen months earlier. Zambello promptly rebranded the company as the Glimmerglass Festival and used her Rolodex to bring in stars like Deborah Voigt and Eric Owens as resident artists who would work with the apprentices and perform cabaret shows in addition to starring in operas. She also staged classic musicals without amplification, founded a children's chorus, and commissioned operas for its members to perform. She made new rela-tionships with local merchants and visitor attractions, and brought in food trucks to enhance the summer outdoor picnicking experience on the theater's rolling acres of lakeside grounds. (Outdoor dining is a much-loved tradition at summer opera festivals from Glyndebourne's mead-ows to Santa Fe's parking lots to OTSL's gaily striped tents.)

An important aspect of the festival model, particularly at Santa Fe and Saint Louis, and especially in the new Philadelphia endeavor, was the commitment to contemporary opera. John Crosby, an iconoclast, believed that presenting contemporary operas and novelties would attract the curious rather than drive them away; at OTSL, Richard Gaddes adhered to a similar philosophy. Both companies were outliers in an industry built on standard repertoire; both were regular commissioners of new operas. As contemporary opera crept gradually into the schedules of the more mainstream opera companies, the festivals continued to lead the way in demonstrating how new work could be not just an obligation or a way to attract press attention but an asset.

Under Timothy O'Leary, who took over OTSL in 2008, the company expanded its commitment with its New Works, Bold Voices series of commissions and revivals of recent work. With the goal of keeping opera relevant, these contemporary operas would be focused on current issues and stories: OTSL commissioned, for example, Terence Blanchard's *Champion*, based on a true story about a gay black boxer, and Jack Perla's *Shalimar the Clown*, taken from Salman Rushdie's novel, an anguished metaphor for the destruction of Kashmir. In 2011, OTSL went out on a limb with a production of John Adams's *The Death of Klinghoffer*, a work that had been vigorously protested at the time of its premiere in 1991. Based on the true story of an elderly Jewish tourist on a cruise ship who was murdered by Palestinian hijackers, the opera was considered overly sympathetic to the cause of the killers and became untouchable.

OTSL took an active approach to the potential controversy, bringing together representatives of different faiths in St. Louis to discuss the issues raised. As a result, *Klinghoffer* was a hit at the box office. That community network was expanded and strengthened and became key piece of OTSL's community engagement for all of its operas, and particularly its new ones. Contemporary operas at OTSL now regularly sell more single tickets than the traditional titles.

The attitude toward new opera had undergone a remarkable change since the 1950s, when the Ford Foundation's American works subsidy rescued City Opera. Ford's attempt to expand the program with its commissioning grants had not caught on in the subsequent decades, and only a handful of pioneers, like Santa Fe, OTSL, Houston Grand Opera, and City Opera regularly tackled contemporary scores. But during the '80s, two other national funding programs had started to move the needle: the National Endowment for the Arts' Musical Theater Program and Opera America's "Opera for the 80s and Beyond." The first helped bring some of the energy of the avant-garde theater world into opera;

the second, in addition to providing commissioning and production funds, helped opera company representatives travel to see new work and thus understand how it could be incorporated into their own production systems. By the mid-1990s, there were many more world premieres of operas by American composers. Many were still taking place in colleges and universities, but the raw numbers had multiplied, from a handful in the early 1980s to an average of thirty a year in the late 1990s.

The number and significance of premieres continued to grow. By the second decade of the twenty-first century, productions of new operas began springing up regularly in major companies around the United States, not just colleges and universities. The decline in audiences had made abundantly clear to opera companies the need for novelty in programming; new operas attracted press attention, and companies could see that a new generation of composers and librettists were producing pieces that audiences found more relatable, both in their musical language and their subject matter. New operas could also be potent fodder for community engagement and conversation, as OTSL found with *Klinghoffer.*

One reason for this change is that the subjects of these new works represented an enormous shift in what was considered appropriate for opera. In 1987, John Adams's *Nixon in China* was one of the first American operas to explore a recent historical event. At the time, *Nixon* and some of its successors, like *Klinghoffer* and Stewart Wallace's *Harvey Milk* were mockingly called "CNN Opera"—seemingly absurd, attention-seeking anomalies in an art form that was considered the province of long-ago stories featuring tragic kings, gods, and courtesans. Otello or Wotan could sing, but Nixon?

The landscape has now changed: anyone can sing their story. Today, up-to-the-minute subjects are considered prime operatic material, from Jake Heggie's *Dead Man Walking*, which deals with capital punishment, to Kamala Sankaram's *Thumbprint*, based on a true story about a Pakistani rape victim who brought her attackers to justice, to Laura Kaminsky's *As One*, a two-singer chamber opera based on the story of the transgender filmmaker Kimberly Reed, who also served as its co-librettist.

Kaminsky's opera was an instant hit, and has had numerous productions since its premiere in 2014.

The definition of what an opera could be, formally and musically speaking, also began to change. In the 1970s, Philip Glass and Robert Wilson expanded the form by introducing their long, hallucinatory, nonnarrative theater spectacles like *Einstein on the Beach* and *Satyagraha* into the body of operatic work, attracting enthusiastic young audiences. In the twenty-first century, streamlined budgets and shorter audience attention spans helped send creators in the opposite direction in terms of length and performing forces. The composer David Lang challenged the boundaries regularly: was his sixty-minute work, *The Loser*, really an opera? The piece featured just one singer and a mostly invisible chamber ensemble who performed on a platform placed in the darkened auditorium of BAM's opera house, at eye level with the mezzanine. In commissioning new operas, companies routinely asked for pieces that would run no more than two hours, with one intermission. An opera wasn't necessarily a four-hour evening in a foreign language anymore, and that shift was helping to rebrand its image as a contemporary art form.

Donors were interested as well. The Mellon Foundation's music program, under the leadership of Susan Feder, had long been providing significant support to opera companies in their efforts to commission and present contemporary operas—and now other funders joined in. Individual patrons, responding to the excitement around new works, were starting to become interested. OTSL was able to establish several endowment funds specifically for new works. At Opera Colorado, which gave the world premiere of Lori Laitman's *The Scarlet Letter* in 2016, general director Greg Carpenter found that patrons who were approached about funding specific productions wanted to fund new operas, not the warhorses.

In 2016 alone, numerous high-profile contemporary operas were staged across the country: in addition to *Shalimar the Clown, JFK,* and *The Scarlet Letter*, there was an opera based on Stephen King's horror tale *The Shining*, which premiered at the Minnesota Opera, and an operatic version of the classic Chinese novel, *Dream of the Red Chamber*, in San Francisco. Du Yun's *Angel's Bone*, a savage, cacophonous allegory about modern-day slavery, won the Pulitzer Prize for Music. *Breaking the Waves*, a stunning reimagining of the Lars von Trier film by Missy Mazzoli and Royce Vavrek, premiered in Philadelphia; and *Fellow Travelers*, a haunting piece by Gregory Spears about the 1950s Lavender Scare, in which gay employees in the US government were outed and persecuted, was done in Cincinnati. The Brevard Music Center Summer Festival in North Carolina, a summer training program, offered its first world premiere, *Falling Angel*, a detective story with a voodoo subtext. Brevard's logic was that its young professional students were now most likely to be offered parts in new operas and that preparing them for such assignments was an important part of its role.

As traditionally structured opera companies struggled to reinvent themselves, new entities sprang up around them. Smaller, nimbler, and often focused on particular kinds of repertory or presentation, they offered audiences a different slant on opera. One of the most influential was New York's Prototype Festival, which, since its founding by Beth Morrison Projects (BMP) and HERE Arts Center in 2013, had become a national focal point for the latest in contemporary opera-theater work. Each January, Prototype's two weeks were packed with unusual new works, from *Angel's Bone* to the enigmatic *Sunken Cathedral*, a multimedia performance piece by composer and sonic artist Bora Yoon. Some of Prototype's projects were developed by Morrison and HERE, while others were curated from artists around the United States and abroad. Prototype became a New York showcase for BMP co-commissions that had premieres elsewhere in the United States—*Breaking the Waves* came to Prototype in 2017 after playing Philadelphia. New York City had always been the home of small-scale groups doing new opera. Prototype, with its fully staged presentations in an annual festival format, helped establish new work as a central feature of New York's opera scene rather than a fringe activity.

Prototype also became important to forward-looking presenters elsewhere in the United States. Christopher Koelsch of LA Opera quickly recognized that Morrison and Prototype could supply edgy, contemporary fare for his REDCAT series, and they established an ongoing partnership, beginning with *Dog Days* and continuing with such works as David Lang's *anatomy theater*, Kamala Sankaram's *Thumbprint*, and Ted Hearne's *The Source*, a multimedia oratorio about Private Chelsea Manning's leak of classified military documents from Iraq and Afghanistan.

Other new opera companies, many expressly designed to attract younger audiences put off by the perceived formality—and expense—of the Metropolitan Opera, began to spring up at the same time. These companies, for the most part, offered fresh takes on old operas, in intimate settings. LoftOpera, founded in 2013, was all about making opera attractive to millennials. The fledgling company's productions of both traditional works (Verdi's *Macbeth*) and less familiar ones (Rossini's *Le Comte Ory*) were staged exclusively in "cool" spaces, like a converted factory at the Brooklyn Navy Yard or a circus school in Bushwick. Beer and wine were sold for consumption during the performance, loud rock music was played during the intervals and afterward, and tickets cost $30. Production values were rudimentary but effective—a few platforms, modern-dress costumes, and, for *Le Comte Ory*, some trapezes—and the operas were performed by capable singers and full orchestras. Also in the pop-up category were On Site Opera, which specialized in matching the venue to the work—Mozart's *The Secret Gardener* in a Manhattan community garden—and Heartbeat Opera, the brainchild of a group of Yale graduates, offering classic titles, ingeniously rescored for smaller forces (*Carmen*, for example, with a sextet that included saxophone) and presented in intimate settings. In a way, these smaller-scale groups were fulfilling two functions that were central to the mission of the departed New York City Opera—presenting new work and keeping prices low—but in radically different models.

The nimbleness of these small companies was an asset—with minimal overhead, they could charge low prices and attract new audiences. The flip side of that equation was that their professional orchestras and singers were, for the most part, paid very little. The model could be sustainable, but only at the expense of the artists. Players and singers, even piecing together a lot of these small engagements, would find it hard to earn enough to survive in today's expensive New York City. And small is not necessarily a guarantee of survival. Gotham Chamber Opera folded in 2014. And in 2017, LoftOpera, out of money, canceled its fall production.

Grander opera projects could also be found in New York, mounted by presenting organizations and festivals. The Brooklyn Academy of Music had long imported significant productions, like the baroque spectacles of Les Arts Florissants, from Europe, and the Lincoln Center Festival ventured still further afield, sometimes even creating its own extravaganzas, like the eighteen-hour Chinese opera, *The Peony Pavilion*. In 2008, a new player arrived on the scene: the Park Avenue Armory teamed up with the Lincoln Center Festival to import an enormous production of *Die Soldaten* from the Ruhrtriennale. The vast Drill Hall of the facility thus became *the* place for spectacular events, most notably the Berlin Philharmonic's staging of Bach's *St. Matthew Passion* in 2014. The terraced, in-the-round seating arrangement of Berlin's home concert hall was re-created on bleachers in the Armory and when the two performances, directed by Peter Sellars and featuring Mark Padmore as the anguished Evangelist, sold out as soon as they went on sale, the Armory sold tickets for the dress rehearsal.

The "event" quality of the Berlin *St. Matthew* drove its box office—two performances, limited seating, see it now or never. How many Metropolitan Opera productions could possibly generate that kind of enthusiasm, let alone sustain it over five or more performances with thirty-eight hundred seats each? William Kentridge's multimedia production of Shostakovich's *The Nose* was one. During its premiere run in 2010, it generated huge excitement, particularly in the art world, aided by a comprehensive retrospective of Kentridge's work at the Museum of Modern Art. But when the production returned in 2013, the box office magic was gone—it was no longer a must-see event and was instead an example of how difficult it is for a repertory house to maintain a competitive edge in a thrill-seeking market. It is also worth noting that the *St. Matthew* would not have existed without the generous state subsidy that pays for the fifty-two-week operation of the Berlin Philharmonic's orchestra, chorus, and overhead; the DVD of the show, produced by the orchestra itself and thus also a result of European funding, helped drive the excitement behind its New York appearance. The tiny amount of government subsidy allotted to American arts groups, although symbolically important, amounts to a very small portion of their operating budgets. And ironically, for a city that considers itself a world capital of classical music, some of the snob appeal of the event derived from its European origins.

For today's opera companies, one of the most frustrating realities is that the new finance and tech billionaires *are* committed to philanthropy, but they are putting very little of their substantial donations toward the arts. In New York, the billionaires who do offer major support for culture direct their largesse primarily to the tangible cause of arts-related construction rather than operating costs. In 2015, the entertainment mogul David Geffen gave $100 million to jump-start the renovation of Lincoln Center's Avery Fisher Hall, home of the New York Philharmonic; the hall was renamed for him. Two years later, former New York mayor Michael Bloomberg announced that he was giving $75 million to the $500 million Culture Shed, part of the giant Hudson Yards development on Manhattan's Far West Side. It was not Bloomberg's first indication of interest: In the spring of 2013, a few months before the New York City Opera filed for bankruptcy, his administration released its budget for the next year. It included $50 million in capital funds for the Culture Shed. That appropriation was later increased.

The Shed (as it was renamed in 2016), scheduled to open in spring 2019, is an eight-story flexible space, designed by "starchitects" and envisioned as a place for the art of the future—whatever that may be. It has a moveable shell, enabling the building to expand and contract for differently sized events, or even to be entirely open-air, as well as a black box theater and gallery space. The center's artistic director, Alex Poots, who made his mark at the Manchester Festival in England, calls the Shed "a tool kit for artists of all kinds." It remains to be seen who will foot the bill for the ongoing work of those artists once the building opens and its shiny newness wears off.

But there is a larger point: as the Shed demonstrates, there is plenty of money around. Why shouldn't opera get some of it? The challenge in America, unlike in Europe, is that culture has long been perceived as optional—and even worse, important only to elites. In the second decade of the twenty-first century, interest in opera remained strong among devotees and newcomers alike, but the financial conundrum has continued to afflict the institutions committed to presenting it. How could the economics of the Metropolitan Opera, with fifty-two-week labor contracts and a thirty-eight-hundred-seat house, work out in the long run? The Met is still selling hundreds of thousands of tickets every season, so clearly people want what it is selling. Peter Gelb's HD innovation has provided one new income stream, but it is nowhere near enough to offset the rising costs of the repertory model, as currently constructed.

Some are pessimistic. In his 2015 book, *Curtains?: The Future of the Arts in America*, the arts administrator and consultant Michael M. Kaiser, who had once insisted that arts organizations could spend their way out of trouble, changed his tune and painted a grim picture, forecasting the gradual dwindling of American performing arts organizations. The economic downturn of 2008, he said, had not caused the problems but rather revealed the structural weaknesses of the arts organization model. By 2035, he projected, the biggest organizations would dominate the landscape through video streaming (sponsorship revenues for that would defray the costs of the institution, much like television advertising); high-quality live performance would become an expensive luxury, available only to the wealthy in a few population-dense areas; and there would be a downward spiral for the regional arts groups unable to compete with the higher-quality streaming from the biggest ones.

In this scenario, the Metropolitan Opera and its ilk would live. Tiny operations like On Site Opera would likely survive as well, on the economic fringes, employing a handful of the thousands of musicians and singers who graduate from conservatories every year, as long as they were willing or able to work for very little. For all but a very few, it would be the end of independent artistic companies, with their own distinctive personalities.

However, forward-looking institutions and individuals are resisting that outcome, questioning old assumptions and structures to come up with new ones that will allow them to survive. Making sure everyone within an institution is aligned about its mission is an essential first step, and that is only possible when the company fosters a climate of trust. "Mission is the thing that motivates the donors, the board and the staff," says Timothy O'Leary of Opera Theatre of Saint Louis. "You've got to take the time regularly to clarify it, debate it, celebrate it." Accountability in governance is another. Opera Philadelphia reconfigured its board structure in 2011, disbanding the executive committee in order to do away with two-tiered decision-making. "Everybody on the board [of twenty-eight members] has equal legal obligations, so all decisions happen at the board level," says David Devan. "The whole board is engaged. You can't check your brains at the door because some committee of six people has already decided what is going to happen."

Opera has never been a logical economic proposition, yet it is an art form with profound resonance. The trick today is to make that value clear to a much larger audience. The struggle to demonstrate that "high" culture in all its forms—music, dance, art, literature—is not just for the rich but, like health care and education, an essential component of civil society has taken on a new urgency. Forward-looking people in the opera world have worked to make their art and their institutions engage the wider world, whether through new subject matter, new media, or new voices. As entities like the Prototype Festival and others have demonstrated, opera is an art form of the present as well as of the past. The idea of a People's Opera in the twenty-first century is considerably more complex than it was in 1943, but on a basic level, it is the same—a profound artistic expression that knows no boundaries of age, class, or privilege.

Perhaps the greatest hope for the future of opera lies with the artists themselves. One of the most often cited effects of the death of the New

York City Opera was the loss of the proving ground that the company had long provided for young singers. The trajectory a fledgling singer might follow—from conservatory, to a Young Artist Program or two, and then a few years at NYCO—was fatally interrupted. Where else would the young singer get to try out her Violetta and get the New York review that would help launch her career?

Yet the loss of all those slots for the hopeful young Violettas and Rodolfos may be symptomatic of an even larger change in the opera of the future. American conservatories are still turning out thousands of graduates, young people who want to sing, play, conduct, direct, and compose. The wisest of them recognize that if they plan to work, they will have to play a role in shaping or even creating the institutions that will enable them to do so.

One of the most unusual and inventive operatic creations of the last several years took place in Los Angeles in the fall of 2015, the brainchild of the director Yuval Sharon. Sharon ran the New York City Opera's Vox program from 2006 to 2009, where he was most interested in operas by composers like Christopher Cerrone and Anne LeBaron that did not fit into the traditional format. In 2010, he moved to Los Angeles and started his own company, The Industry, specifically to produce that kind of work. The Industry's 2013 world premiere of Cerrone's *Invisible Cities*, experienced via headphones at Los Angeles's Union Station, was a runaway hit, selling out all thirteen performances, and was a finalist for the Pulitzer Prize.

Sharon's 2015 project, *Hopscotch: A Mobile Opera for 24 Cars*, was an even greater technological and logistical challenge, and it defied operatic convention in almost every way. Twenty-four ten-minute segments of the story were performed in moving limousines and in different, undisclosed locations around Los Angeles. All these chapters were occurring simultaneously: in groups of four, the audience moved from car to car and from place to place, watching fragments of the tale unfold unchronologically. Audience members could read a synopsis or watch ten animated, expository chapters online in advance and get a sense of the overall arc of the story, but the experience of surrendering to the moment, rather than knowing the end, was really the point.

In fact, the most fascinating thing about *Hopscotch* was how it made the fundamental materials of opera—story told in song—new again. The materials were there: ten composers and six writers created the chapters; the story was easily recognizable as a modern, hallucinatory version of the most classic of opera plots, Orpheus and Eurydice, albeit with the male and female roles reversed; it featured over 120 performers. But a story told out of order forces the listener to pay attention, particularly when one is sharing a very intimate space with several singers and instrumentalists. The dislocation of not knowing where you are going means that you must abandon control. A scene may take place on the shore of the rushing Los Angeles River, on the top tier of an ornate old downtown theater, on a rooftop—and every new location means a shift in perspective. And you start to wonder: who else is part of the show? The mariachi guys on the corner? The other people driving by? It could be anyone. *Hopscotch* made you suddenly, physically conscious of all the lives and sorrows and joys going on in all those cars driving past on the freeway all the time. It not only freed opera from the opera house but made its heightened expression the sound of real, everyday, and inner life.

Hopscotch took a year and $1 million in donations to create and earned another $500,000 in ticket sales. When the scheduled performances sold out quickly, another weekend was added, so a total of three thousand people were able to experience it. More could watch the chapters being live streamed—for free—on twenty-four televisions in the Central Hub, a structure set up in a parking lot in the Arts District. Some of the music was later recorded and released in a digital format, but *Hopscotch* is not really replicable in the way that *La Bohème* and *La Traviata* are.

Yet the originality of Sharon's artistic vision, and the way he was able to successfully realize it, offers a glimpse of how radically rethinking basic assumptions might just be the way of the future for opera. Giant opera houses were built for another age; so were American opera companies, with their constant repetitions of those canonical works of the past. Especially in an era of virtual everything, live performance remains a value to be cherished. But perhaps we don't need quite as many *Bohème*s and *Traviata*s—and the most creative minds may well revolutionize not just the repertoire but the institutions that present it.

The Resurrection

AS THEY SAY in the infomercials, "But wait! There's more!" In January 2016, more than two years after its abrupt demise, the New York City Opera suddenly reappeared, presenting four performances of *Tosca* at the Time Warner Center's Rose Theater at Columbus Circle. The resurrection had been orchestrated by two longtime City Opera fans: Michael Capasso, an opera producer, and Roy Niederhoffer, a hedge fund manager who had been on the company's board during its last years.

Their journey to this moment had been lengthy, complex, and expensive. City Opera's bankruptcy had barely been announced in the press when Capasso approached the company's attorneys with a proposal to resurrect it. Capasso, who had founded the small-scale Dicapo Opera on Manhattan's East Side and run it successfully for thirty-two years, was something of a maverick in the New York opera world. Raised in Long Island, part of an Italian American family with a construction business, Capasso had fallen in love with opera early. He started his own company, directing some of the shows himself, while still keeping a hand in the family business. Thanks to his construction background, he was able to build a tiny, two-hundred-seat opera house for Dicapo in the basement of the St. Jean Baptiste Roman Catholic Church; it was both a home base for the company and a vital source of income through rentals. But even so, Capasso's company had fallen on hard times and had recently filed for bankruptcy as well, leaving some of its artists and vendors unpaid.

Nevertheless, the attorneys were willing to listen, and they suggested that Capasso enlist a City Opera insider to help his case, so Capasso immediately contacted Roy Niederhoffer, who was still on the company's board. The two had been acquainted for decades: they attended the same high school, Great Neck South, and when Capasso, the elder by seven years, had returned to direct a school production of *Carmen*, Niederhoffer was the student concertmaster of the orchestra. Both were shocked by the sudden death of City Opera, which had played so important a role in their lives, and both wanted to bring it back. Capasso had, in fact, been so influenced by City Opera that he modeled his own company after it.

It took Capasso and Niederhoffer over two years to finally gain control of the New York City Opera. It was a complicated process for several reasons. First, unusually, there were other competitors, the most persistent of whom was Gene Kaufman, an architect and opera fan. The terms of the resurrection changed as well. Initially, Capasso and Niederhoffer, operating as a newly incorporated entity called NYCO Renaissance, had planned to simply purchase the company's name and its few remaining assets. By January 2015, the field of competition had narrowed to just two contenders, NYCO Renaissance and Kaufman—and the City Opera board awarded the name to NYCO Renaissance.

But the situation changed abruptly in the spring of 2015, when it came to light that a longtime City Opera patron, Pierre DeMenasce, had died in September 2013, and left 10 percent of his estate to City Opera—a sum that amounted to approximately $5.5 million. However, the money would only be available if the company reorganized and came out of Chapter 11. With such a large amount at stake, the City Opera board decided against a simple sale, and a new legal process was begun, with both NYCO Renaissance and Kaufman's organization again submitting plans for reorganization.

Then, in December 2015, Kaufman withdrew his bid in exchange for the payment of his legal fees, and in January 2016, the federal bank-ruptcy court awarded Capasso and Niederhoffer control of the reorga-nized New York City Opera along with the remaining endowment funds, the DeMenasce bequest, and several other smaller bequests, total-ing over $11 million. (Some of the reorganized company's funds were to be used to pay off its creditors, including full refunds to the ticket buyers of the 2013–14 season.) When the decision was announced, Capasso and Niederhoffer were already in the midst of their first opera presentation—*Tosca*—still using the name NYCO Renaissance (since they were not yet in official possession of the name). Along with paying for the legal battle, Niederhoffer had put up the funds for the produc-tion so it could begin before their case was settled. Like the rest of the resurrection odyssey, the *Tosca* had its own hiccups: a blizzard dropped twenty-eight inches of snow on New York City during its five-day run, forcing the cancellation of two of the six scheduled performances.

From the beginning, Capasso's vision was to revive the company in the image of the Julius Rudel years, which he saw as its golden era and the most representative of its historical mission. He and Niederhoffer had met with Rudel on Easter Sunday 2014, a few months before the for-mer City Opera general director died, at ninety-three. According to Rudel's son, Anthony, who was present, the conductor called their plans "workable" and wished them luck. In a lengthy business plan, they spelled out their ambitions to reestablish a home theater at the Rose, which is part of Lincoln Center, and produce both standard repertoire and contemporary American operas. City Opera had historically been a lean operation, and the new City Opera would follow in that tradition, producing on a careful budget, with overhead costs kept to a minimum. The budget for the first full season in 2016–17—with thirty-two per-formances including four main-stage productions in the Rose, two smaller productions, and several concerts in other venues, spread out over the year—was $5.5 million. (The expenses for the old City Opera's final 2012–13 season of sixteen performances were $14.4 million.)

Though the company hoped to grow, it had no plans to ever again be a repertory operation with over one hundred performances a year. And the union relationships would be dramatically different. One of Capasso's earliest acts during the process of acquiring the company was to make a five-year agreement with the City Opera orchestra for a 30 percent reduction in wages and the elimination of minimums and guarantees. Local 802, whose pension fund was also one of the principal creditors in the bankruptcy, proved eager to put its members back to work. Having come to terms with the new reality, the musicians decided that they would rather have some City Opera work for less money than have no work at all. In the end, the union supported Capasso and Niederhoffer's plan throughout the process.

In Capasso's view, there is always a deal to be made. He was interviewed for the City Opera general director job in the post-Mortier period in 2008, and says that he recommended making new deals at that time. "That was the time to restructure. The company was closed, they are renovating the theater, there are no performances, so why are we paying pay-or-play contracts? I would have threatened the [New York City] Ballet and CCMD with leaving the theater, and been aggressive in renegotiating the lease and the contracts."

The new, flexible City Opera labor agreements reflected its stagione production format, the fact that it put on significantly fewer performances than it had in the New York State Theater, and its plan to produce works of different sizes, some in small theaters that seated only two hundred, cutting down on their earned income potential. Productions in small theaters, for instance, had a different pay scale and employed fewer musicians than those in the Rose, a contract provision that would have been unthinkable under the old Lincoln Center agreements. "The unions became our partner," Capasso said. As a result of this partnership, he was able to mount a project like the big production of *La Campana Sommersa*, an obscure Respighi opera, which he acquired from an Italian opera house for just the cost of shipping. Under a special deal with Local 802, thirty-five musicians from the Italian company's orchestra—paid for by the Italian government—played the New York run, making up half the pit orchestra of seventy and slashing City Opera's orchestra costs. "It was a good deal for the company," Capasso says.

I've got a lot of experience dealing with unions from growing up in the construction business. I understand how they work, and I understand the union mentality. You [need to] walk in and be completely transparent. You say, here's the budget, here are the numbers, and here's where you figure, and this is what we can do for you. You don't try to get cute—no smoke and mirrors.

The new City Opera format—multiple venues, diverse repertory, flexible performing personnel, half a dozen operas each year—was, in many respects, the same model that David Gockley proposed when asked about the future of opera production. But the revived City Opera was doing it at about half the cost that Gockley cited. Niederhoffer, who was footing the bills, appreciated Capasso's deal-making prowess and his ability to produce inexpensively, an ability that he honed in his years running Dicapo. All of NYCO's productions were evaluated from a business perspective, including their expense, possible partnerships, and what could be done with them afterward—such as tours or rentals. The plan is for the company to earn 50 percent of its operating budget.

Institutionally, Capasso and Niederhoffer looked to what they feel City Opera did right. "In its first few decades, it was always very lean, with a very small number of people," Niederhoffer says.

It had an institutional importance, so you didn't have to attract people by paying huge amounts of money. For singers, it was their New York City debut—you get a rave review on the front page of the arts section of the *New York Times*, and you're made as a singer. We don't have to attract those singers by paying as much as the top company does. We look to the past for inspiration about what to do and what not to do, but we recognize that there are random forces, and industry changes, and we have to have a defined presence in the opera world.

The program for the company's first full season reflected Capasso and Niederhoffer's desire to evoke City Opera's history. Indeed, its biggest hit was Bernstein's *Candide*, for which the eighty-eight-year-old Hal

Prince re-created his 1982 City Opera production (the sets and costumes were built anew) with a few tweaks. Despite—or perhaps because of— its rather old-fashioned aura, the production sold out all ten performances and was, for the most part, positively reviewed. The production, though expensive for the company, was built with the idea that it would eventually pay for itself and actually make money through rentals and tours.

The People's Opera tradition was revived with lower prices than those at the Met and through several production initiatives. In the company's early history, it served New York's Italian- and German-speaking immigrant population; since today's primary immigrant language is Spanish, NYCO announced an Ópera en Español series. The 2017 chamber staging of an obscure eighteenth-century baroque piece seemed unlikely to attract that target audience, and it did not; the 2018 offering went more populist, with Houston Grand Opera's well-traveled mariachi piece *Cruzar la Cara de la Luna*. Capasso also folded gay rights into the People's Opera tradition by planning a work dealing explicitly with LGBTQ issues each June, which is Pride Month. The first was the New York premiere of Péter Eötvös's *Angels in America* in 2017; for 2018, the company scheduled Charles Wuorinen's *Brokeback Mountain*. This choice was doubly significant: Mortier had commissioned *Brokeback* for City Opera but left before it was even written. He had then taken it with him when he took over the Teatro Real in Madrid, where it finally had its premiere in 2014. Now the work would finally see its New York premiere.

City Opera has planned some world premieres—Tobias Picker, its composer in residence, has been commissioned to write *American Venus*, about the tragic life of Audrey Munson, an artist's model of the early twentieth century, for 2019. However, the resurrected company's most significant contribution may be in another nod to City Opera's history: giving New York presentations to important, large-scale new works that have been premiered elsewhere—pieces like *Angels in America* and *Brokeback Mountain*. Apart from the Prototype Festival, which presents chamber-size pieces, New Yorkers have not been able to experience much of the current explosion of contemporary opera around the United States. Companies like the Minnesota Opera, Santa Fe, Dallas, Houston, San Francisco, Opera Theatre of Saint Louis, Washington National Opera,

Opera Philadelphia, and others have become a network, both commissioning operas and giving many of them—like Jake Heggie's *Moby Dick* (premiered in Dallas) and Kevin Puts's *Silent Night* (premiered in Minnesota)—additional hearings around the country.

Other than the Metropolitan Opera, City Opera is the only New York entity with the resources to mount these bigger new works with full-size orchestras. The Met has shown little interest in this body of work, although, under Gelb, it has stepped up its commitment to contemporary opera. However, the Met has focused on a few major contemporary names: it has presented the operas of John Adams and Philip Glass, and looked abroad to Thomas Adès (partnering with European and UK houses to commission *The Exterminating Angel*) and Kaija Saariaho, whose *L'Amour de loin*, presented in 2016, was only the second work by a woman to be given there; the previous one had been over a century earlier. The Met/LCT New Works Program, founded in 2006 in collaboration with Lincoln Center Theater, which provides commissioning funds and workshop support to selected teams of composers and librettists but does not guarantee a production, has so far resulted in only one staging at the house: Nico Muhly's *Two Boys* in 2013. City Opera thus seems to have this part of the field to itself.

Indeed, hoping to avoid the trap their predecessors had fallen victim to, Capasso and Niederhoffer have explicitly designed their City Opera to complement, rather than compete with, the Met. Their offerings, for the most part, steer clear of anything the Met would be likely to do, whether new or old. Of the 2017–18 season's offerings, the only title that has ever appeared on the Met stage is *La Fanciulla del West*. Capasso, a Puccini devotee, is unlikely to cede that ground entirely.

As a showcase for young talent, another historical City Opera realm, the company had mixed results in its first year and a half. A few interesting new voices emerged, but much of the casting was lackluster. Nor were the productions consistently high quality. *Angels in America*, staged by Sam Helfrich, was fresh and lively, but the double bill of *Pagliacci* paired with Rachmaninoff's *Aleko* looked cheap, with flat, generic sets (the same railroad yard for both operas) and, like *La Campana Sommersa*, was directed for traffic-cop-style efficiency rather than theatrical impact.

Campana Sommersa was also a forgettable score; Capasso's predilection for obscure Italian operas may not serve him well in the long run, no matter how good a deal he gets on the production. The company's initial *Tosca*, which re-created the original designs for the opera's world premiere in Rome, was a poor advertisement for the company's stated approach to standard repertory pieces, which prescribes representational stagings in order to contrast with the "director's theater" now in vogue at the Met. (This Gelb-initiated trend, for Capasso and other traditionalists, was exemplified by the bleakly minimalist 2009 Luc Bondy staging of *Tosca*, which replaced the Met's beloved Franco Zeffirelli version from 1985, a lavish production so literal and detailed that its settings appeared to be exact replicas of the opera's locations.) There is some irony here—City Opera, which once tried to distinguish itself with cutting-edge production styles, now felt that its role was to provide the opposite. In any case, with its painted, representational drops, gesticulating, bellowing singers, and coarse orchestral playing, this *Tosca* looked disturbingly like low-level regional opera of forty years ago.

And who is the audience for the new New York City Opera? Capasso and Niederhoffer believe that company's old audience evaporated with the move out of Lincoln Center. Some returned for *Candide*, but, for the most part, City Opera is now building its following anew. In the company's first full year, it filled its small theater shows, and got respectable attendance, beyond just the *Candide* sellouts, at the Rose. Niederhoffer sees the Rose as an attractive option for all kinds of opera fans, including well-to-do ones. With around a thousand seats, it is more intimate than the Met, more comfortable than the folding chairs of LoftOpera's warehouses, more centrally located than BAM. Forward-looking opera companies have begun to consider the importance of their customers' experience beyond the performance itself, and Niederhoffer views the Time Warner Center's proximity to fancy restaurants and easy taxi access as an important asset.

Building an audience is critical for survival. Dedicated audience members become donors; an enthusiastic audience attracts other financial support. City Opera's relaunch included money in the bank from the bequest and the endowment, and a single, dedicated funder in Niederhoffer, but a legitimate, ongoing arts organization needs more check-writing board members and a wider circle of supporters.

Niederhoffer has learned a few things from the company's previous debacles, not least the need for all board members to pay close attention to what is actually happening on the stage and in the office. "Non-profit boards have to act like for-profit boards and make the tough decisions that a for-profit company would make." A more engaged board, he thinks, would have made radically different choices after Mortier pulled out in 2008. For example: "You hire a turnaround specialist like Michael Capasso to get you out of the hole. You let people go, you renegotiate all your contracts, you threaten people with bankruptcy and maybe you even go bankrupt. Look at the airlines."

The airline analogy resonates for him in other ways. "George Steel had a vision for the company that was certainly unique," Niederhoffer says.

> I think he executed it without a full appreciation for the business of opera, and thus, the side effects of that vision were not obvious until it was too late. I liken running an opera company to filling an A380 [the world's largest passenger airplane]. You've got a lot of seats to fill. You've got a lot of people in the bottom deck, your coach class. Maybe they will subscribe; a few might be premium economy. On your top deck, you've got to fill your $20,000-a-ticket suite that only the richest people in the world can do. And then you have a lot of first-class seats. You have to run a business that has the enthusiasm of everyone. You can't run an all-coach airline. It's very tough to run an all-coach opera company. To have that broad appeal, it can't just be the vision of the general director. It has to take into account the people that want to pay for the opera, and that's the audiences, the funders, and the foundations. Everyone has to be on board, and if you deviate too far from that, you run a tremendous organizational risk.

And so the New York City Opera has been reinvented once again. The built-in financial fragility that finally knocked the company off its tight-rope has been addressed in this new model—but can it earn an ongoing place in the ecosystem of the arts in New York, and find that broad appeal? Today all arts institutions must have a niche—what will City Opera's be?

In its first seventy years, the New York City Opera's identity shifted numerous times. It was born as the People's Opera—informal and inexpensive, for opera lovers who couldn't afford the Met. It added to that its identity as an ensemble company, a place for American singers to be heard and a showcase for contemporary opera. For a while, it was the place to hear America's homegrown diva, Beverly Sills; later, it offered classic and contemporary American musicals, baroque operas, and cutting-edge stagings. Overall, from 1966 through 2008, it was a large repertory company, performing a mix of standard and unusual works with a full standing orchestra and chorus—and, most essentially, it was not the Met. Yet, because it was at Lincoln Center and also a repertory company, it was expected to reach high artistic standards on a fraction of the Met's budget. Perhaps the most important reason for City Opera's continued existence was the fact that it provided a living for its orchestra and chorus in a city that was teeming with musicians. But the employment of musicians is not an artistic, marketing, or fund-raising strategy.

The decadelong struggle that ended in City Opera's 2013 bankruptcy filing coincided with a seismic upheaval in the way the performing arts were presented and consumed. The change was driven by generational, economic, and technological forces. It is now clear that the landscape will never be the same. City Opera, caught in the maelstrom as it was unfolding, could not see the big picture and was, in any case, singularly ill-equipped to face it and make the necessary changes. It was too big and too poor, saddled with a weak board and the wrong leadership.

Reborn in 2016, City Opera still has a full orchestra and chorus (though they are now paid per service) and the intention to be "not the Met." Other elements from the company's history have been cannily repurposed for the present, as with the People's Opera Spanish-language and LGBTQ initiatives and the focus on contemporary works. Beyond that, the company reflects the artistic vision of Capasso and resembles an expanded, somewhat better-resourced version of his old Dicapo Opera, which he had fashioned in the image of City Opera in the first place.

While it remains to be seen whether grand opera on the cheap is a viable artistic or business proposition, some of the can-do City Opera spirit lives on in this new incarnation. It represents an alternative—scrappier than the Met but more comfortable and middle-brow than the edgy start-ups like On Site Opera and the Prototype Festival—and is positioned to capture a piece of the audience that still responds to the visceral appeal of sung theater.

When City Opera declared bankruptcy in 2013, there was an outpouring of sorrow and reminiscence. Invited to contribute memories to a *New York Times* column, City Opera fans wrote of their life-changing experiences with the company, right up through its final years. "My first opera performance ever, 'Bohème,' from the balcony," one wrote. "The start of my classical music education, in my teens," said another. Citing favorite performances, one writer chose *La Clemenza di Tito* with "the incandescent Lorraine Hunt Lieberson, the greatest artist I've had the privilege to witness live on stage." Another picked *Moses und Aron*, saying, "It was the first time I'd really sensed the depth of feeling that somewhat less-comfortable music can bring to a familiar story, and I treasure that memory. That's a few hours of discovery that I wish I could live over and over."

For many, the company's affordable prices had opened a new world. "In the 1990s, when my wife and I were out of college and childless, it was NYCO that made us fans of this wonderful art form. We were too poor to attend the Met more than once or twice a year, but the City Opera was within our reach financially. . . . It's sad to see an institution that blazed so many trails disappear from the New York arts scene. For many like us, the City Opera was the gateway to an enduring love of the opera. Now that it's gone, it's hard to see what will take its place."

As Opera Philadelphia discovered during its in-depth audience research, the contemporary counterparts of these writers are out there. Perhaps now more than ever, given the enormous wealth disparity in the United States and in New York in particular, there is a need for the People's Opera, where the young, the (relatively) poor, the adventurous, and the inquisitive can discover the extraordinary power of opera, both the old titles and the new ones. But producing the People's Opera in the twenty-first century is a different proposition from what it was in 1943 or even 2003. It requires a high level of subsidy from individuals and institutions (be they foundations or governments) that believe the classical arts are worth preserving. And just as important, it needs leaders—board members, executives, artists—with a strong, shared vision, a realistic understanding of the marketplace, and the imagination to develop the art form as well as preserve it.

The crucible of the last fifteen years has produced some strong leaders who are remaking the institutions and tweaking the four-hundred-year-old art form so that it can survive and thrive for another century. It will be up to them to capture the imagination of the next generations of opera lovers with the artistic verve and adventurous spirit that exemplified the old City Opera at its finest.

ACKNOWLEDGMENTS

The New York City Opera was part of my life for decades, and the opportunity to tell its story was a wonderful gift. My thanks go to my publishers—Steve Rubin, for his deep commitment to opera and music criticism, including the groundbreaking Rubin Institute, and Sara Bershtel, for her patience and insight—and to my editor, Connor Guy, for his careful reading and shaping of the manuscript. Thanks also to Holt's excellent editors and designers: Kenn Russell, Muriel Jorgensen, Rick Pracher, and Kelly Too. My agent, Will Lippincott, believed in the book from the first, helped me turn an idea into a concrete project, and supported me tirelessly along the way.

Many City Opera veterans and observers generously shared their experiences and thoughts with me, as well as supplying documents and memorabilia. I am especially grateful to Susan Woelzl, who, as the company's longtime press director and, briefly, archivist, was enormously helpful in providing direction, contacts, materials, and context, to say nothing of the complete list of the company's repertoire and productions.

The *Wall Street Journal* has allowed me to experience and write about the American opera landscape in depth for many years. As music criticism fades away at many traditional media outlets, the *Journal* has remained steadfast in its belief in the importance of chronicling the cultural landscape. As a result, I am one of the few critics who still has the opportunity to see and write about new operas, wherever they may take place. I am eternally grateful to Ray Sokolov, who launched our page at the *Journal* and invited me to write for it in 1985; to Eric Gibson, who ably succeeded him; and to the indefatigable Arts in Review staff, Barbara Phillips and Brian Kelly.

My opera-loving parents planted the seed early, and waited out my teenage apostasy in the church of Joni Mitchell. My wonderful daughters, Hannah and Lily, inspire me every day. Surely it was fate that my husband, Andy Manshel, and I met again, nearly a decade after our last encounter (in high school), at a New York City Opera performance of *The Makropulos Affair* in April 1981. Since then, he has been my rock, my reader, and my cheerleader, as well as my constant companion at hundreds of opera performances, thrilling and dire alike. I couldn't do it without him.

SOURCES

As the following attests, I had cooperation from a large number of individuals in the opera community. There were, however, some exceptions who declined to speak with me or did not respond to my inquiries. These included: Susan Baker, Mary Sharp Cronson, Nomi Ghez, Mark Newhouse, George Steel, and Charles Wall.

CHAPTER 1

For the early history of the New York City Opera, I have relied on several books.

Martin L. Sokol, *The New York City Opera: An American Adventure* (New York: Macmillan, 1981) is a detailed history of the company covering the years 1943–1966; it is less comprehensive for 1966–1979. Also extremely useful are the *Annals*, included in the book, which list every performance, with casts and creative teams, through spring 1981. Also important were: Julius Rudel and Rebecca Paller, *First and Lasting Impressions: Julius Rudel Looks Back on a Life in Music* (Rochester, NY: University of Rochester Press, 2013) and Jean Dalrymple, *From the Last Row* (Clifton, NJ: James T. White, 1975). For details about the history of the Metropolitan Opera, Charles Affron and Mirella Jona Affron, *Grand Opera: The Story of the Met* (Oakland: University of California Press, 2014);

John Dizikes, *Opera in America: A Cultural History* (New Haven, CT: Yale University Press, 1993) is a more general history. A collection of unpublished oral history interview transcripts (1993), created for City Opera's fiftieth anniversary, supplied lively personal viewpoints from company veterans, especially Frances Bible, Phyllis Curtin, Brenda Lewis, Julius Rudel, and John White.

CHAPTER 2

For the Rudel years, I have consulted the same books: Sokol, Rudel, Dalrymple, and Affron, the oral histories (Curtin, Rudel, White), as well as: Beverly Sills, *Bubbles: A Self-Portrait* (Indianapolis, IN: Bobbs-Merrill, 1976) and Beverly Sills and Lawrence Linderman, *Beverly: An Autobiography* (New York: Bantam Books, 1987). For information about the Ford Foundation and its role in funding the arts in the United States, Rachel S. Vandagriff, *American Foundations for the Arts* (Oxford Handbooks Online, April 2015) provided a good outline, as did articles in the *New York Times*, such as Howard Taubman, "How Ford's Aid to the Arts Grew" (December 7, 1971). Philip Hart, *Orpheus in the New World: The Symphony Orchestra as an American Cultural Institution* (New York: W. W. Norton, 1973) offered a detailed study of the mid-century growth of orchestras in the United States, particularly with regard to labor issues, Ford funding, and the Baumol and Bowen study. William J. Baumol, *The Cost Disease: Why Computers Get Cheaper and Health Care Doesn't* (New Haven, CT: Yale University Press, 2012) updated the 1966 Baumol and Bowen economic study. The *New York Times* exhaustively covered the stories of the labor actions during the Rudel years. I consulted dozens of news articles, editorials, and think pieces, such as Emanuel Perlmutter, "Musicians' Strike Forces City Opera Cancellations" (September 2, 1973); Editorial, "City Opera Saved" (September 25, 1973); and Donal Henahan, "City Opera Cancels Shows in Dispute with Musicians" (September 28, 1976). Reporting on fiscal crises at Lincoln Center more generally included Fred Ferretti, "Endowment Points Up Fiscal Crises at All Components of Lincoln Center" (September 21, 1973); and Allen Hughes, "Met Cancels New *Giovanni* in Worst Fund Crisis Since '32" (September 14, 1973). The *Times* covered the City Opera/City Center financial problems that came to a head in 1972, and the Ford Foundation loan and matching grant: Peter Kiess, "City Center Reports a $1.3 Million Deficit" (October 4, 1972); Richard F. Shepard, "City Ballet and Opera Get a $6.3 Million Ford Grant" (June 27, 1974); also the reorganization of the City Center board: Richard F. Shepard, "City Center Undertakes a Reorganization" (May 21, 1975), and the appointment of John Samuels as chair in Grace Glueck, "John S. Samuels 3rd to Head City Center" (July 26, 1975); the changes at the Fifty-Fifth Street Theater, Heidi Waleson, "Turning City Center into a First-Rate Dance Space" (August 29, 1982); and the Rudel-Sills transition, for example, Donal Henahan, "Beverly Sills Will Retire in 1980 to Be Co-director of City Opera."

The *Times* also published several pieces about City Opera's "identity crisis," including Dale Harris, "The Identity Crisis of City Opera" (May 4, 1975); the response from Rudel, Julius Rudel, "Back Talk" (June 1, 1974); Harold C. Schonberg, "The City Opera Comes Back Singing" (October 22, 1976); Donal Henahan, "New York Without City Opera? Unthinkable!" (February 19, 1978). Useful features about the company included: Martin Mayer, "New York City Opera Sings for 'Julius'" (September 29, 1963); Stephen E. Rubin, "But She's Not Italian!" (May 14, 1972); Julius Rudel, "Modern Operas? You Write 'Em, We'll Produce 'Em" (August 12, 1973).

CHAPTER 3

I moved to New York and began attending City Opera performances regularly in 1979, and I wrote several feature articles about Beverly Sills and the company for different publications. I consulted transcripts of my interviews with Sills from April 1983, June 1985, and September 1986. Published pieces include Heidi Waleson, "New York City Opera Is Hot," *Connoisseur* (July 1984), and several *New York Times* features. Thoughts about City Opera performances during the Sills era are drawn from my own recollections as well as *New York Times* reviews.

During 2014–18, I interviewed many people who worked at, performed at, or were connected to City Opera. In this chapter, I used material from my interviews with: Joyce Castle, Joseph Colaneri, Cori Ellison, Chuck Giles, Beth Greenberg, Nathaniel Leventhal, Anthony J. Rudel, Marc Scorca, David Titcomb, Carol Vaness, Mark Weinstein, and Susan Woelzl.

Books consulted include the second Sills autobiography, *Beverly*; Damian Fowler, *American Impresario: David Gockley's Life in Opera* (San Francisco: Chronicle, 2016). Other sources include the Sills oral history interview transcript (1993), a script from the Sills Tribute (October 27, 2007), and minutes from board meetings in 1986 and 1987. The Jerry Hadley debut story is chronicled in F. Paul Driscoll, "Trial by Fire," *Opera News* (February 8, 1997). Mark Weinstein's July 1995 deposition in the class action suit provided additional details about the costume warehouse fire.

Financial information is drawn from the company's year-end audited financial statements, from 1980 on. Opera America supplied a list of all its company members and their founding dates. Susan Woelzl's compilation of all company performances from fall 1969 through the 2009–10 season was invaluable, as was her master list of the company's repertoire, with production teams and revivals specified, from 1943 through the 2007–08 season.

The *New York Times* provided a helpful framework with reporting and interviews, and in assessing the state of the company. Among the dozens of articles consulted: Donal Henahan, "A Tough New Role for Beverly" (September 23, 1979); Harold C. Schonberg, "City Opera Cuts Prices 20% to Spur Attendance" (November 11, 1981); John Rockwell, "City Opera Searches for Stability" (February 21, 1982); Donal Henahan, "Music View: City Opera's Season—the High Hopes Were Its Sopranos" (May 2, 1982); John Rockwell, "New York City Opera to Overhaul Schedule" (July 9, 1982); John Rockwell, "City Opera Proposes a Year's Wage Freeze" (July 29, 1982); Bernard Holland, "Opera Opening Renovated State Theater" (September 7, 1982); John Rockwell, "Opera Board Firm on Strike, But Appears Split Internally" (August 1, 1983); John Rockwell, "Gloom at City Opera" (August 20, 1983); Bernard Holland, "Met Opera Contract May Have Long-Term Effect" (December 11, 1983); John Rockwell, "City Opera Boasts a Smash Season" (November 15, 1984); John Rockwell, "City Opera Costumes Lost in Fire" (September 4, 1985); Donal Henahan, "Music View: City Opera's Astonishing Good Health" (November 17, 1985); John Rockwell, "City Opera Raises the Curtain on Better Times" (June 29, 1986); Heidi Waleson, "Costume Hunting After the Warehouse Fire" (September 14, 1986); John Rockwell, "Met Narrows Repertory Plans" (May 27, 1987); John Rockwell, "Beverly Sills Announces She Will Retire on Jan. 1" (May 11, 1988); Donal Henahan, "Music View: Whither City Opera Now?" (September 18, 1988).

CHAPTER 4

In 1988, I began reviewing opera for the *Wall Street Journal*, with an emphasis on festivals and companies outside New York City. I reviewed several City Opera productions during that time, and in 1995, I became the regular opera critic for the *Journal*; my reviews during the Keene years included coverage of *Midsummer Marriage, Mathis der Maler,* and *Kinkakuji.* My articles for *Opera Now* included "City Opera at Fifty" (1993) and an obituary for Christopher Keene (1995). My accounts of performances during this period are also drawn from *New York Times* reviews.

The 2014–18 interview subjects for this chapter are Amy Burton, Joseph Colaneri, Chuck Giles, Beth Greenberg, Nathaniel Leventhal, David Titcomb, Mark Weinstein, and Susan Woelzl.

Financial details are from the company's year-end audited financials. Keene's letter to the City Opera board (October 26, 1993) sets out his objections to the hiring of Mark Weinstein. Valuable articles included: Peter G. Davis, "Voice of America: City Opera Director Christopher Keene Champions the New and the Homegrown," *New York Magazine* (July 30, 1990); and Robin Pogrebin, "The Fat Lady May Sing for City Opera; Company Wobbles Under Sills' Successor," *New York Observer* (September 20, 1993).

The many *New York Times* articles consulted include: Will Crutchfield, "Whither City Opera? The Chairman of the Board Has Some Ideas, Too" (October 27, 1988); Bernard Holland, "City Opera Musicians Set Strike Vote for Thursday" (September 7, 1989); John Rockwell, "New York City Opera Cancels the Rest of Season" (October 13, 1989); Donal Henahan, "Music View; An Opera Company in Search of Itself" (October 22, 1989); John Rockwell, "New York City Opera Union Ratifies a Five-Year Contract" (November 19, 1989); John Rockwell, "City Opera Announces Some Changes of Plan" (November 28, 1989); Allan Kozinn, "The Joys and Woes of Running the City Opera" (March 8, 1990); John Rockwell, "The City Opera Considers a Move to 42nd St." (May 29, 1991); Allan Kozinn, "Keene and the '3 Giant Fears' He Overcame at City Opera" (November 18, 1991); Allan Kozinn, "First Deficit in a Decade at Troubled City Opera" (November 26, 1992); Allan Kozinn, "City Opera Chairman Is Stepping Down" (April 16, 1993); Allan Kozinn, "City Opera Turns 50, But Who's Counting?" (July 25, 1993); Allan Kozinn, "City Opera Chief Takes Leave of Absence" (September 24, 1993); Allan Kozinn, "City Opera and Orchestra Settle Contract" (April 15, 1994); James R. Oestreich, "The Job Is Undoable, and That Is the Easy Part" (August 27, 1995); Bernard Holland, "Classical View: This Riverboat Gambler Was Also a Giver of Gifts" (October 15, 1995). The *Times* also chronicled, in its obituaries, the rising toll of City Opera artists and employees who died of AIDS.

Will Crutchfield, "Critic's Notebook; Opera in Brooklyn: A Preliminary Bravo" (July 27, 1988), discussed the problems of too-large opera houses and the repertory system.

CHAPTER 5

This chapter reflects my assessments of City Opera during the period in my capacity as the opera critic for the *Wall Street Journal*.

The 2014–18 interview subjects are: Amy Burton, Joseph Colaneri, John Conklin, Derek Davis, Cori Ellison, Chuck Giles, Sherwin Goldman, Beth Greenberg, Jane Gullong, Claudia Keenan, Paul Kellogg, Gail Kruvand, Nathaniel Leventhal, George Manahan, James Robinson, Robin Thompson, David Titcomb, Stephen Wadsworth, and Susan Woelzl.

Financial details are from the company's year-end audited statements; other information is from board meeting minutes in 2000–01. Some details about the transfer of the Wallace endowment came from Ralph Blumenthal, "13 Institutions Obtain Control of Vast Bequest," *New York Times* (May 4, 2001); and the Federal form 990 (2001) of the Lila Acheson and DeWitt Wallace Fund for Lincoln Center.

Paul Kellogg's arrival and early years were extensively covered in the press; in addition to the *Times*, articles include Justin Davidson, "City Opera's

Second Act" *Newsday* (April 21, 1996); and Martin Mayer, "Upstate, Down-state," *Opera Magazine* (Festival 1999). There were numerous *Times* stories about the acoustical fixes, such as Anthony Tommasini, "Critic's Notebook; Visionary of the Opera Inspires a Turnaround" (May 16, 2000); and Vox, including John Rockwell, "Critic's Notebook; Reviewing New Opera? Not Quite" (May 15, 2002). The Lincoln Center redevelopment plan, and Kellogg's quest for a new theater, was also extensively covered. Key stories include Ralph Blumenthal and Robin Pogrebin, "Lincoln Center Renovation Plan Has Opera Houses at Odds," *New York Times* (January 25, 2001); and Leslie Bennetts, "The Metropolitan Soap Opera," *New York Magazine* (February 4, 2002). Joshua Kosman, "Touring Opera Closes Down," *SFGate* (March 2, 2003), covers the demise of Western Opera Theater. Judith Miller, "As Patrons Age, Future of Arts Is Uncertain," *New York Times* (February 12, 1996), was an early warning sign.

CHAPTER 6

This chapter reflects my assessments of City Opera during the period in my capacity as the opera critic for the *Wall Street Journal*.

The 2014–18 interviewees are Emilie Corey, Mark Moorman, and Kara Unterberg, in addition to those listed for Chapter 5. I referred to company documents, which, in addition to the year-end audited financials, include the Boston Consulting Group (BCG) Report, in PowerPoint form, for the September 14, 2005, board meeting; the AEA Consulting survey results of the Opera for All project; board minutes for 2004–05; and some internal marketing and financial summaries.

The continuing saga of City Opera's search for a new theater is detailed in the *New York Times*, including: Robin Pogrebin, "To Stay or to Go? City Opera Is Deciding on Its Home" (December 19, 2001); Robin Pogrebin, "Beverly Sills and the Future of City Opera" (March 30, 2002); Edward Wyatt and Robin Pogrebin, "Trade Center Decisions Affected by What's Best for Lincoln Center" (June 15, 2004); and Robin Pogrebin, "New York City Opera in Talks to Build Its Own Home" (October 29, 2004).

CHAPTER 7

This chapter reflects my assessments of City Opera during the period in my capacity as the opera critic for the *Wall Street Journal*.

The 2014–18 interviewees include Robert Meya, Alexander Neef, Timothy O'Leary, and Marc Scorca in addition to those listed in Chapters 5 and 6. I referred to company documents, which, in addition to year-end audited financials, include the Boston Consulting Group (BCG) Report, board minutes for

2005–07, some internal marketing and financial summaries, and artistic planning documents.

In the *New York Times*, City Opera's woes after the last new theater prospect fell through are detailed in Robin Pogrebin, "City Opera, After a Frustrating Year, Still Longs for a New Home" (July 4, 2006). The excitement over the appointment of Mortier began with Daniel J. Wakin, "City Opera Lures Director from Paris" (February 28, 2007), and continued with Anthony Tommasini, "Which Is the People's Opera? Let the Fireworks Begin" (March 11, 2007). Not everyone was as delighted at the prospect as Tommasini was, and would remain: Charles Michener, "City Opera's Bad Boy," *New York Observer* (March 13, 2007), and Frank Cadenhead, "Critics Notebook: Mortier's Regime in Paris," MusicalAmerica.com (March 6, 2007), took a more jaundiced view of the impresario's accomplishments. Mortier outlined his aesthetic in a radio interview with Gilbert Kaplan, "Mad About Music," WNYC.org (October 7, 2007), which City Opera distributed as a promotional CD.

CHAPTER 8

The 2014–18 interviewees include Michael Gary, in addition to those already listed for Chapters 5–7. I referred to company documents, including year-end audited financials, board minutes, the cy pres application, and some company internal documents and memos.

The unraveling of the Mortier appointment was covered in the *New York Times*, including Daniel J. Wakin, "City Opera Director Has Eyes on Bayreuth" (August 26, 2008): Anthony Tommasini, "At City Opera, Concern over a Visionary Whose Eye Seems to Wander" (October 3, 2008); Daniel J. Wakin, "City Opera Lays Off 11 Members of Its Staff" (October 3, 2008); and, on page 1, Daniel J. Wakin, "Bold Impresario and Opera Part Ways" (November 7, 2008). Fred Cohn, "Reinventing New York City Opera," *Opera News* (January 2012), was a valuable chronicle of the company's history and travails.

CHAPTER 9

This chapter reflects my assessments of City Opera during the period in my capacity as the opera critic for the *Wall Street Journal*.

The 2014–18 interviewees include Amy Burton, Emilie Corey, Cori Ellison, Michael Gary, Chuck Giles, Gail Kruvand, George Manahan, Robert Meya, Mark Moorman, Allen Moyer, Kevin Murphy, David Titcomb, Kara Unterberg, Susan Woelzl, Edward Yim, and Francesca Zambello. I referred to company documents, including year-end audited financials, board minutes, the cy pres application, and some company internal documents and memos, including the Kaiser "Turnaround Plan." Michael M. Kaiser, *The Art of the Turnaround* (Hanover, NH:

University Press of New England, 2008), spells out his techniques for rescuing arts organizations. Reynold Levy, *They Told Me Not to Take That Job: Tumult, Betrayal, Heroics, and the Transformation of Lincoln Center* (New York: PublicAffairs, 2015), supplies the ex-president of Lincoln Center's point of view on the City Opera departure. The July 10, 2011, Letter from Opera Stars protesting the Lincoln Center departure has an entire page of names.

Articles about opera companies hit by the 2008–09 downturn include Barry Singer, "Opera in the Age of Anxiety," *Opera News* (September 2009); and Daniel J. Wakin, "Metropolitan Opera Faces Cuts, Its Leader Says" (January 16, 2009). *New York Times* coverage of the post-Mortier period include Daniel J. Wakin, "Turnaround Specialist Talks of City Opera Plans" (November 19, 2008); Daniel J. Wakin, "New Leader Is Named for Embattled City Opera" (January 15, 2009); Robin Pogrebin, "Beleaguered City Opera Tries to Hold Off the Ultimate Finale" (June 18, 2009). Bloomberg.com energetically tracked the company's fortunes in this period, particularly its endowment invasion, including Zita Lundberg, "Board Eats Endowment, Gloom Deepens at City Opera: Commentary" (April 22, 2009). The *Times* chronicled the departure from Lincoln Center and its fallout. Pieces included the op-ed, Julius Rudel, "The People's Opera in Peril" (June 6, 2011); Daniel J. Wakin, "Stars Sign Letter Protesting City Opera's Move" (July 7, 2011); Robin Pogrebin and Daniel J. Wakin, "How the People's Opera Orchestrated Its Peril" (June 15, 2011); an editorial, "An Opera on the Loose" (July 15, 2011); Daniel J. Wakin, "Unions Say City Opera Offer Would Gut Chorus and Orchestra" (July 11, 2011).

CHAPTER 10

This chapter reflects my assessments of City Opera and other opera companies during this period in my capacity as the opera critic for the *Wall Street Journal*.

The 2014–18 interviewees include Emilie Corey, Michael Gary, Chuck Giles, Gail Kruvand, Robert Meya, and Roy Niederhoffer. I referred to company documents, including year-end audited financials, Federal Form 990s, some board minutes, and internal documents.

The *Times* chronicled the company's last years: Daniel J. Wakin, "City Opera Is to Shed Its Past, Not Store It" (October 2, 2012, "For City Opera, the Talk Turns to a Shutdown" (September 26, 2013); Michael Cooper and Kate Taylor, "Bloomberg Says City Opera Is on Its Own" (September 30, 2013); Michael Cooper and Robin Pogrebin, "The Frenzied Last-Act Effort to Save City Opera" (October 4, 2013). The endowment depletion was explored by James B. Stewart, "A Ransacked Endowment at New York City Opera" (October 12, 2013).

CHAPTER 11

A City Opera "identity" story from an earlier period was Donal Henahan, "Music View; An Opera Company in Search of Itself," *New York Times* (October 22, 1989).

Articles about opera companies adapting to the pressures of the new age include Joshua Kosman, "David Gockley Seeks to Overhaul S.F. Opera Funding," SFGate.com, (May 7, 2011); Lisa Bertagnoli, "Can Lyric Opera Survive the 21st Century?" *Crain's Chicago Business* (March 3, 2017); opera in Texas is explored in Christopher Kelly, "The Texans," *Opera News* (October 2014). Fred Cohn, "Revised Ending," *Opera News* (September 2014), is an excellent account of the San Diego story. James Chute, "San Diego Opera Stands Behind New Director," *San Diego Union-Tribune* (October 6, 2015) and Michael Cooper, "Gotham Opera's Liabilities Bring Scrutiny," *New York Times* (October 16, 2015) discuss the Gotham closing. I interviewed David Gockley about the changing landscape for opera in November 2014. The Met labor battle of 2014 was covered extensively in the *Wall Street Journal*, including Jennifer Maloney, "Opera to Seek Pay Cutbacks from Unions" (February 28, 2014); and the *New York Times*, Michael Cooper, "Not Over Till Overtime's Due? Met Labor Strife Bares Secrets" (July 7, 2014); and Michael Cooper, "Metropolitan Opera Clears Last Major Hurdle in Labor Talks" (August 21, 2014). James B. Stewart, "A Fight at the Opera," *New Yorker* (March 23, 2015), goes into the Met's problems in detail. The musicians' detailed accusations of Met overspending made for fascinating reading, as did the company's rebuttal.

My research in philanthropy includes looks at younger philanthropists and conversations with such people as philanthropy adviser Nick Tedesco at JPMorgan Private Bank in San Francisco; my most recent publication in the field is *Atlantic Insights: Giving While Living* (New York: Atlantic Philanthropies, 2017).

CHAPTER 12

As the *Wall Street Journal*'s opera critic, I have focused a lot of attention on companies around the United States, particularly in the area of contemporary opera. This chapter reflects many years of visits to such companies as Houston, Los Angeles, Boston, Fort Worth, Philadelphia, Minnesota, Cincinnati, and others, as well as the festival companies Santa Fe, Opera Theatre of Saint Louis, and Glimmerglass, and conversations with such leaders as Christopher Koelsch, Timothy O'Leary, Beth Morrison, and Yuval Sharon. I spoke with David Devan about Philadelphia's new festival format before and after O17. Matthew Sigman, "On the Town," *Opera News* (August 2017), is a thorough advance story about O17; three other stories in the same issue examine individual works and artists; my *Wall Street Journal* review is "An Opera Festival to Binge On" (September 19, 2017).

Two articles with a wealth of detail about the growth of contemporary opera in the United States are by Sasha Metcalf, "How Opera America Has Supported New Works," www.newmusicbox.org (July 26, 2017), including a link to a 2015 Opera America study covering new operas by North American composers from 1995 to 2015; and Sasha Metcalf, "Project MUSE—Funding 'Opera for the 80s and Beyond': The Role of Impresarios in Creating a New American Repertoire," *American Music* 35, no. 1 (Spring 2017): 7–28. An older publication, Alan Rich, *An American Voice: Houston Grand Opera Celebrates Twenty-Five World Premieres* (Houston, TX: Houston Grand Opera, 2000), as well as the 2016 Gockley book listed under Chapter 3, recount Gockley's role in championing new work at both HGO and San Francisco.

Craig A. Smith, *A Vision of Voices: John Crosby and the Santa Fe Opera* (Albuquerque: University of New Mexico Press, 2015), is an excellent history. Michael M. Kaiser, *Curtains?: The Future of the Arts in America* (Waltham, MA: Brandeis University Press, 2015), chronicles Kaiser's retreat from optimism. Robin Pogrebin, "Michael Bloomberg Gives $75 Million to Shed Arts Center," *New York Times* (May 24, 2017), shows one billionaire's cultural priorities.

CODA

I attended and reviewed most of the resurrected New York City Opera's productions for the *Wall Street Journal*. I interviewed Michael Capasso and Roy Niederhoffer in February 2017. I consulted the lengthy business plan that they submitted to the court. The saga of their acquisition of the name was chronicled in the *Wall Street Journal*, including Jennifer Smith, "Two Visions for Bringing New York City Opera Back to Life" (November 2, 2015), and the *New York Times*, including Michael Cooper, "Group Cedes Bid to Revive City Opera to Its Rival" (December 3, 2015). Brian Kellow, "Revival Meeting," *Opera News* (March 2015), explored it as well. The *New York Times Arts Beat* blog asked readers to "Share Your City Opera Memories" (October 1, 2013); there were 130 comment responses. The Met's much-maligned Luc Bondy *Tosca* was replaced on New Year's Eve 2017 with a more traditional staging by David McVicar. Less purely decorative and more thoughtful than the Zeffirelli, it was greeted happily by the audience, though some critics felt that the Met had capitulated. My positive review ran in the *Wall Street Journal* on January 3, 2018.

INDEX

278

ABOUT THE AUTHOR

HEIDI WALESON has been the opera critic of the *Wall Street Journal* for twenty-five years. In addition to her regular criticism, her work has also focused more broadly on the changing profiles of musical institutions, new models for opera presentation, and the broader significance of opera and culture. She is a faculty member of the Rubin Institute for Music Criticism at the San Francisco Conservatory of Music.